# VISUAL
# FACTFINDER

First published by Bardfield Press in 2005
Copyright © Miles Kelly Publishing 2005

Bardfield Press is an imprint of
Miles Kelly Publishing Ltd,
Bardfield Centre, Great Bardfield, Essex, CM7 4SL

This material also appears in the *1000 Facts* series

4 6 8 10 9 7 5 3

Editorial Director: Belinda Gallagher

Art Director: Jo Brewer

Editorial Assistant: Bethanie Bourne

Picture Researcher: Liberty Newton

Production Manager: Elizabeth Brunwin

Reprographics: Anthony Cambray, Mike Coupe, Ian Paulyn

British Library Cataloguing-in-Publication Data
A catalogue record for this book is available from the British Library

ISBN 1-84236-591-6

Printed in China

www.mileskelly.net
info@mileskelly.net

# VISUAL
# FACTFINDER

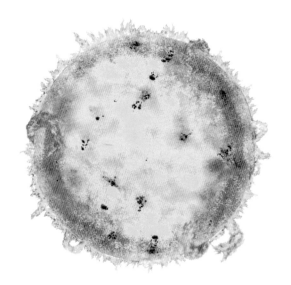

**BARDFIELD
PRESS**

# Contents

# History

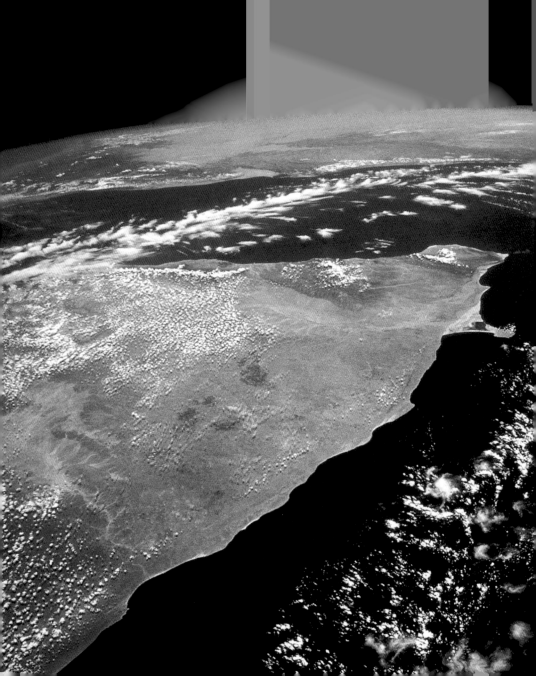

# EARTH & SPACE

**Why did the Big Bang happen?**

**What causes volcanoes and earthquakes?**

**Which  lake holds one-fifth of all the world's freshwater?**

The answers to these and many other questions can be found in this amazing section. *Earth & Space* is split into two parts. The first part spans the depths of the Universe in great detail. Subjects such as planets and stars are presented alongside fascinating information about space travel and exploration.

The second part takes a closer look at our planet. Starting with the formation of the Earth, there are hundreds of facts about volcanoes and earthquakes, rivers and swamps, and climate and oceans. Countries of the world are also covered, along with hundreds of statistics about famous cities and well-known landmarks.

# The Universe

- **The Universe is everything** that we can ever know – all of space and time.

- **The Universe is almost entirely empty**, with small clusters of matter and energy.

- **The Universe is probably** about 15 billion years old, but estimates vary.

- **One problem with working out** the age of the Universe is that there are stars in our galaxy which are thought to be 14 to 18 billion years old – older than the estimated age of the Universe. So either the stars must be younger, or the Universe older.

- **The furthest galaxies yet detected** are about 13 billion light-years away (130 billion trillion km).

- **The Universe is getting bigger** by the second. We know this because all the galaxies are zooming away from us. The further away they are, the faster they are moving.

- **The very furthest galaxies** are spreading away at more than 90 percent of the speed of light.

- **The Universe was once thought** to be everything that could ever exist, but recent theories about inflation suggest our Universe may be just one of countless bubbles of space-time.

- **The Universe may have neither** a centre nor an edge, because according to Einstein's theory of relativity, gravity bends all of space-time around into an endless curve.

▲ *The Universe is getting bigger and bigger all the time, as galaxies rush outwards in all directions.*

▼ *Most astronomers believe that the Universe was created in a huge explosion called 'The Big Bang', seen here as a flash in the middle of the image. It occurred in just a fraction of a second, and sent matter flying out in all directions.*

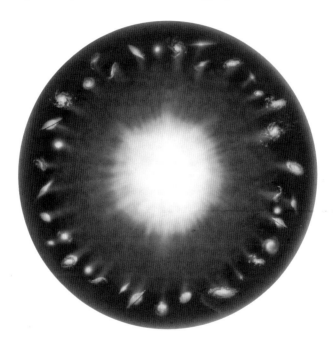

...FASCINATING FACT...
Recent theories suggest there may
be many other universes which we can
never know.

# The Big Bang

- **The Big Bang explosion** is how scientists think the Universe began some 15 billion years ago.

- **First there was a hot ball** tinier than an atom. This cooled to 10 billion billion °C as it grew to football size.

- **A split second later,** a super-force swelled the infant Universe a thousand billion billion billion times. Scientists call this inflation.

- **As it mushroomed out,** the Universe was flooded with energy and matter, and the super-force separated into basic forces such as electricity and gravity.

- **There were no atoms at first,** just tiny particles such as quarks in a dense soup a trillion trillion trillion trillion trillion times denser than water.

- **There was also antimatter,** the mirror image of matter. Antimatter and matter destroy each other when they meet, so they battled it out. Matter just won – but the Universe was left almost empty.

- **After three minutes,** quarks started to fuse (join) to make the smallest atoms, hydrogen. Then hydrogen gas atoms fused to make helium gas atoms.

- **After one million years** the gases began to curdle into strands with dark holes between them.

- **After 300 million years,** the strands clumped into clouds, and then the clouds clumped together to form stars and galaxies.

- **The afterglow of the Big Bang** can still be detected as microwave background radiation coming from all over space (see picture above).

▼ *Before the Big Bang all the material that existed was contained in one small lump. The material was forced out causing the Universe to expand rapidly. The galaxies are still moving away from one another and some scientists believe that they will continue to move apart forever.*

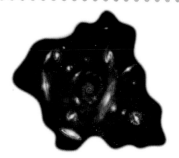

*1. The Big Bang was a massive explosion that created the Universe.*

*4. The millions of stars that are visible in the night sky are still just a tiny part of the Universe.*

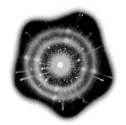

*3. The clouds formed together to form galaxies.*

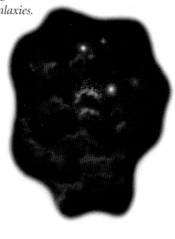

*2. Millions of years later, gases clustered into clouds.*

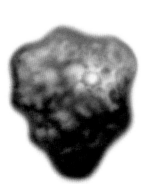

**17**

# Black holes

- **Black holes** are places where gravity is so strong that it sucks everything in, including light.

- **If you fell** into a black hole you'd stretch like spaghetti.

- **Black holes** form when a star or galaxy gets so dense that it collapses under the pull of its own gravity.

- **Black holes** may exist at the heart of every galaxy.

- **Gravity shrinks** a black hole to an unimaginably small point called a singularity.

- **Around a singularity,** gravity is so intense that space-time is bent into a funnel.

▲ *This is an artist's impression of what a black hole might look like, with jets of electricity shooting out from either side.*

- **Matter spiralling** into a black hole is torn apart and glows so brightly that it creates the brightest objects in the Universe – quasars.

- **The swirling gases** around a black hole turn it into an electrical generator, making it spout jets of electricity billions of kilometres out into space.

- **The opposite of black holes** may be white holes which spray out matter and light like fountains.

▼ *No light is able to escape from a black hole. Scientists know where they are because they affect the light emitted by nearby stars.*

⋅⋅⋅FASCINATING FACT⋅⋅⋅
Black holes and white holes may join to
form tunnels called wormholes – and
these may be the secret to time travel.

# Dark matter

- **Dark matter** is space matter we cannot see because, unlike stars and galaxies, it does not give off light.

- **There is much more dark matter** in the Universe than bright. Some scientists think 90 percent of matter is dark.

- **Astronomers know about dark matter** because its gravity pulls on stars and galaxies, changing their orbits and the way they rotate (spin round).

- **The visible stars in the Milky Way** are only a thin central slice, embedded in a big bun-shaped ball of dark matter.

- **Dark matter** is of two kinds – the matter in galaxies (galactic), and the matter between them (intergalactic).

- **Galactic dark matter** may be much the same as ordinary matter. However, it burnt out (as black dwarf stars do) early in the life of the Universe.

- **Intergalactic dark matter** is made up of WIMPs (Weakly Interacting Massive Particles).

- **Some WIMPs** are called cold dark matter because they are travelling slowly away from the Big Bang.

- **Some WIMPs** are called hot dark matter because they are travelling very fast away from the Big Bang.

- **The future of the Universe** may depend on how much dark matter there is. If there is too much, its gravity will eventually stop the Universe's expansion – and make it shrink again.

▲ A galaxy's bright stars may be only a tiny part of its total matter. Much of the galaxy may be invisible dark matter.

▲ *Astronomers determined the amount of dark matter in clusters of galaxies by measuring arcs of light. These arcs occur when the gravity of a cluster bends light from distant galaxies.*

# Stars

- **Stars are balls** of mainly hydrogen and helium gas.

- **Nuclear reactions** in the heart of stars generate heat and light.

- **The heart of a star** reaches 16 million°C. A grain of sand this hot would kill someone 150 km away.

- **The gas in stars** is in a special hot state called plasma, which is made of atoms stripped of electrons.

- **In the core of a star,** hydrogen nuclei fuse (join together) to form helium. This nuclear reaction is called a proton-proton chain.

- **Stars twinkle** because we see them through the wafting of the Earth's atmosphere.

- **Astronomers work out how big a star is** from its brightness and its temperature.

- **The size and brightness** of a star depends on its mass – that is, how much gas it is made of. Our Sun is a medium-sized star, and no star has more than 100 times the Sun's mass or less than 6–7% of its mass.

▲ *The few thousand stars visible to the naked eye are just a tiny fraction of the trillions in the Universe.*

- **The coolest stars**, such as Arcturus and Antares, glow reddest. Hotter stars are yellow and white. The hottest are blue-white.

- **The blue supergiant Zeta Puppis** has a surface temperature of 40,000°C, while Rigel's is 10,000°C.

▲ *A swarm, or large cluster of stars known as M80 (Nac 6093), from The Milky Way galaxy. This swarm, 28,000 light-years from Earth, contains hundreds of thousands of stars, 'attracted' to each other by gravity.*

# Constellations

- **Constellations are patterns** of stars in the sky which astronomers use to help them pinpoint individual stars.

- **Most of the constellations** were identified long ago by the stargazers of Ancient Babylon and Egypt.

- **Constellations are simply patterns** – there is no real link between the stars whatsoever.

- **Astronomers today** recognize 88 constellations.

- **Heroes and creatures** of Greek myth, such as Orion the Hunter and Perseus, provided the names for many constellations, although each name is usually written in its Latin form, not Greek.

- **The stars in each constellation** are named after a letter of the Greek alphabet.

- **The brightest star** in each constellation is called the Alpha star, the next brightest Beta, and so on.

- **Different constellations** become visible at different times of year, as the Earth travels around the Sun.

- **Southern hemisphere constellations** are different from those in the north.

- **The constellation of the Great Bear** – also known by its Latin name Ursa Major – contains an easily recognizable group of seven stars called the Plough or the Big Dipper.

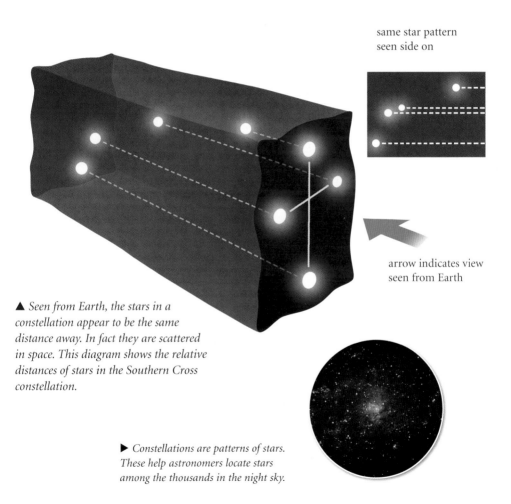

same star pattern
seen side on

arrow indicates view
seen from Earth

▲ *Seen from Earth, the stars in a constellation appear to be the same distance away. In fact they are scattered in space. This diagram shows the relative distances of stars in the Southern Cross constellation.*

▶ *Constellations are patterns of stars. These help astronomers locate stars among the thousands in the night sky.*

# Zodiac

- **The zodiac** is the band of constellations the Sun appears to pass in front of during the year, as the Earth orbits the Sun. It lies along the ecliptic.

- **The ecliptic** is the plane (level) of the Earth's orbit around the Sun. The Moon and all planets but Pluto lie in the same plane.

- **The Ancient Greeks** divided the zodiac into 12 parts, named after the constellation they saw in each part. These are the signs of the zodiac.

- **The 12 constellations of the zodiac** are Aries, Taurus, Gemini, Cancer, Leo, Virgo, Libra, Scorpio, Sagittarius, Capricorn, Aquarius and Pisces.

- **Astrologers** are people who believe that the movements of planets and stars have an effect on people's lives. They are not scientists.

- **For astrologers**, all the constellations of the zodiac are equal in size. The ones used by astronomers are not.

- **The Earth has tilted** slightly since ancient times and the constellations no longer correspond to the zodiac.

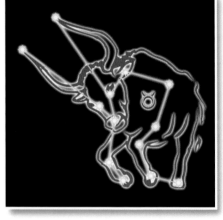
▲ *Taurus, the bull*

- **A 13th constellation, Ophiuchus,** now lies within the zodiac, but astrologers ignore it.

- **The dates that the Sun** seems to pass in front of each constellation no longer match the dates astrologers use.

◀ *Leo, the lion*

▼ *Libra, the scales*

◀ *Aries, the ram*

▲ *The zodiac signs are imaginary symbols that ancient astronomers linked to star patterns.*

**...FASCINATING FACT...**
Some people think that the position of the zodiac stars affects our behaviour.

27

# Galaxies

- **Galaxies are giant groups** of millions or even trillions of stars. Our own local galaxy is the Milky Way.

- **There may be 20 trillion** galaxies in the Universe.

- **Only three galaxies** are visible to the naked eye from Earth besides the Milky Way – the Large and Small Magellanic clouds, and the Andromeda galaxy.

- **Although galaxies are vast,** they are so far away that they look like fuzzy clouds. Only in 1916 did astronomers realize that they are huge star groups.

- **Spiral galaxies** are spinning, Catherine-wheel-like galaxies with a dense core and spiralling arms.

- **Barred spiral galaxies** have just two arms. These are linked across the galaxy's middle by a bar from which they trail like water from a spinning garden sprinkler.

- **Elliptical galaxies** are vast, very old, egg-shaped galaxies, made up of as many as a trillion stars.

- **Irregular galaxies** are galaxies with no obvious shape. They may have formed from the debris of galaxies that crashed into each other.

- **Galaxies are often** found in groups called clusters. One cluster may have 30 or so galaxies in it.

> ... FASCINATING FACT ...
> Galaxies like the Small Magellanic Cloud
> may be the debris of mighty collisions
> between galaxies.

▲ *Like our own Milky Way and the nearby Andromeda galaxy, many galaxies are spiral in shape, with a dense core of stars and long, whirling arms made up of millions of stars.*

# The Milky Way

▲ *The spiralling Milky Way galaxy looks much like a Catherine wheel firework.*

- **The Milky Way** is the faint, hazy band of light that you can see stretching right across the night sky.

- **Looking through binoculars,** you would see that the Milky Way is made up of countless stars.

- **A galaxy** is a vast group of stars, and the Milky Way is the galaxy we live in.

- **There are billions** of galaxies in space.

- **The Milky Way** is 100,000 light-years across and 1000 light-years thick. It is made up of 100 billion stars.

- **All the stars** are arranged in a spiral (like a giant Catherine wheel), with a bulge in the middle.

- **Our Sun** is just one of the billions of stars on one arm of the spiral.

- **The Milky Way** is whirling rapidly, spinning our Sun and all its other stars around at 100 million km/h.

- **The Sun** travels around the galaxy once every 200 million years – a journey of 100,000 light-years.

- **The huge bulge** at the centre of the Milky Way is about 20,000 light-years across and 3000 thick. It contains only very old stars and little dust or gas.

- **There may be a huge black hole** in the very middle of the Milky Way.

▼ *To the naked eye, the Milky Way looks like a hazy, white cloud, but binoculars show it to be a blur of countless stars.*

# Nebulae

- **Nebula** (plural nebulae) was the word once used for any fuzzy patch of light in the night sky. Nowadays, many nebulae are known to be galaxies instead.

- **Many nebulae** are gigantic clouds of gas and space dust.

- **Glowing nebulae** are named because they give off a dim, red light, as the hydrogen gas in them is heated by radiation from nearby stars.

- **The Great Nebula of Orion** is a glowing nebula just visible to the naked eye.

- **Reflection nebulae** have no light of their own. They can only be seen because starlight shines off the dust in them.

- **Dark nebulae** not only have no light of their own, they also soak up light. They are seen as patches of darkness, blocking light from the stars behind them.

▲ *This is a glowing nebula called the Lagoon nebula, which glows as hydrogen and helium gas in it is heated by radiation from stars.*

- **The Horsehead nebula** in Orion is the best-known dark nebula. As its name suggests, it is shaped like a horse's head.
- **Planetary nebulae** are thin rings of gas cloud which are thrown out by dying stars. Despite their name, they have nothing to do with planets.
- **The Ring nebula** in Lyra is the best-known of the planetary nebulae.
- **The Crab nebula** is the remains of a supernova that exploded in AD1054.

▲ *There are two general types of nebulae. Diffuse nebulae, the larger of the two, can contain enough dust and gases to form 100,000 stars the size of the Sun. Planetary nebulae form when a dying star throws off the outer layers of its atmosphere.*

# Star birth

- **Stars are being born** and dying all over the Universe, and by looking at stars in different stages of their life, astronomers have worked out their life stories.

- **Medium-sized stars** last for about ten billion years. Small stars may last for 200 billion years.

- **Big stars** have short, fierce lives of ten million years.

- **Stars start life** in clouds of gas and dust called nebulae.

- **Inside nebulae**, gravity creates dark clumps called dark nebulae, each clump containing the seeds of a family of stars.

- **As gravity squeezes** the clumps in dark nebulae, they become hot.

- **Smaller clumps** never get very hot and eventually fizzle out. Even if they start burning, they lose surface gas and shrink to wizened, old white dwarf stars.

- **If a larger clump** reaches 10 million °C, hydrogen atoms in its core begin to join together in nuclear reactions, and the baby star starts to glow.

- **In a medium-sized star** like our Sun, the heat of burning hydrogen pushes gas out as fiercely as gravity pulls inwards, and the star becomes stable (steady).

- **Medium-sized stars** burn steadily until all of their hydrogen fuel is used up.

▶ *Stars are born within clouds of gas and dust (nebulae).*

# Supernova

- **A supernova** (plural supernovae) is the final, gigantic explosion of a supergiant star at the end of its life.

- **A supernova** lasts for just a week or so, but shines as bright as a galaxy of 100 billion ordinary stars.

- **Supernovae happen** when a supergiant star uses up its hydrogen and helium fuel and shrinks, boosting pressure in its core enough to fuse heavy elements such as iron.

- **When iron begins to fuse** in its core, a star collapses instantly – then rebounds in a mighty explosion.

- **Seen in 1987, supernova 1987A** was the first viewed with the naked eye since Kepler's 1604 sighting.

- **Supernova remnants** (leftovers) are the gigantic, cloudy shells of material swelling out from supernovae.

- **A supernova** seen by Chinese astronomers in AD184 was thought to be such a bad omen that it sparked off a palace revolution.

- **A dramatic supernova** was seen by Chinese astronomers in AD1054 and left the Crab nebula.

- **Elements heavier** than iron were made in supernovae.

> ...FASCINATING FACT...
> Many of the elements that make up your
> body were forged in supernovae.

▼ *Seeing a supernova is rare, but at any moment in time there is one happening somewhere in the Universe.*

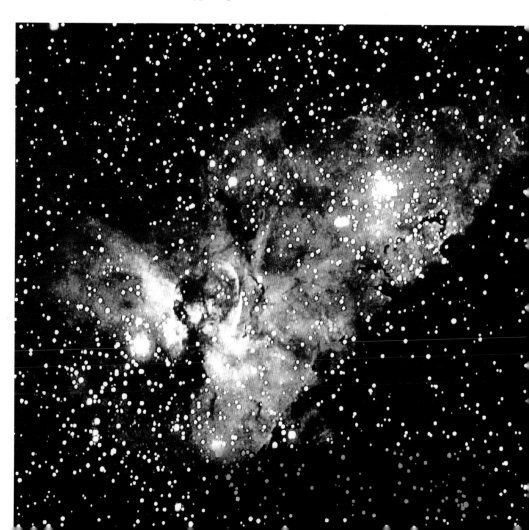

# Celestial sphere

- **Looking at the stars,** they seem to move across the night sky as though they were painted on the inside of a giant, slowly turning ball. This is the celestial sphere.

- **The northern tip** of the celestial sphere is called the North Celestial Pole.

- **The southern tip** is the South Celestial Pole.

- **The celestial sphere rotates** on an axis which runs between its two celestial poles.

- **There is an equator** around the middle of the celestial sphere, just like Earth's.

- **Stars are positioned** on the celestial sphere by their declination and their right ascension.

- **Declination** is like latitude. It is measured in degrees and shows a star's position between pole and equator.

- **Right ascension** is like longitude. It is measured in hours, minutes and seconds, and shows how far a star is from a marker called the First Point of Aries.

- **The Pole Star,** Polaris, lies very near the North Celestial Pole.

- **The zenith** is the point on the sphere directly above your head as you look at the night sky.

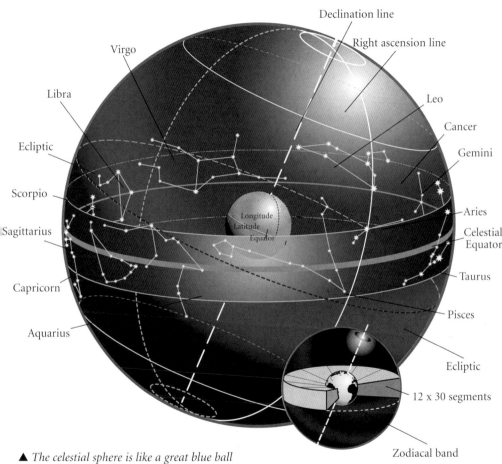

Declination line

Right ascension line

Virgo

Libra

Leo

Ecliptic

Cancer

Gemini

Scorpio

Sagittarius

Longitude
Latitude
Equator

Aries

Celestial
Equator

Capricorn

Taurus

Aquarius

Pisces

Ecliptic

12 x 30 segments

Zodiacal band

▲ *The celestial sphere is like a great blue ball
dotted with stars, with the Earth in the middle. It
is imaginary, but makes it easy to locate stars and
constellations. The zodiac is shown on the inset.*

**39**

# Planets

- **Planets** are globe-shaped space objects that orbit a star.

- **Planets begin life** at the same time as their star, from the left over clouds of gas and dust.

- **Planets are never** more than 20 percent of the size of their star. If they were bigger, they would have become stars.

- **Some planets,** called terrestrial planets, have a surface of solid rock. Others, called gas planets, have a surface of liquid or airy gas.

- **The solar system** has nine planets including Pluto. But Pluto may be an escaped moon or an asteroid, not a planet.

- **Giant planets** have now been detected orbiting stars other than the Sun. These are called extra-solar planets.

- **Extra-solar planets** are too far away to see, but can be detected because they make their star wobble.

- **One extra-solar planet** has now been photographed.

- **Among the nine stars** so far known to have planets are 47 Ursae Majoris, 51 Pegasi, and 70 Virginis.

- **Four of the new planets** – called 51 Peg planets, after the planet that circles 51 Pegasi – seem to orbit their stars in less than 15 days. The planet orbiting Tau Bootis gets around in just 3.3 days!

*◀ Most of the nine planets in our Solar System have been known since ancient times, but in the last few years planets have been found orbiting other, faraway stars.*

▲ *The planets of our Solar System: from the front, Neptune, Uranus, Saturn, Jupiter, Mars, Earth and its moon, Venus and Mercury. Pluto (not shown) is the furthest out from the Sun.*

# Mercury

- **Mercury is the nearest planet** to the Sun – during its orbit it is between 45.9 and 69.7 million km away.

- **Mercury is the fastest orbiting** of all the planets, getting around the Sun in just 88 days.

- **Mercury takes 58.6 days** to rotate once, so a Mercury day lasts nearly 59 times as long as ours.

- **Temperatures** on Mercury veer from -180°C at night to over 430°C during the day (enough to melt lead).

- **The crust and mantle** are made largely of rock, but the core (75 percent of its diameter) is solid iron.

▲ *Mercury is a tiny planet with a thin atmosphere and a solid core.*

- **Mercury's dusty surface** is pocketed by craters made by space debris crashing into it.

- **With barely 20 percent of Earth's mass,** Mercury is so small that its gravity can only hold on to a very thin atmosphere of sodium vapour.

- **Mercury is so small** that its core has cooled and become solid (unlike Earth's). As this happened, Mercury shrank and its surface wrinkled like the skin of an old apple.

- **Craters on Mercury** discovered by the USA's *Mariner* space probe have names like Bach, Beethoven, Wagner, Shakespeare and Tolstoy.

The largest feature on Mercury is a huge impact crater called the Caloris Basin, which is about 1300 km across and 2 km deep

Mercury's surface is covered with impact craters Most were formed by the impact of debris left over from the birth of the Solar System, about 4 billion years ago

The surface is wrinkled by long, low ridges which probably formed as the core cooled and shrunk

▲ *Mercury is a planet of yellow dust, as deeply dented with craters as the Moon. It does have small polar icecaps, but the ice is pure acid.*

FASCINATING FACT
Twice during its orbit, Mercury gets very close to the Sun and speeds up so much that the Sun seems to go backwards in the sky.

# Venus

- **Venus** is the second planet from the Sun – its orbit makes it 107.4 million km away at its nearest and 109 million km away at its furthest.

- **Venus shines like a star** in the night sky because its thick atmosphere reflects sunlight amazingly well. This planet is the brightest thing in the sky, after the Sun and the Moon.

- **Venus is called the Evening Star** because it can be seen from Earth in the evening, just after sunset. It can also be seen before sunrise, though. It is visible at these times because it is quite close to the Sun.

- **Venus's cloudy atmosphere** is a thick mixture of carbon dioxide gas and sulphuric acid.

- **Venus is the hottest planet** in the Solar System, with a surface temperature of over 470°C.

- **Venus is so hot** because the carbon dioxide in its atmosphere works like the panes of glass in a greenhouse to trap the Sun's heat. This overheating is called a runaway greenhouse effect.

- **Venus's thick clouds** hide its surface so well that until space probes detected the very high temperatures some people thought there might be jungles beneath the clouds.

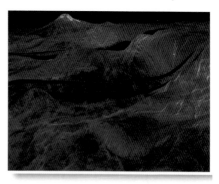

▲ *This is a view of a 6 km-high volcano on Venus' surface called Maat Mons. It is not an actual photograph, but was created on computer from radar data collected by the* Magellan *orbiter, which reached Venus in the 1980s. The colours are what astronomers guess them to be from their knowledge of the chemistry of Venus.*

- **Venus's day** (the time it takes to spin round once) lasts 243 Earth days – longer than its year, which lasts 224.7 days. But because Venus rotates backwards, the Sun comes up twice during the planet's yearly orbit – once every 116.8 days.

- **Venus is the nearest** to Earth in size, measuring 12,102 km across its diameter.

▶ *Venus's thick clouds of carbon dioxide gas and sulphuric acid reflect sunlight and make it shine like a star, but none of its atmosphere is transparent like the Earth's. This makes it very hard to see what is happening down on its surface.*

...**FASCINATING FACT**...
Pressure on the surface of Venus is
90 times greater than that on Earth!

# Mars

- **Mars** is the nearest planet to Earth after Venus, and it is the only planet to have either an atmosphere or a daytime temperature close to ours.

- **Mars is called the red planet** because of its rusty red colour. This comes from oxidized (rusted) iron in its soil.

- **Mars is the fourth planet** out from the Sun, orbiting it at an average distance of 227.9 million km. It takes 687 days to complete its orbit.

- **Mars is 6786 km** in diameter and spins round once every 24.62 hours – almost the same time as the Earth takes to rotate.

- **Mars's volcano Olympus Mons** is the biggest in the Solar System. It covers the same area as Ireland and is three times higher than Mount Everest.

- **In the 1880s,** American astronomer Percival Lowell was sure that the dark lines he saw on Mars' surface through his telescope were canals built by Martians.

- **The *Viking* probes** found no evidence of life on Mars, but the discovery of a possible fossil of a micro-organism in a Mars rock means the hunt for life on Mars is on. Future missions to the planet will hunt for life below its surface.

- **The evidence is growing** that Mars was warmer and wetter in the past, although scientists cannot say how much water there was, or when and why it dried up.

▲ *Mars' surface is cracked by a valley called the Vallis Marineris – so big it makes the Grand Canyon look tiny.*

- **Mars has two tiny moons** called Phobos and Deimos. Phobos is just 27 km across, while Deimos is just 15 km across and has so little gravity that you could reach escape velocity riding a bike up a ramp!

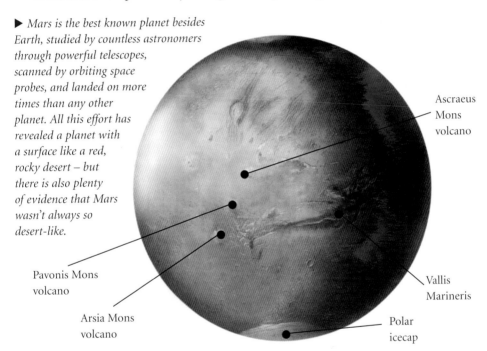

▶ *Mars is the best known planet besides Earth, studied by countless astronomers through powerful telescopes, scanned by orbiting space probes, and landed on more times than any other planet. All this effort has revealed a planet with a surface like a red, rocky desert – but there is also plenty of evidence that Mars wasn't always so desert-like.*

Ascraeus Mons volcano

Pavonis Mons volcano

Arsia Mons volcano

Vallis Marineris

Polar icecap

. . . **FASCINATING FACT** . . .
The 1997 *Mars Pathfinder* mission showed that many of the rocks on Mars' surface were dumped in their positions by a huge flood at least two billion years ago.

# Jupiter

- **Jupiter** is the biggest planet in the Solar System – twice as heavy as all the other planets put together.

- **Jupiter has no surface** for a spacecraft to land on because it is made mostly from helium gas and hydrogen. The massive pull of Jupiter's gravity squeezes the hydrogen so hard that it is liquid.

- **Towards Jupiter's core,** immense pressure turns the hydrogen to solid metal.

- **The Ancient Greeks** originally named the planet Zeus, after the king of their gods. Jupiter was the Romans' name for Zeus.

- **Jupiter spins right round** in less than ten hours, which means that the planet's surface is moving at nearly 50,000 km/h.

- **Jupiter's speedy spin makes** its middle bulge out. It also churns up the planet's metal core until it generates a hugely powerful magnetic field, ten times as strong as the Earth's.

- **Jupiter has a Great Red Spot** – a huge swirl of red clouds measuring more than 40,000 km across. The scientist Robert Hooke first noticed the spot in 1644.

- **Jupiter's four biggest moons** were first spotted by Galileo in the 17th century. Their names are Io, Europa, Callisto and Ganymede.

- **Jupiter also has 17 smaller moons** – Metis, Adastrea, Amalthea, Thebe, Leda, Himalia, Lysithea, Elara, Ananke, Carme, Pasiphaë, Sinope as well as five recent discoveries.

- **Jupiter is so massive** that the pressure at its heart makes it glow very faintly with invisible infrared rays. Indeed, it glows as brightly as four million billion 100-watt light bulbs. But it is not quite big enough for nuclear reactions to start, and make it become a star.

▼ *Jupiter is a gigantic planet, 142,984 km across. Its orbit takes 11.86 years and varies between 740.9 and 815.7 million km from the Sun. Its surface is often rent by huge lightning flashes and thunderclaps, and temperatures here plunge to −150°C. Looking at Jupiter's surface, all you can see is a swirling mass of red, brown and yellow clouds of ammonia, including the Great Red Spot.*

Great Red Spot

...FASCINATING FACT...
The Galileo space probe reached Jupiter
and its moons in the year 1995.

# Saturn

- **Saturn is the second biggest planet** in the Solar System – 815 times as big in volume as the Earth, and measuring 120,000 km around its equator.

- **Saturn takes 29 and a half years** to travel round the Sun, so Saturn's year is 29.46 Earth years. The planet's complete orbit is a journey of more than 4.5 billion km.

- **Winds ten times stronger than** a hurricane on Earth swirl around Saturn's equator, reaching up to 1100 km/h – and they never let up, even for a moment.

- **Saturn is named after Saturnus,** the Ancient Roman god of seed-time and harvest. He was celebrated in the Roman's wild, Christmas-time festival of Saturnalia.

- **Saturn is not solid,** but is made almost entirely of gas – mostly liquid hydrogen and helium. Only in the planet's very small core is there any solid rock.

- **Because Saturn is so massive,** the pressure at its heart is enough to turn hydrogen solid. That is why there is a layer of metallic hydrogen around the planet's inner core of rock.

- **Saturn is one of the fastest spinning** of all the planets. Despite its size, it rotates in just 11.5 hours – which means it turns round at over 10,000 km/h.

- **Saturn's surface appears** to be almost completely smooth, though *Voyager 1* and *2* did photograph a few small, swirling storms when they flew past.

- **Saturn has a very powerful magnetic field** and sends out strong radio signals.

...FASCINATING FACT...
Saturn is so low in density that if you could find a bath big enough, you would be able to float the planet in the water.

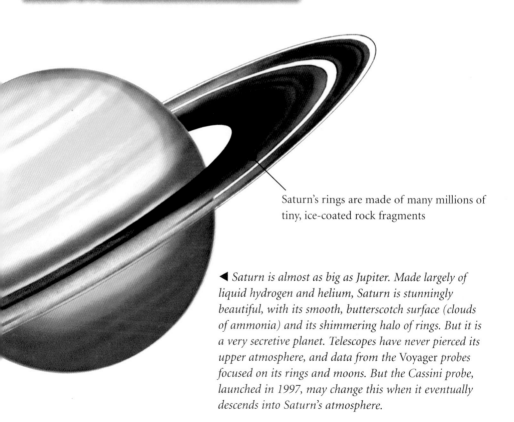

Saturn's rings are made of many millions of tiny, ice-coated rock fragments

◀ *Saturn is almost as big as Jupiter. Made largely of liquid hydrogen and helium, Saturn is stunningly beautiful, with its smooth, butterscotch surface (clouds of ammonia) and its shimmering halo of rings. But it is a very secretive planet. Telescopes have never pierced its upper atmosphere, and data from the* Voyager *probes focused on its rings and moons. But the Cassini probe, launched in 1997, may change this when it eventually descends into Saturn's atmosphere.*

51

# Uranus

- **Uranus is the seventh planet** out from the Sun. Its orbit keeps it 1784 million km away on average and takes 84 years to complete.

- **Uranus tilts so far on its side** that it seems to roll around the Sun like a gigantic bowling ball. The angle of its tilt is 98°, in fact, so its equator runs top to bottom. This tilt may be the result of a collision with a meteor or another planet a long time ago.

- **In summer on Uranus,** the Sun does not set for 20 years. In winter, darkness lasts for over 20 years. In autumn, the Sun rises and sets every nine hours.

- **Uranus has 17 moons,** all named after characters in William Shakespeare's plays. There are five large moons – Ariel, Umbriel, Titania, Oberon and Miranda. The ten smaller ones were discovered by the *Voyager 2* space probe in 1986.

- **Uranus' moon Miranda** is the weirdest moon of all. It seems to have been blasted apart, then put itself back together again!

- **Because Uranus is so far from the Sun,** it is very, very cold, with surface temperatures dropping to -210°C. Sunlight takes just eight minutes to reach Earth, but 2.5 hours to reach Uranus.

- **Uranus' icy atmosphere** is made of hydrogen and helium. Winds whistle around the planet at over 2000 km/h – ten times as fast as hurricanes on Earth.

Uranus has its own, very faint set of rings

● **Uranus' surface** is an ice-cold ocean of liquid methane (natural gas), thousands of kilometres deep, which gives the planet its beautiful colour. If you fell into this ocean even for a fraction of a second, you would freeze so hard that you would shatter like glass.

● **Uranus is only faintly visible** from Earth. It looks no bigger than a star through a telescope, and was not identified until 1781.

● **Uranus was named** after Urania, the ancient Greek goddess of astronomy.

Uranus has an atmosphere of hydrogen and helium gas

◀ *Uranus is the third largest planet in the Solar System – 51,118 km across and with a mass 14.54 times that of the Earth's. The planet spins round once every 17.24 hours, but because it is lying almost on its side, this has almost no effect on the length of its day. Instead, this depends on where the planet is in its orbit of the Sun. Like Saturn, Uranus has rings, but they are much thinner and were only detected in 1977. They are made of the darkest material in the Solar System.*

The planet's surface of liquid methane gives it a stunning blue colour

. . . .FASCINATING FACT. . . .
On Uranus in spring, the Sun sets
every nine hours – backwards!

# Neptune

- **Neptune is the eighth** planet out from the Sun, varying in distance from 4456 to 4537 million km.

- **Neptune was discovered** in 1846 because two mathematicians, John Couch Adams in England and Urbain le Verrier in France, worked out that it must be there because of the effect of its gravity on the movement of Uranus.

- **Neptune is so far** from the Sun that its orbit lasts 164.79 Earth years. Indeed, it has not yet completed one orbit since it was discovered in 1846.

- **Like Uranus,** Neptune has a surface of icy cold liquid methane (-210°C), and an atmosphere of hydrogen and helium.

- **Unlike Uranus,** which is almost perfectly blue, Neptune has white clouds, created by heat inside the planet.

- **Neptune has the strongest winds** in the Solar System, blowing at up to 700 m per second.

- **Neptune has eight moons,** each named after characters from Ancient Greek myths – Naiad, Thalassa, Despoina, Galatea, Larissa, Proteus, Triton and Nereid.

- **Neptune's moon Triton** looks like a green melon, while its icecaps of frozen nitrogen look like pink ice cream. It also has volcanoes that erupt fountains of ice.

- **Triton is the only moon** to orbit backwards.

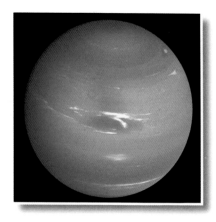

▲ *This photo of Neptune was taken by the* Voyager 2 *spacecraft in 1989. The Great Dark Spot, and the little white tail of clouds, named Scooter by astronomers, are both clearly visible.*

▼ Neptune is the fourth largest planet. At 49,528 km across, it is slightly smaller than Uranus – but it is actually a little heavier. Like Uranus, its oceans of incredibly cold liquid methane make it a beautiful shiny blue, although Neptune's surface is a deeper blue than that of Uranus. Again like Uranus, Neptune has a thin layer of rings. But Neptune's are level, and not at right angles to the Sun. Neptune has a Great Dark Spot, like Jupiter's Great Red Spot, where storms whip up swirling clouds.

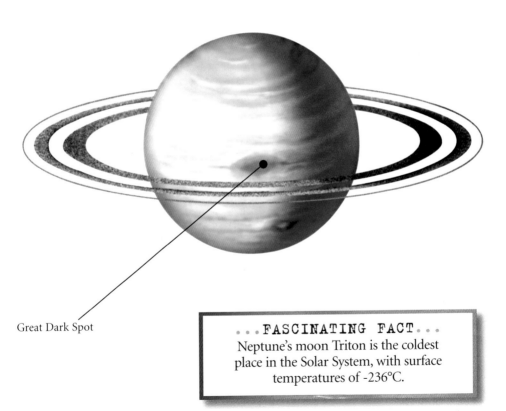

Great Dark Spot

...FASCINATING FACT...
Neptune's moon Triton is the coldest place in the Solar System, with surface temperatures of -236°C.

55

# Pluto

- **Pluto was the last** of all the planets to be discovered, and it was only found because it has a slight effect on the orbits of Neptune and Uranus.

- **Pluto is the furthest out** of the planets, varying from 4730 to 7375 million km from the Sun.

- **The Sun is so far from Pluto** that if you could stand on the planet's surface, the Sun would look no bigger than a star in Earth's sky and shine no more brightly than the Moon does.

- **Pluto's orbit** is so far from the Sun that it takes 248.54 years just to travel right around once. This means that a year on Pluto lasts almost three Earth centuries. A day, however, lasts just under a week.

- **Pluto has a strange elliptical (oval) orbit** which actually brings it closer to the Sun than Neptune for a year or two every few centuries.

- **Unlike all the other planets** which orbit on exactly the same plane (level) as the Earth, Pluto's orbit cuts across diagonally.

▲ *Pluto is tiny in comparison to the Earth, which is why it was so hard to find. Earth is five times bigger and 500 times as heavy. This illustration shows the relative sizes of the Earth and Pluto.*

- **While studying** a photo of Pluto in 1978, American astronomer James Christy noticed a bump. This turned out to be a large moon, which was later named Charon.

- **Charon** is about half the size of Pluto and they orbit one another, locked together like a weightlifter's dumbbells.

- **Charon** always stays in the same place in Pluto's sky, looking three times as big as our Moon.

● **Unlike the other outer planets,** Pluto is made from rock. But the rock is covered in water, ice and a thin layer of frozen methane.

Daytime temperatures on Pluto's surface are -220°C or less, so the surface is thought to be coated in frozen methane.

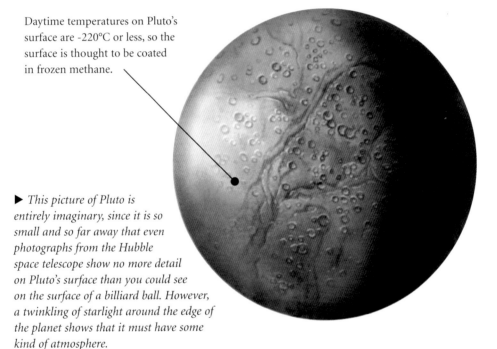

▶ *This picture of Pluto is entirely imaginary, since it is so small and so far away that even photographs from the Hubble space telescope show no more detail on Pluto's surface than you could see on the surface of a billiard ball. However, a twinkling of starlight around the edge of the planet shows that it must have some kind of atmosphere.*

> . . . **FASCINATING FACT** . . .
> Pluto was discovered on 18 February 1930 by young American astronomer Clyde Tombaugh.

57

# Asteroids

- **Asteroids** are lumps of rock that orbit the Sun. They are sometimes called the minor planets.

- **Most asteroids** are in the Asteroid Belt, which lies between Mars and Jupiter.

- **Some distant asteroids** are made of ice and orbit the Sun beyond Neptune.

- **A few asteroids** come near the Earth. These are called Near Earth Objects.

- **The first asteroid to be discovered** was Ceres in 1801. It was detected by Giuseppi Piazzi, one of the Celestial Police whose mission was to find a 'missing' planet.

- **Ceres** is the biggest asteroid – 940 km across, and 0.0002 percent the size of the Earth.

- **The *Galileo* space probe** took close-up pictures of the asteroids Ida and Gaspra in 1991 and 1993.

- **There are half a million or so** asteroids bigger than 1 km across. More than 200 asteroids are over 100 km across.

- **The Trojan asteroids** are groups of asteroids that follow the same orbit as Jupiter. Many are named after warriors in the ancient Greek tales of the Trojan wars.

Jupiter

Mars

▲ *Most asteroids – more than half a million – orbit the Sun in the Asteroid Belt, between Mars and Jupiter.*

...FASCINATING FACT...
Every 50 million years, the Earth is hit by an asteroid measuring over 10 km across.

# Comets

- **Comets are bright objects** with long tails, which we sometimes see streaking across the night sky.

- **They may look spectacular,** but a comet is just a dirty ball of ice a few kilometres across.

- **Many comets orbit the Sun,** but their orbits are very long and they spend most of the time in the far reaches of the Solar System. We see them when their orbit brings them close to the Sun for a few weeks.

- **A comet's tail** is made as it nears the Sun and begins to melt. A vast plume of gas millions of kilometres across is blown out behind by the solar wind. The tail is what you see, shining as the sunlight catches it.

- **Comets called periodics** appear at regular intervals.

- **Some comets reach speeds** of two million km/h as they near the Sun.

- **Far away from the Sun,** comets slow down to 1000 km/h or so – that is why they stay away for so long.

- **The visit of the comet Hale-Bopp** in 1997 gave the brightest view of a comet since 1811, visible even from brightly lit cities.

- **The Shoemaker-Levy 9 comet** smashed into Jupiter in July 1994, with the biggest crash ever witnessed.

- **The most famous comet** of all is Halley's comet.

▲ *The tail of a comet always points away from the Sun.*

▶ *Comet Kahoutek streaks through the night sky.*

# The Moon

- **The Moon** is 384,400 km from the Earth and about 25 percent of Earth's size.

- **The Moon** orbits the Earth once every month, with each orbit taking 27.3 days. It spins round once on its axis every 720 hours.

- **The Moon** is the brightest object in the night sky, but it does not give out any light itself. It shines only because its light-coloured surface reflects sunlight.

- **Only the side of the Moon** lit by the Sun is bright enough to see. And because we see more of this side each month as the Moon orbits the Earth, and then less again, the Moon seems to change shape. These changes are called the Moon's phases.

- **During the first half of each monthly cycle,** the Moon waxes (grows) from a crescent-shaped new moon to a full moon. During the second half, it wanes (dwindles) back to a crescent-shaped old moon.

▲ *The Moon is the only other world that humans have ever set foot on. Because the Moon has no atmosphere or wind, the footprints planted in its dusty surface in 1969 by the* Apollo *astronauts are still there today, perfectly preserved.*

- **A lunar month** is the time between one full moon and the next. This is longer than the time the Moon takes to orbit the Earth because the Earth is moving.

- **The Moon has no atmosphere** and its surface is simply grey dust, pitted with craters created by meteorites smashing into it early in its history.

- **On the Moon's surface** are large, dark patches called seas – because that is what people once believed they were. They are, in fact, lava flows from ancient volcanoes.

- **One side of the Moon** is always turned away from us and is called its dark side. This is because the Moon spins round on its axis at exactly the same speed that it orbits the Earth.

▶ *Unlike the Earth's surface, which changes by the hour, the Moon's dusty, crater-pitted surface has remained much the same for billions of years. The only change happens when a meteorite smashes into it and creates a new crater.*

...FASCINATING FACT...
The Moon's gravity is 17 percent of the Earth's, so astronauts in space suits can jump 4 m high!

# The Sun

- **The Sun** is a medium-sized star measuring 1,392,000 km across.

- **The Sun weighs** 2000 trillion trillion tonnes – about 300,000 times as much as the Earth – even though it is made almost entirely of hydrogen and helium, the lightest gases in the Universe.

- **The Sun's interior** is heated by nuclear reactions to temperatures of 15 million °C.

- **The visible surface layer of the Sun** is called the photosphere. This sea of boiling gas sends out the light and heat we see and feel on Earth.

- **Above the photosphere** is the chromosphere, a thin layer through which dart tongues of flame called spicules, making the chromosphere look like a flaming forest.

- **Above the chromosphere** is the Sun's halo-like corona.

- **The heat from the Sun's interior** erupts on the surface in patches called granules, and gigantic, flame-like tongues of hot gases called solar prominences.

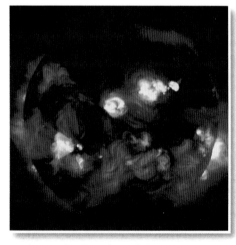

▲ *This artificially coloured photo was taken by a space satellite and shows the Sun's surface to be a turbulent mass of flames and tongues of hot gases – very different from the even, yellowish ball we see from Earth.*

- **The Sun gets hot** because it is so big that the pressure in its core is tremendous – enough to force the nuclei of hydrogen atoms to fuse (join together) to make helium atoms. This nuclear fusion reaction is like a gigantic atom bomb and it releases huge amounts of heat.

- **Halfway out from its centre** to its surface, the Sun is about as dense as water. Two-thirds of the way out, it is as dense as air.

- **The nuclear fusion reactions** in the Sun's core send out billions of light photons every minute – but they take 10 million years to reachits surface.

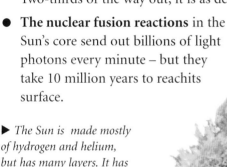

prominence

sunspot

▶ *The Sun is made mostly of hydrogen and helium, but has many layers. It has a core, where most heat is made, then a number of layers building to the flaming chromosphere on its surface.*

....FASCINATING FACT....
The temperature of the Sun's surface is 6000°C. Each centimetre burns with the brightness of 250,000 candles!

# Space exploration

- **Space is explored** in two ways – by studying it from Earth using powerful telescopes, and by launching spacecraft to get a closer view.

- **Most space exploration** is by unmanned space probes.

- **The first pictures** of the far side of the Moon were sent back by the *Luna 3* space probe in October 1959.

- **Manned missions** have only reached as far as the Moon, but there may be a manned mission to Mars in 2020.

- **Apollo astronauts** took three days to reach the Moon.

- **No space probe** has ever come back from another planet.

- **Travel to the stars** would take hundreds of years, but one idea is that humans might go there inside gigantic spaceships made from hollowed-out asteroids.

- **Another idea is that spacecraft** on long voyages of exploration may be driven along by pulses of laser light.

- **The *Pioneer 10* and *11* probes** carry metal plaques with messages for aliens telling them about us.

> ....FASCINATING FACT....
> NASA may fund research on spacecraft
> that jump to the stars through wormholes.

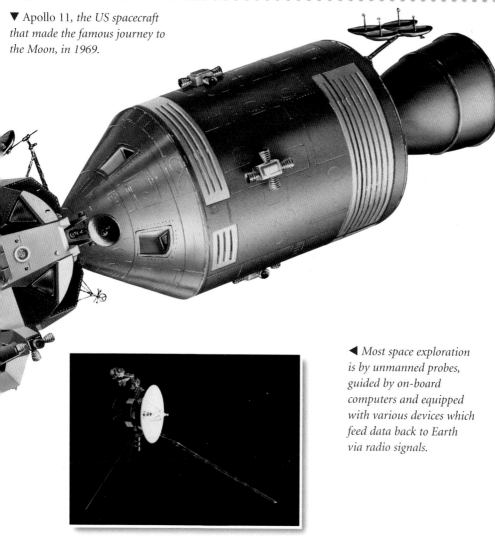

▼ Apollo 11, *the US spacecraft that made the famous journey to the Moon, in 1969.*

◀ *Most space exploration is by unmanned probes, guided by on-board computers and equipped with various devices which feed data back to Earth via radio signals.*

# Satellites

- **Satellites are objects** that orbit planets and other space objects. Moons are natural satellites. Spacecraft sent up to orbit the Earth and the Sun are artificial satellites.

- **The first artificial satellite** was *Sputnik 1*, launched on 4 October 1957.

- **About 100 artificial satellites** are now launched every year. A few of them are space telescopes.

- **Communications satellites** beam everything from TV pictures to telephone calls around the world.

- **Observation satellites** scan the Earth and are used for purposes such as scientific research, weather forecasting and spying.

▲ *One of the many hundreds of satellites now in Earth's orbit.*

- **Navigation satellites** such as the Global Positioning System (GPS) are used by people such as airline pilots to work out exactly where they are.

- **Satellites are launched** at a particular speed and trajectory (path) to place them in just the right orbit.

- **The lower a satellite's orbit,** the faster it must fly to avoid falling back to Earth. Most satellites fly in low orbits, 500 km above the Earth.

- **A geostationary orbit** is 35,786 km up. Satellites in geostationary orbit over the Equator always stay in exactly the same place above the Earth.

- **Polar orbiting satellites** circle the Earth from pole to pole about 850 km up, covering a different strip of the Earth's surface on each orbit.

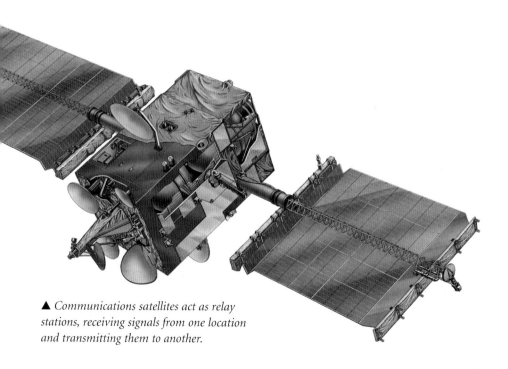

▲ *Communications satellites act as relay stations, receiving signals from one location and transmitting them to another.*

# Space shuttle

- **The space shuttle** is a reusable spacecraft, made up of a 37.2-m-long orbiter, two big Solid Rocket Boosters (SRBs), three main engines and a tank.

- **The shuttle orbiter is launched** into space upright on SRBs, which fall away to be collected for reuse. When the mission is over the orbiter lands like a glider.

- **The orbiter can go** as high as a near-Earth orbit, some 300 km above the Earth.

- **The maximum crew** is eight, and a basic mission is seven days, during which the crew work in shirtsleeves.

- **Orbiter toilets** use flowing air to suck away waste.

- **The orbiter can carry** a 25,000 kg-load in its cargo bay.

- **The first four orbiters** were named after old sailing ships – *Columbia*, *Challenger*, *Discovery* and *Atlantis*.

- **The three main engines** are used only for lift-off. In space, the small Orbital Manoeuvring System (OMS) engines take over. The Reaction Control System (RCS) makes small adjustments to the orbiter's position.

◀ *In future, faster space planes may take over from shuttles, so that humans can visit other planets.*

● **The shuttle programme** was brought to a temporary halt in 1986, when the *Challenger* exploded shortly after launch, killing its crew of seven.

● **In 1994 the crew of *Discovery*** mended the Hubble space telescope in orbit.

▲ *The entire centre section of the orbiter is a cargo bay which can be opened in space so satellites can be placed in orbit.*

# The Earth

- **The Earth is the third planet** out from the Sun, 149.6 million km away on average. On 3 January, at the nearest point of its orbit (called the perihelion), the Earth is 147,097,800 km away from the Sun. On 4 July, at its furthest (the aphelion), it is 152,098,200 km away.

- **The Earth is the fifth largest planet** in the Solar System, with a diameter of 12,756 km and a circumference of 40,024 km at the Equator.

- **The Earth is one of four rocky planets,** along with Mercury, Venus and Mars. It is made mostly of rock, with a core of iron and nickel.

- **No other planet in the solar system** has water on its surface, which is why Earth is uniquely suitable for life. Over 70 percent of Earth's surface is under water.

- **The Earth's atmosphere** is mainly harmless nitrogen and life-giving oxygen, and it is over 700 km deep. The oxygen has been made and maintained by plants over billions of years.

- **The Earth formed 4.65 billion years** ago from clouds of space dust whirling around the Sun. The planet was so hot that it was molten at first. Only slowly did the surface cool into a hard crust.

- **The Earth's orbit** around the Sun is 939,886,400 km long and takes 365.242 days.

▲ *The Earth from space. It is the only planet known to support life.*

- **The Earth is tilted** at an angle of 23.5°. Even so, it orbits the Sun in a level plane, called the plane of the ecliptic.

- **The Earth is made up** of the same basic materials as meteorites and the other rocky planets – mostly iron (35 percent), oxygen (28 percent), magnesium (17 percent), silicon (13 percent) and nickel (2.7 percent).

◄ *Most of the Earth's rocky crust is drowned beneath oceans, formed from steam belched out by volcanoes early in the planet's history. The Earth is just the right distance from the Sun for surface temperatures to stay an average 15°C, and keep most of its water liquid.*

... **FASCINATING FACT** ...
The Earth is protected from the Sun's radiation by a magnetic field, which stretches 60,000 km out into space.

# Formation of the Earth

- **The Solar System** was created when the gas cloud left over from a giant supernova explosion started to collapse in on itself and spin.

- **About 4.55 billion years ago** there was just a vast, hot cloud of dust and gas circling a new star, our Sun.

- **The Earth probably began** when tiny pieces of space debris (called planetesimals) began to clump together, pulled together by each other's gravity.

- **As the Earth formed,** more space debris kept on smashing into it, adding new material. This debris included ice from the edges of the Solar System.

- **About 4.5 billion years ago,** a rock the size of Mars crashed into Earth. Splashes of material from this crash clumped together to form the Moon.

- **The collision** that formed the Moon made the Earth very hot.

- **Radioactive decay** heated the Earth even further.

- **For a long time** the surface of the Earth was a mass of erupting volcanoes.

- **Iron and nickel melted** and sank to form the core.

▲ *Earth and the Solar System formed from a cloud of gas and dust.*

- **Aluminium,** oxygen and silicon floated up and cooled to form the crust.

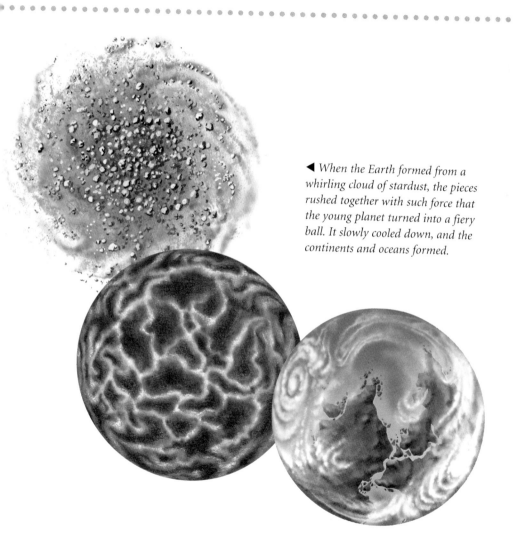

◀ When the Earth formed from a whirling cloud of stardust, the pieces rushed together with such force that the young planet turned into a fiery ball. It slowly cooled down, and the continents and oceans formed.

# The ages of the Earth

- **The Earth formed 4570 million years ago** (mya) but the first animals with shells and bones appeared less than 600 million years ago. It is mainly with the help of their fossils that geologists have learned about the Earth's history since then. We know very little about the 4000 million years before, known as Precambrian Time.

- **Just as days are divided** into hours and minutes, so geologists divide the Earth's history into time periods. The longest are eons, thousands of millions of years long. The shortest are chrons, a few thousand years long. In between come eras, periods, epochs and ages.

- **The years since Precambrian Time** are split into three eras: Palaeozoic, Mesozoic and Cenozoic.

- **Different plants and animals** lived at different times, so geologists can tell from the fossils in rocks how long ago the rocks formed. Using fossils, they have divided the Earth's history since Precambrian Time into 11 periods.

2 mya

Quaternary Period: many mammals die out in Ice Ages; humans evolve

65 mya

Tertiary Period: first large mammals; birds flourish; widespread grasslands

144 mya

Cretaceous Period: first flowering plants; the dinosaurs die out

213 mya

Jurassic Period: dinosaurs widespread; Archaeopteryx, earliest known bird

248 mya

Triassic Period: first mammals; seed-bearing plants spread; Europe is in the tropics

286 mya

Permian Period: conifers replace ferns as big trees; deserts are widespread

- **Layers of rock** form on top of each other, so the oldest rocks are usually at the bottom and the youngest at the top, unless they have been disturbed. The order of layers from top to bottom is known as the geological column.

- **By looking for certain fossils** geologists can tell if one layer of rock is older than another.

- **Fossils can only show** if a rock is older or younger than another; they cannot give a date in years. Also, many rocks contain no fossils. To give an absolute date, radiocarbon dating is used.

- **Radiocarbon dating** allows the oldest rocks to be dated. After certain substances, such as uranium and rubidium, form in rocks, their atoms. This sends out rays, or radioactivity. By assessing how many atoms in a rock have changed, geologists work out the rock's age.

- **Breaks in the sequence** of the geological column are called unconformities.

360 mya

Carboniferous Period: vast warm swamps of fern forests which form coal; first reptiles

408 mya

Devonian Period: first insects and amphibians; ferns and mosses as big as trees

438 mya

Silurian Period: first land plants; fish with jaws and freshwater fish

505 mya

Ordovician Period: early fish-like vertebrates appear; the Sahara is glaciated

590 mya

Cambrian Period: no life on land, but shellfish flourish in the oceans

Precambrian Time: the first life forms (bacteria) appear, and give the air oxygen

# Shape of the Earth

- **The study of the shape of the Earth** is called geodesy. In the past, geodesy depended on ground-based surveys. Today, satellites play a major role.

- **The Earth is not a perfect sphere.** It is a unique shape called a geoid, which means 'Earth shaped'.

- **The Earth spins** faster at the Equator than at the Poles, because the Equator is farther from the Earth's spinning axis.

- **The extra speed** of the Earth at the Equator flings it out in a bulge, while it is flattened at the Poles.

- **Equatorial bulge** was predicted in 1687 by Isaac Newton.

- **The equatorial bulge** was confirmed 70 years after Newton – by French surveys in Peru by Charles de La Condamine, and in Lapland by Pierre de Maupertuis.

- **The Earth's diameter** at the Equator is 12,758 km. This is larger, by 43 km, than the vertical diameter from North Pole to South Pole.

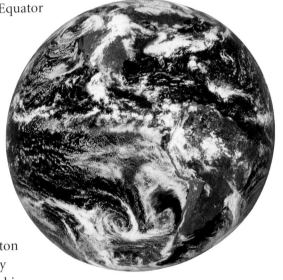

▲ *The ancient Greeks realized that the Earth is a globe. Satellite measurements show that it is not quite perfectly round.*

- **The official measurement** of the Earth's radius at the Equator is 6,376,136 m plus or minus 1 m.

- **The Lageos** (Laser Geodynamic) satellite launched in 1976 has measured gravitational differences with extreme precision. It has revealed bumps up to 100 m high, notably just south of India.

- **The Seasat** satellite confirmed the ocean surfaces are geoid. It took millions of measurements of the height of the ocean surface, accurate to within a few centimetres.

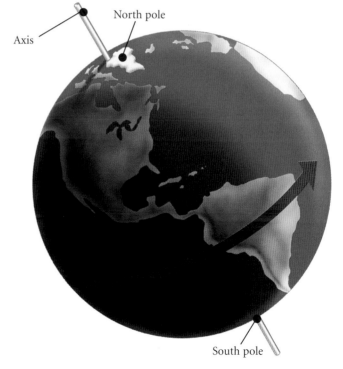

▶ *The Earth rotates around its axis, the imaginary line running through the centre of the planet from pole to pole at an angle of 23.5°.*

North pole

Axis

South pole

# The Earth's chemistry

- **The bulk of the Earth** is made from iron, oxygen, magnesium and silicon.

- **More than 80 chemical elements** occur naturally in the Earth and its atmosphere.

- **The crust** is made mostly from oxygen and silicon, with aluminium, iron, calcium, magnesium, sodium, potassium, titanium and traces of 64 other elements.

- **The upper mantle** is made up of iron and magnesium silicates; the lower is silicon and magnesium sulphides and oxides.

- **The core** is mostly iron, with a little nickel and traces of sulphur, carbon, oxygen and potassium.

- **Evidence for the Earth's chemistry** comes from analysing densities with the help of earthquake waves, and from studying stars, meteorites and other planets.

- **When the Earth** was still semi-molten, dense elements such as iron sank to form the core. Lighter elements such as oxygen floated up to form the crust.

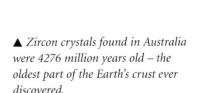

▲ *Zircon crystals found in Australia were 4276 million years old – the oldest part of the Earth's crust ever discovered.*

- **Some heavy elements,** such as uranium, ended up in the crust because they easily make compounds with oxygen and silicon.

- **Large blobs of elements** that combine easily with sulphur, such as zinc and lead, spread through the mantle.

- **Elements that combine with iron,** such as gold and nickel, sank to the core.

▼ *This diagram shows the percentages of the chemical elements that make up the Earth.*

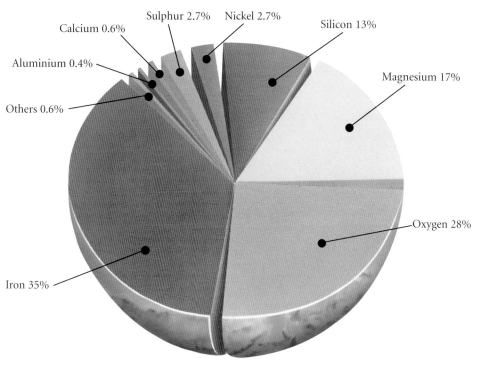

Sulphur 2.7%  Nickel 2.7%

Calcium 0.6%

Silicon 13%

Aluminium 0.4%

Magnesium 17%

Others 0.6%

Oxygen 28%

Iron 35%

# Earth's interior

- **The Earth's crust** is a thin hard outer shell of rock which is a few dozen kilometres thick.

- **Under the crust,** there is a deep layer of hot soft rock called the mantle.

- **The crust and upper mantle** can be divided into three layers according to their rigidity – the lithosphere, the asthenosphere and the mesosphere.

- **Beneath the mantle** is a core of hot iron and nickel. The outer core is so hot – climbing from 4500°C to 6000°C – that it is always molten. The inner core is even hotter (up to 7000°C) but it stays solid because the pressure is 6000 times greater than on the surface.

- **The inner core** contains 1.7 percent of the Earth's mass, the outer core 30.8 percent; the core–mantle boundary 3 percent; the lower mantle 49 percent; the upper mantle 15 percent; the ocean crust 0.099 percent and the continental crust 0.374 percent.

- **Satellite measurements** are so accurate they can detect slight lumps and dents in the Earth's surface. These indicate where gravity is stronger or weaker because of differences in rock density. Variations in gravity reveal things such as mantle plumes.

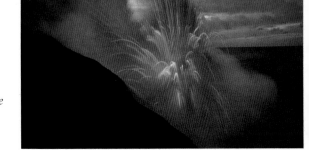

▶ *Hot material from the Earth's interior often bursts on to the surface from volcanoes.*

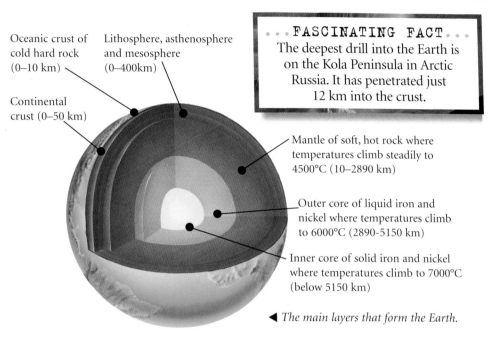

Oceanic crust of cold hard rock (0–10 km)

Lithosphere, asthenosphere and mesosphere (0–400km)

Continental crust (0–50 km)

**FASCINATING FACT**
The deepest drill into the Earth is on the Kola Peninsula in Arctic Russia. It has penetrated just 12 km into the crust.

Mantle of soft, hot rock where temperatures climb steadily to 4500°C (10–2890 km)

Outer core of liquid iron and nickel where temperatures climb to 6000°C (2890-5150 km)

Inner core of solid iron and nickel where temperatures climb to 7000°C (below 5150 km)

◀ *The main layers that form the Earth.*

- **Our knowledge of the Earth's interior** comes mainly from studying how earthquake waves move through different kinds of rock.

- **Analysis of how earthquake waves** are deflected reveals where different materials occur in the interior. S (secondary) waves pass only through the mantle. P (primary) waves pass through the core as well. P waves passing through the core are deflected, leaving a shadow zone where no waves reach the far side of the Earth.

- **The speed of earthquake waves** reveals how dense the rocky materials are. Cold, hard rock transmits waves more quickly than hot, soft rock.

# Crust

- **The Earth's crust** is its hard outer shell.

- **The crust** is a thin layer of rock that floats on the mantle. It is made mainly of silicate minerals (minerals made of silicon and oxygen) such as quartz.

- **There are two kinds of crust** – oceanic and continental.

- **Oceanic crust** is the crust beneath the oceans. It is much thinner – just 7 km thick on average. It is also young, with none being over 200 million years old.

- **Continental crust** is the crust beneath the continents. It is up to 80 km thick and mostly old.

- **Continental crust** is mostly crystalline 'basement' rock up to 3800 million years old. Some geologists think at least half of this rock is over 2500 million years old.

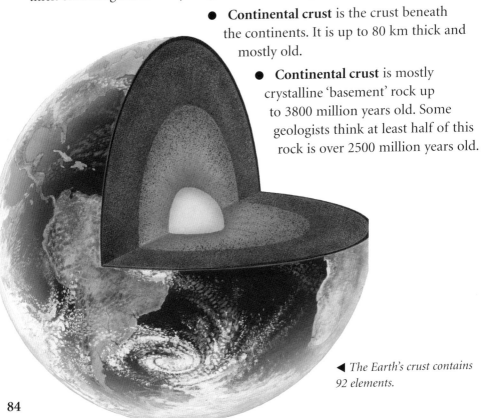

◄ *The Earth's crust contains 92 elements.*

- **It is estimated** that approximately one cubic kilometre of new continental crust is probably being created each year.

- **The 'basement' rock** has two main layers – an upper half of silica-rich rocks such as granite, schist and gneiss, and a lower half of volcanic rocks such as basalt which have less silica. Ocean crust is mostly basalt.

- **Continental crust** is created in the volcanic arcs above subduction zones. Molten rock from the subducted plate oozes to the surface over a period of a few hundred thousand years.

- **The boundary** between the crust and the mantle beneath it is called the Mohorovicic discontinuity.

▶ *The Horn of Africa and the Red Sea is one of the places where the Earth's thin oceanic crust is cracked and moving. It is gradually widening the Red Sea.*

# Tectonic plates

- **The Earth's surface** is divided into slabs called tectonic plates. Each plate is a fragment of the Earth's rigid outer layer, or lithosphere.

- **There are 16 large plates** and several smaller ones. Plates are approximately 100 km thick but can vary in thickness from 8 km to 200 km.

- **The biggest plate** is the Pacific plate, which underlies the whole of the Pacific Ocean. The Pacific Ocean represents half of the world's ocean area.

- **Tectonic plates** are moving all the time – by about 10 cm a year. Over hundreds of millions of years they move vast distances. Some have moved halfway round the globe.

- **The continents** are embedded in the tops of the plates, so as the plates move the continents move with them.

- **The Pacific plate** is the only large plate with no part of a continent situated on it.It represents more than one-third of the Earth's surface area.

- **The movement** of tectonic plates accounts for many things, including the pattern of volcanic and earthquake activity around the world.

▲ *Beneath the Pacific Ocean lies the Pacific plate, the largest of the tectonic plates.*

- **There are three kinds** of boundary between plates: convergent, divergent and transform.

- **Tectonic plates** are probably driven by convection currents of molten rock that circulate within the Earth's mantle.

- **The lithosphere** was too thin for tectonic plates until 500 million years ago.

▼ *This map shows some of the jagged boundaries between plates.*

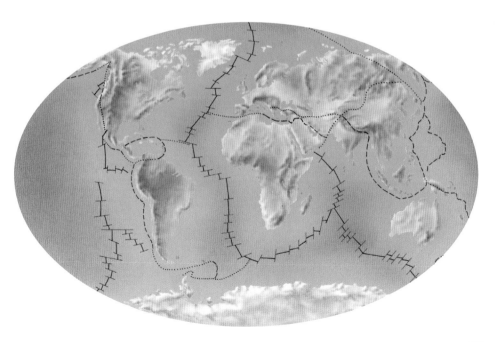

# Rocks

▲ *The Kent coast near Dover is famous for its white cliffs which are made of chalk.*

- **The oldest known rocks** on Earth are 3900 million years old – they are the Acasta gneiss rocks from Canada.

- **There are three main kinds of rock** – igneous rock, sedimentary rock and metamorphic rock.

- **Igneous rocks** (igneous means 'fiery') are made when hot molten magma or lava cools and solidifies.

- **Volcanic rocks,** such as basalt, are igneous rocks that form from lava that has erupted from volcanoes.

- **Metamorphic rocks** are rocks that have changed over time, such as limestone which is made into marble because of the heat generated by magma.

- **Sedimentary rocks** are rocks that are made from the slow hardening of sediments into layers, or strata.

- **Some sedimentary rocks,** such as sandstone, are made from sand and silt. Other rocks are broken down into these materials by weathering and erosion.

- **Most sediments** form on the seabed. Sand is washed down onto the seabed by rivers.

- **Limestone and chalk** are sedimentary rocks made mainly from the remains of sea creatures.

▶ *Rocks are continually recycled. Whether they form from volcanoes or sediments, all rocks are broken down into sand by weathering and erosion. The sand is deposited on seabeds and riverbeds where it hardens to form new rock. This process is the rock cycle.*

# Fossils

- **Fossils** are the remains of living things preserved for millions of years, usually in stone.

- **Most fossils** are the remains of living things such as bones, shells, eggs, leaves and seeds.

- **Trace fossils** are fossils of signs left behind by creatures, such as footprints and scratch marks.

- **Paleontologists** (scientists who study fossils) tell the age of a fossil from the rock layer in which it is found. Also, they measure how the rock has changed radioactively since it was formed (radiocarbon dating).

- **The oldest fossils** are called stromatolites. They are fossils of big, pizza-like colonies of microscopic bacteria over 3500 million years old.

▼ *Scientists study fossils to learn about the Earth's history and about the animals and plants that lived millions of years ago.*

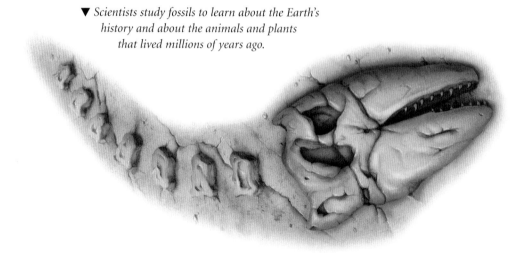

▶ When an animal dies, its soft parts rot away quickly. If its bones or shell are buried quickly in mud, they may turn to stone. When a shellfish such as this ancient trilobite dies and sinks to the sea-bed, its shell is buried. Over millions of years, water trickling through the mud may dissolve the shell, but minerals in the water fill its place to make a perfect cast.

- **The biggest fossils** are conyphytons, 2000-million-year-old stromatolites over 100 m high.

- **Not all fossils** are stone. Mammoths have been preserved by being frozen in the permafrost of Siberia.

- **Insects** have been preserved in amber, the solidified sap of ancient trees.

- **Certain widespread, short-lived fossils** are very useful for dating rock layers. These are known as index fossils.

- **Index fossils** include ancient shellfish such as trilobites, graptolites, crinoids, belemnites, ammonites and brachiopods.

1. A trilobite dies on the ocean floor long ago.

2. The trilobite's soft parts eventually rot away.

3. The shell is slowly buried by mud.

4. Mineral-rich waters dissolve the shell.

5. New minerals fill the mould to form a fossil.

# Minerals

- **Minerals** are the natural chemicals from which rocks are made.

- **All but a few minerals** are crystals.

- **Some rocks are made** from crystals of just one mineral; many are made from half a dozen or more minerals.

- **Most minerals** are combinations of two or more chemical elements. A few minerals, such as gold and copper, are made of just one element.

- **There are over 2000** minerals, but around 30 of these are very common.

- **Most of the less common** minerals are present in rocks in minute traces. They may become concentrated in certain places by geological processes.

- **Silicate minerals** are made when metals join with oxygen and silicon. There are more silicate minerals than all the other minerals together.

- **The most common** silicates are quartz and feldspar, the most common rock-forming minerals. They are major constituents in granite and other volcanic rocks.

Quartz

Galena

Pyrite

▶ *Minerals include common substances such as rock salt and rare ones such as gold and gems.*

▶ *The rich range of colours in each layer is evidence of traces of different minerals within the rocks.*

● **Other common minerals** are oxides such as haematite and cuprite, sulphates such as gypsum and barite, sulphides such as galena and pyrite, and carbonates such as calcite and aragonite.

● **Some minerals** form as hot, molten rock from the Earth's interior, some from chemicals dissolved in liquids underground, and some are made by changes to other minerals.

Gypsum

Barite

Calcite

93

# Gems and crystals

- **Gems** are mineral crystals that are beautifully coloured or sparkling.

- **There are over 3000 minerals** but only 130 are gemstones. Only about 50 of these are commonly used.

- **The rarest gems** are called precious gems and include diamonds, emeralds and rubies.

- **Less rare gems** are known as semi-precious gems.

- **Gems** are weighed in carats. A carat is one-fifth of a gram. A 50-carat sapphire is very large and very valuable.

- **In the ancient world** gems were weighed with carob seeds. The word 'carat' comes from the Arabic for seed.

▶ *Many minerals are made as magma cools. When this happens crystals, such as amethyst crystals, are formed.*

Diamond

Garnet

▶ *There are more than 100 different kinds of gemstone.*

- **Gems** often form in gas bubbles called geodes in cooling magma. They can also form when hot magma packed with minerals seeps up through cracks in the rock to form a vein.

- **When magma** cools, minerals with the highest melting points crystallize first. Unusual minerals are left behind to crystallize last, forming rocks called pegmatites. These rocks are often rich in gems such as emeralds, garnets, topazes and tourmalines.

- **Some gems** with a high melting point and simple chemical composition form directly from magma, such as diamond, which is pure carbon, and rubies.

Topaz

Emerald

> ...FASCINATING FACT...
> Diamonds are among the oldest mineral crystals, over 3000 million years old.

95

# Seasons

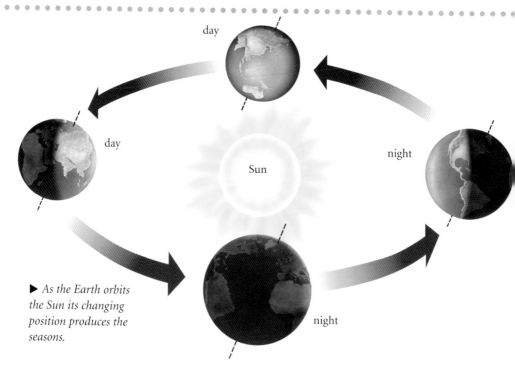

day

day

Sun

night

night

▶ As the Earth orbits the Sun its changing position produces the seasons.

- **Seasons** are periods in a year that bring changes in weather and temperature.

- **Outside the tropics** there are four seasons each year. Each one lasts about three months.

- **The changes in the seasons** occur because the tilt of the Earth's axis is always the same as it circles the Sun.

- **When the Earth** is on one side of the Sun, the Northern Hemisphere (half of the world) is tilted towards the Sun. It is summer in the north of the world and winter in the south.

- **As the Earth moves** a quarter way round the Sun, the northern half begins to tilt away. This brings cooler autumn weather to the north and spring to the south.

- **When the Earth** moves another quarter round to the far side of the Sun, the Northern Hemisphere is tilted away from the Sun. It is winter in the north of the world, and summer in the south.

- **As the Earth moves** three-quarters of the way round the Sun, the north begins to tilt towards the Sun again. This brings the warmer weather of spring to the north, and autumn to the south.

- **Around March 21** and September 21, the night is exactly 12 hours long all over the world. These times are called the vernal (spring) equinox and the autumnal equinox.

- **The day when** nights begin to get longer again is called the summer solstice. This is around June 21 in the north and December 21 in the south.

- **Many places** in the tropics have just two six-month seasons – wet and dry.

▲ *In autumn, the leaves of deciduous trees change colour then drop off ready for winter. Nights grow cooler, and a mist will often develop by morning.*

97

# Volcanoes

- **Volcanoes** are places where magma (red-hot liquid rock from the Earth's interior) emerges through the crust and onto the surface.

- **The word 'volcano'** comes from Vulcano Island in the Mediterranean. Here Vulcan, the ancient Roman god of fire and blacksmith to the gods, was supposed to have forged his weapons in the fire beneath the mountain.

- **There are many types** of volcano. The most distinctive are the cone-shaped composite volcanoes, which build up from alternating layers of ash and lava in successive eruptions.

- **Beneath a composite volcano** there is typically a large reservoir of magma called a magma chamber. Magma collects in the chamber before an eruption.

- **From the magma chamber** a narrow chimney, or vent, leads up to the surface. It passes through the cone of debris from previous eruptions.

- **When a volcano erupts,** the magma is driven up the vent by the gases within it. As the magma nears the surface, the pressure drops, allowing the gases dissolved in the magma to boil out. The expanding gases – mostly carbon dioxide and steam – push the molten rock upwards and out of the vent.

> **...FASCINATING FACT...**
> At Urgüp, Turkey, volcanic ash has been
> blown into tall cones by gas fumes
> bubbling up. The cones have hardened
> like huge salt cellars. People have dug
> them out to make homes.

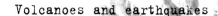

- **If the level of magma** in the magma chamber drops, the top of the volcano's cone may collapse into it, forming a giant crater called a caldera. Caldera is Spanish for 'boiling pot'. The world's largest caldera is Toba on Sumatra, Indonesia, which is 1775 sq km.

- **When a volcano** with a caldera subsides, the whole cone may collapse into the old magma chamber. The caldera may fill with water to form a crater lake, such as Crater Lake in Oregon, USA.

- **All the magma** does not gush up the central vent. Some exits through branching side vents, often forming their own small 'parasitic' cones on the side of the main one.

Volcanic bombs, or tephra, are fragments of the shattered volcanic plug flung out far and wide

Before each eruption, the vent is clogged by old volcanic material from previous eruptions. The explosion blows the plug into tiny pieces of ash and cinder, and blasts them high into the air

Central vent

Side vent

Magma chamber where magma collects before an eruption

# Earthquakes

- **Earthquakes** are a shaking of the ground. Some are slight tremors that barely rock a cradle. Others are so violent they can tear down mountains.

- **Small earthquakes** may be set off by landslides, volcanoes or even just heavy traffic. Big earthquakes are set off by the grinding together of the vast tectonic plates that make up the Earth's surface.

- **Tectonic plates** are sliding past each other all the time, but sometimes they stick. The rock bends and stretches for a while and then snaps. This makes the plates jolt, sending out the shock waves that cause the earthquake's effects to be felt far away.

- **Tectonic plates** typically slide 4 or 5 cm past each other in a year. In a slip that triggers a major quake they can slip more than 1 m in a few seconds.

- **In most quakes** a few minor tremors (foreshocks) are followed by an intense burst lasting just one or two minutes. A second series of minor tremors (aftershocks) occurs over the next few hours.

- **The starting point** of an earthquake below ground is called the hypocentre, or focus. The epicentre of an earthquake is the point on the surface directly above the hypocentre.

- **Earthquakes are strongest** at the epicentre and become gradually weaker farther away.

- **Certain regions** called earthquake zones are especially prone to earthquakes. Earthquake zones lie along the edges of tectonic plates.

- **A shallow earthquake** originates 0–70 km below the ground. These are the ones that do the most damage. An intermediate quake begins 70–300 km down. Deep quakes begin over 300 km down. The deepest-ever recorded earthquake began over 720 km down.

▼ *During an earthquake, shock waves radiate in circles outwards and upwards from the focus of the earthquake. The damage caused is greatest at the epicentre, where the waves are strongest, but vibrations may be felt 400 km away.*

Isoseismic lines show where the quake's intensity is equal

As two tectonic plates jolt past each other, they send out shock waves

The quake's intensity is reduced away from the epicentre

Epicentre

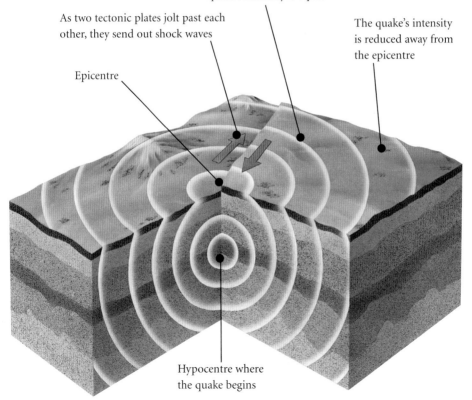

Hypocentre where the quake begins

# Mountain ranges

▲ *Mountain ranges are thrown up by the crumpling of rock strata (layers) as the tectonic plates of the Earth's surface crunch together.*

- **Great mountain ranges** such as the Andes in South America usually lie along the edges of continents.

- **Most mountain ranges** are made by the folding of rock layers as tectonic plates move slowly together.

- **High ranges** are geologically young because they are soon worn down. The Himalayas are 25 million years old.

- **Many ranges** are still growing. The Himalayas grow a few centimetres each year as the Indian plate pushes into Asia.

- **Mountain-building** is slow because rocks flow like thick treacle. Rock is pushed up like a bow wave in front of a boat as one tectonic plate pushes into another.

- **Satellite techniques** show that the central peaks of the Andes and Himalayas are rising. The outer peaks are sinking as the rock flows slowly away from the 'bow wave'.

- **Mountain-building** is very active during orogenic (mountain-forming) phases that last millions of years.

- **Different orogenic phases** occur in different places, for example the Alpine, Caledonian, Hercynian in Europe and the Huronian, Nevadian and Pasadenian in North America. The Caledonian was about 550 million years ago.

- **Mountain-building** makes the Earth's crust especially thick under mountains, giving them very deep 'roots'.

- **As mountains** are worn down, their weight reduces and the 'roots' float upwards. This is called isostasy.

▼ There are different types of mountain ranges including volcano mountains (1), fold mountains (2) and fault mountains (3).

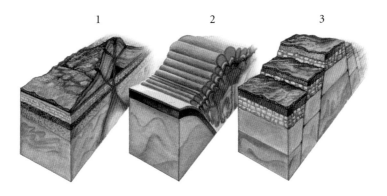

# Rivers

- **Rivers** are filled with water from rainfall running directly off the land, from melting snow or ice or from a spring bubbling out water that is soaked into the ground.

▲ *A river typically tumbles over boulders high up near its source.*

- **High up in mountains** near their source (start), rivers are usually small. They tumble over rocks through narrow valleys which they carved out over thousands of years.

- **All the rivers** in a certain area, called a catchment area, flow down to join each other, like branches on a tree. The branches are called tributaries. The bigger the river, the more tributaries it is likely to have.

- **As rivers flow downhill,** they are joined by tributaries and grow bigger. They often flow in smooth channels made not of big rocks but of fine debris washed down from higher up. River valleys are wider and gentler lower down, and the river may wind across the valley floor.

- **In its lower reaches** a river is often wide and deep. It winds back and forth in meanders across floodplains made of silt from higher up.

- **Rivers flow fast** over rapids in their upper reaches. On average, they flow as fast in the lower reaches where the channel is smoother because there is much less turbulence.

- **Rivers wear away** their banks and beds, mainly by battering them with bits of gravel and sand and by the sheer force of the moving water.

- **Every river** carries sediment, which consists of large stones rolled along the riverbed, sand bounced along the bed and fine silt that floats in the water.

- **The discharge of a river** is the amount of water flowing past a particular point each second.

- **Rivers that flow** only after heavy rainstorms are 'intermittent'. Rivers that flow all year round are 'perennial' – they are kept going between rains by water flowing from underground.

▼ *Some of the ways in which a river changes as it flows from its source high up in the hills downwards to the sea.*

In its upper reaches, a river tumbles over rocks through steep valleys

The neck of a meander may in time be worn through to leave an oxbow lake

In its lower reaches, a river winds broadly and smoothly across flat floodplains

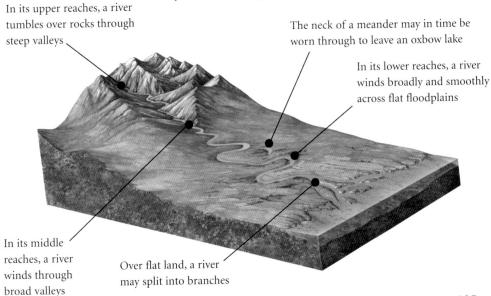

In its middle reaches, a river winds through broad valleys

Over flat land, a river may split into branches

**105**

# Weathering

- **Weathering** is the gradual breakdown of rocks when they are exposed to the air.

- **Weathering affects** surface rocks the most, but water trickling into the ground can weather rocks 200 m down.

- **The more extreme** the climate, the faster weathering takes place, whether the climate is very cold or very hot.

- **In tropical Africa** the basal weathering front (the lowest limit of weathering underground) is often 60 m down.

- **Weathering** works chemically (through chemicals in rainwater), mechanically (through temperature changes) and organically (through plants and animals).

- **Chemical weathering** is when gases dissolve in rain to form weak acids that corrode rocks such as limestone.

▲ Weathering is the breaking up of rocks by agents such as water, ice, chemicals and changing temperature.

- **The main form of mechanical weathering** is frost shattering – when water expands as it freezes in cracks in the rocks and so shatters the rock.

- **Thermoclastis** is when desert rocks crack as they get hot and expand in the day, then cool and contract at night.

- **Exfoliation** is when rocks crack in layers as a weight of rock or ice above them is removed.

▶ *The desert heat means that both the chemical and the mechanical weathering of the rocks is intense.*

#### . . . FASCINATING FACT . . .
At –22°C, ice can exert a pressure of 3000 kg on an area of rock the size of a postage stamp.

# Caves

- **Caves** are giant holes that run horizontally underground. Holes that plunge vertically are called potholes.

- **The most spectacular caves,** called caverns, are found in limestone. Acid rainwater trickles through cracks in the rock and wears away huge cavities.

- **The world's largest known** single cave is the Sarawak Chamber in Gunung Mulu in Sarawak, Malaysia.

- **The deepest** cave gallery yet found is the Pierre St Martin system, 800 m down in the French Pyrenees.

▲ *Caverns can be subterranean palaces filled with glistening pillars.*

- **The longest** cave system is the Mammoth Cave in Kentucky, USA, which is 560 km long.

- **Many caverns** contain fantastic deposits called speleothems. They are made mainly from calcium carbonate deposited by water trickling through the cave.

- **Stalactites** are icicle-like speleothems that hang from cave ceilings. Stalagmites poke upwards from the floor.

- **The world's longest** stalactite is 6.2 m long. It is in the Poll an Ionain in County Clare, Ireland.

- **The world's tallest column** is the Flying Dragon Pillar in the Nine Dragons Cave, Guizhou, China.

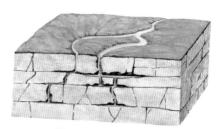

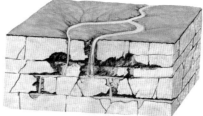

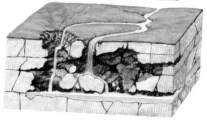

▲ *Surface water flows into layers of limestone and hollows out caves.*

> **...FASCINATING FACT...**
> The Sarawak Chamber is big enough to hold the world's biggest sports stadium three times over.

# Deserts

▲ *Water erosion over millions of years has created these dramatic pillar-like mesas and buttes in Monument Valley in Utah, USA.*

- **Deserts are places** where it rarely rains. Many are hot, but one of the biggest deserts is Antarctica. Deserts cover about one-fifth of the Earth's land.

- **Hamada** is desert that is strewn with boulders. Reg is desert that is blanketed with gravel.

- **About one-fifth** of all deserts are seas of sand dunes. These are known as ergs in the Sahara.

- **The type of sand dune** depends on how much sand there is, and how changeable the wind is.

- **Barchans** are moving, crescent-shaped dunes that form in sparse sand where the wind direction is constant.

- **Seifs** are long dunes that form where sand is sparse and the wind comes from two or more directions.

- **Most streams** in deserts flow only occasionally, leaving dry stream beds called wadis or arroyos. These may suddenly fill with a flash flood after rain.

- **In cool, wet regions**, hills are covered in soil and rounded in shape. In deserts, hills are bare rock with cliff faces footed by straight slopes.

- **Mesas and buttes** are pillar-like plateaux that have been carved gradually by water in deserts.

...FASCINATING FACT...
In the western Sahara, two million dry years have created sand ridges over 300 m high.

▼ *Oases are places in the desert that have water supplies. Plants and animals can thrive in these areas.*

# Swamps and marshes

▲ *Swamps are home to a variety of wildlife including fish, frogs, snakes, alligators and crocodiles.*

- **Wetlands** are areas of land where the water level is mostly above the ground.

- **The main types** of wetland are bogs, fens, swamps and marshes.

- **Bogs and fens** occur in cold climates and contain plenty of partially rotted plant material called peat.

- **Marshes and swamps** are found in warm and cold places. They have more plants than bogs and fens.

- **Marshes** are in permanently wet places, such as shallow lakes and river deltas. Reeds and rushes grow in marshes.

- **Swamps** develop where the water level varies – often along the edges of rivers in the tropics where they are flooded, notably along the Amazon and Congo Rivers. Trees such as mangroves grow in swamps.

- **Half the wetlands** in the USA were drained before most people appreciated their value. Almost half of Dismal Swamp in North Carolina has been drained.

- **The Pripet Marshes** on the borders of Belorussia are the biggest in Europe, covering 270,000 sq km.

- **Wetlands act** like sponges and help to control floods.

- **Wetlands help** to top up supplies of groundwater.

▶ *In the past, wetlands were seen simply as dead areas, ripe for draining. Now their value for both wildlife and water control is beginning to be realized.*

113

# Climate

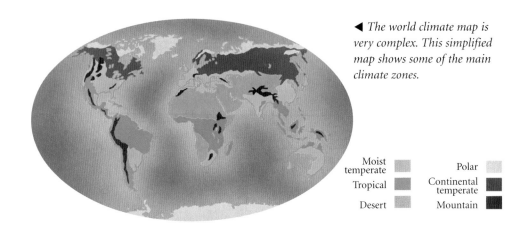

◀ *The world climate map is very complex. This simplified map shows some of the main climate zones.*

Moist temperate     Polar

Tropical     Continental temperate

Desert     Mountain

- **Climate is the typical weather** of a place over a long time.

- **Climates are warm** near the Equator, where the Sun climbs high in the sky.

- **Tropical climates** are warm climates in the tropical zones on either side of the Equator. Average temperatures of 27°C are typical.

- **The climate is cool** near the Poles, where the Sun never climbs high in the sky. Average temperatures of –30°C are typical.

- **Temperate climates** are mild climates in the temperate zones between the tropics and the polar regions. Summer temperatures may average 23°C. Winter temperatures may average 12°C.

- **A Mediterranean climate** is a temperate climate with warm summers and mild winters. It is typical of the Mediterranean, California, South Africa and South Australia.

▶ *The big seasonal difference in temperature is due to the movement of the overhead Sun. The polar regions are too far away from the Equator for the Sun ever to be overhead, or for there to be much seasonal difference in temperature.*

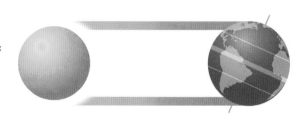

▶ *When the Mediterranean is nearest the Sun in midsummer it is hottest and driest. The coolest time of year comes when the Sun is farthest away from the Mediterranean, and closer to the southern hemisphere.*

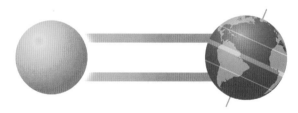

▶ *There is little seasonal variation in temperature near the Equator. Moving away from the Equator, there are seasons. The Sun is directly above the Equator during March and September, and above the Tropics of Cancer and Capricorn in June and December.*

● **A monsoon climate** is a climate with one wet and one very dry season – typical of India and SE Asia.

● **An oceanic climate** is a wetter climate near oceans, with cooler summers and warmer winters.

● **A continental climate** is a drier climate in the centre of continents, with hot summers and cold winters.

● **Mountain climates** get colder and windier with height.

**115**

# Atmosphere

- **The atmosphere** is a blanket of gases about 1000 km deep around the Earth. It can be divided into five layers: troposphere (the lowest), stratosphere, mesosphere, thermosphere and exosphere.

- **The atmosphere** is: 78 percent nitrogen, 21 percent oxygen, 1 percent argon and carbon dioxide with tiny traces of neon, krypton, zenon, helium, nitrous oxide, methane and carbon monoxide.

- **The atmosphere** was first created by the fumes pouring out from the volcanoes that covered the early Earth 4000 million years ago. But it was changed as rocks and seawater absorbed carbon dioxide, and then algae in the sea built up oxygen levels over millions and millions of years.

- **The troposphere** is just 12 km thick yet it contains 75 percent of the weight of gases in the atmosphere. Temperatures drop with height from 18°C on average to about –60°C at the top, called the tropopause.

- **The stratosphere** contains little water. Unlike the troposphere, which is heated from below, it is heated from above as the ozone in it is heated by ultraviolet light from the Sun. Temperatures rise with height from –60°C to 10°C at the top, about 50 km up.

- **The stratosphere** is clear and calm, which is why planes try to fly in this layer.

- **The mesosphere** contains few gases but it is thick enough to slow down meteorites. They burn up as they hurtle into it, leaving fiery trails in the night sky. Temperatures drop from 10°C to –120°C 80 km up.

> ...FASCINATING FACT...
> The stratosphere glows faintly at night because sodium from salty sea spray reacts chemically in the air.

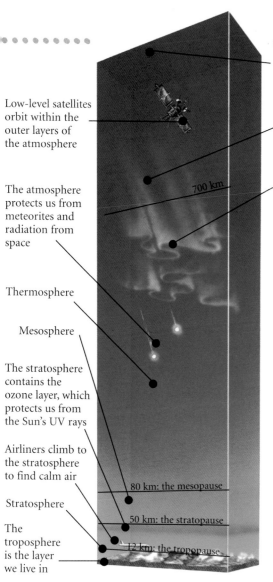

Light gases such as hydrogen and helium continually drift into space from the outer fringes of the atmosphere

Low-level satellites orbit within the outer layers of the atmosphere

Exosphere

The atmosphere protects us from meteorites and radiation from space

700 km

Shimmering curtains of light called auroras appear above the poles. They are caused by the impact of particles from the Sun on the gases in the upper atmosphere

Thermosphere

Mesosphere

The stratosphere contains the ozone layer, which protects us from the Sun's UV rays

Airliners climb to the stratosphere to find calm air

80 km: the mesopause

Stratosphere

50 km: the stratopause

The troposphere is the layer we live in

12 km: the tropopause

- **In the thermosphere** temperatures are very high, but there is so little gas that there is little real heat. Temperatures rise from −120°C to 2000°C 700 km up.

- **The exosphere** is the highest level of the atmosphere where it fades into the nothingness of space.

◀ The atmosphere is a sea of colourless, tasteless, odourless gases, mixed with moisture and fine dust particles. It is about 1000 km deep but has no distinct edge, simply fading away into space. As you move up, each layer contains less and less gas. The topmost layers are very rarefied, which means that gas is sparse.

**117**

# Global warming

▲ *Could global warming make the Mediterranean look like this?*

- **Global warming** is the increase in average temperatures around the world. This increase has been between 0.3°C and 0.8°C over the 20th century.

- **Most scientists** now think that global warming is caused by human activities, which have resulted in an increase in the Earth's natural greenhouse effect.

- **The greenhouse effect** is the way that certain gases in the air – notably carbon dioxide – trap some of the Sun's warmth, like the panes of glass in the walls and roof of a greenhouse.

- **The greenhouse effect** keeps the Earth pleasantly warm – but if it increases, the Earth may become very hot.

- **Many experts** expect a 4°C rise in average temperatures over the next 100 years.

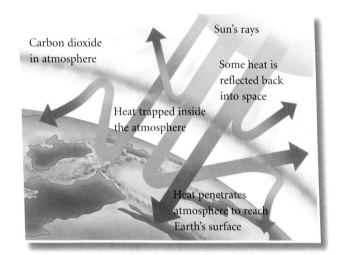

Carbon dioxide in atmosphere

Sun's rays

Some heat is reflected back into space

Heat trapped inside the atmosphere

Heat penetrates atmosphere to reach Earth's surface

▶ *The greenhouse effect occurs when carbon dioxide is released into the atmosphere by burning coal and oil (fossil fuels).*

- **Humans** boost the greenhouse effect by burning fossil fuels, such as coal, oil and natural gas that produce carbon dioxide.

- **Emission of the greenhouse gas** methane from the world's cattle has added to the increase in global warming.

- **Global warming** is bringing stormier weather by trapping more energy inside the atmosphere.

- **Global warming** may melt much of the polar ice caps, flooding low-lying countries such as Bangladesh.

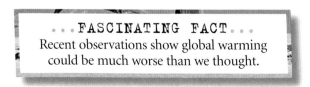

. . . **FASCINATING FACT** . . .
Recent observations show global warming
could be much worse than we thought.

119

# Seas

- **Seas** are small oceans, completely enclosed or partly enclosed by land.

- **Seas** are shallower than oceans and have do not have any major currents flowing through them.

- **In the Mediterranean** and other seas, tides can set up a seiche – a standing wave that sloshes back and forth like a ripple running up and down a bath.

- **If the natural** wave cycle of a seiche is different from the ocean tides, the tides are cancelled out.

- **If the natural** wave cycle of a seiche is similar to the ocean tides, the tides are magnified.

- **Scientists thought that** the Mediterranean was a dry desert 6 million years ago. They believed it was 3000 m lower than it is today, and covered in salts.

▲ *The warm waters of the Mediterranean attract tourists to the coast of Spain.*

- **Recent evidence** from microfossils suggests that the Mediterranean was never completely dry.

- **Warm seas such as the Mediterranean** lose much more water by evaporation than they gain from rivers. So a current of water flows in steadily from the ocean.

- **Warm seas** lose so much water by evaporation that they are usually much saltier than the open ocean.

...FASCINATING FACT...
The Dead Sea is the lowest sea on Earth,
400 m below sea level.

▼ *Waves in enclosed seas tend to be much smaller than those in the open ocean, because there is less space for them to develop.*

# Coasts

- **Coastlines** are changing all the time as new waves roll in and out and tides rise and fall every six hours or so. Over longer periods coastlines are reshaped by the action of waves and the corrosion of salty water.

- **On exposed coasts** where waves strike the high rocks, they undercut the slope to create steep cliffs and headlands. Often waves can penetrate into the cliff to open up sea caves or blast through arches. When a sea arch collapses, it leaves behind tall pillars called stacks which may be worn away to stumps.

- **Waves work** on rocks in two ways. First, the rocks are pounded with a huge weight of water filled with stones. Second, the waves force air into cracks in the rocks with such force that the rocks split apart.

- **The erosive power** of waves is focused in a narrow band at wave height. So as waves wear away sea cliffs, they leave the rock below wave height untouched. As cliffs retreat, the waves slice away a broad shelf of rock called a wave-cut platform. Water left behind in dips when the tide falls forms rockpools.

- **On more sheltered coasts,** the sea may pile up sand into beaches. The sand has been washed down by rivers or worn away from cliffs.

- **When waves hit** a beach at an angle, they fall straight back down the beach at a right angle. Any sand and shingle that the waves carry fall back slightly farther along the beach. In this way sand and shingle are moved along the beach in a zig-zag fashion. This is called longshore drift.

- **On beaches** prone to longshore drift, low fences called groynes are often built to stop the sand being washed away along the beach.

- **Longshore drift** can wash sand out across bays and estuaries to create sand bars called spits.

- **Bays** are broad indents in the coast with a headland on each side. Waves reach the headlands first, focusing their energy here. Material is worn away from the headlands and washed into the bay, forming a bay-head beach.

- **A cove is a small bay.** A bight is a huge bay, such as the Great Australian Bight. A gulf is a long narrow bight. The world's biggest bay is Hudson Bay, Canada, which has a shoreline 12,268 km long. The Bay of Bengal in India is larger in area.

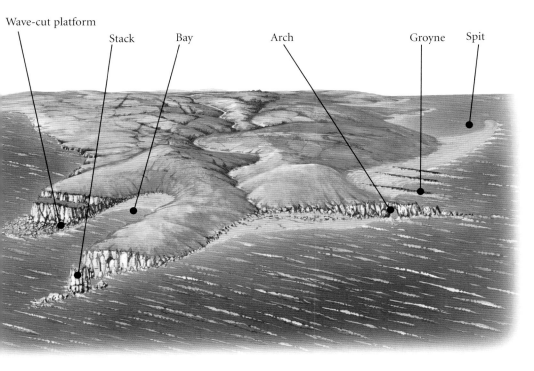

Wave-cut platform

Stack    Bay    Arch    Groyne    Spit

# Tsunamis

- **Tsunamis** are huge waves that begin when the sea floor is violently shaken by an earthquake, a landslide or a volcanic eruption.

- **In deep water** tsunamis travel almost unnoticeably below the surface. However, once they reach shallow coastal waters they rear up into waves 30 m high or higher.

- **Tsunamis** are often mistakenly called 'tidal waves', but they are nothing to do with tides.

- **The word** tsunami (soon-army) is Japanese for 'harbour wave'.

▼ *Tsunamis do little damage in open water but can cause huge amounts of damage in shallow waters and inland.*

A shift in the seabed sends out a pulse of water

As the pulse moves into shallow water it rears into a giant wave

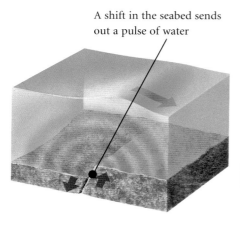
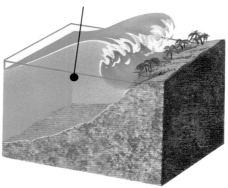

▲ *Tsunamis may be generated underwater by an earthquake, then travel far along the seabed before emerging to swamp a coast.*

- **Tsunamis** usually come in a series of a dozen or more – anything from five minutes to one hour apart.

- **Before a tsunami arrives,** the sea may recede dramatically, like water draining from a bath.

- **Tsunamis can travel** along the seabed as fast as a jet plane, at 700 km/h or more.

- **Tsunamis** arrive within 15 minutes from a local quake.

- **A tsunami** generated by an earthquake in Japan might swamp San Francisco, USA, 10 hours later.

- **Tsunami warnings** are issued by the Pacific Tsunami Warning Centre in Honolulu.

# Ocean deeps

- **The oceans** are over 2000 m deep on average.
- **Along the edge** of the ocean is a ledge of land – the continental shelf. The average sea depth here is 130 m.
- **At the edge of the continental shelf** the sea-bed plunges thousands of metres steeply down the continental slope.
- **Underwater avalanches** roar down the continental slope at over 60 km/h. They carve out deep gashes called submarine canyons.
- **The gently** sloping foot of the continental slope is called the continental rise.
- **Beyond the continental rise** the ocean floor stretches out in a vast plain called the abyssal plain. It lies as deep as 5000 m below the water's surface.

▼ *Under the ocean there are mountains, plateau, plains and trenches similar to those found on land.*

Continental shelf    Continental slope

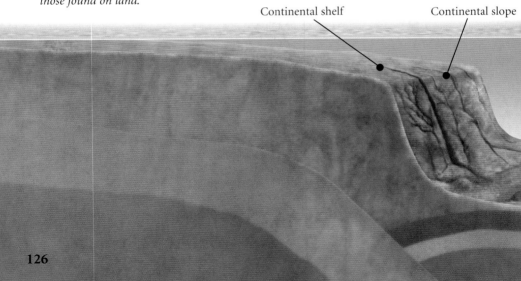

- **The abyssal plain** is covered in a thick slime called ooze. It is made partly from volcanic ash and meteor dust and partly from the remains of sea creatures.

- **The abyssal plain** is dotted with huge mountains, thousands of metres high, called seamounts.

- **Flat-topped seamounts** are called guyots. They may be volcanoes that once projected above the surface.

- **The deepest places** in the ocean floor are ocean trenches – made when tectonic plates are driven down into the mantle. The Mariana Trench is 10,863 m deep.

▶ *Huge numbers of sea creatures live in the pelagic zone – the surface waters of the open ocean beyond the continental shelf.*

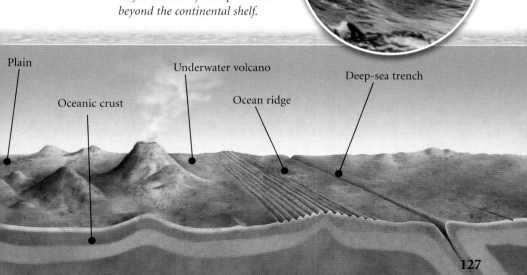

Plain

Oceanic crust

Underwater volcano

Ocean ridge

Deep-sea trench

127

# North America

▶ *North America broke away from Europe about 100 million years ago. It is still moving 2.5 cm farther every year.*

- **North America** is the world's third largest continent. It has an area of 24,230,000 sq km.

- **North America** is a triangle, with its long side bounded by the icy Arctic Ocean and its short side by the tropical Caribbean Sea.

- **The north** of North America lies inside the Arctic Circle and is icebound for much of the year. Death Valley, in the southwestern desert in California and Nevada, is one of the hottest places on the Earth.

- **Mountain ranges** run down each side of North America – the ancient, worn-down Appalachians in the east and the younger, higher Rockies in the west.

- **In between** the mountains lie vast interior plains. These plains are based on very old rocks, the oldest of which are in the Canadian Shield in the north.

- **North America** is the oldest continent on the Earth. It has rocks that are almost 4000 million years old.

- **The Grand Canyon** is one of the world's most spectacular gorges. It is 440 km long, and 1800 m deep in places.

- **The longest river** in North America is the Mississippi–Missouri, at 6019 km long.

- **The highest mountain** is Mt McKinley in Alaska, 6194 m high.

- **The Great Lakes** contain one fifth of the world's fresh water.

▼ *The Grand Canyon covers almost 500,000 hectares. It is one of North America's most popular tourist attractions.*

# South America

▲ *The Amazon rainforest covers an area of about 6 million sq km .*

- **South America** is the world's fourth largest continent. It has a total area of 17,814,000 sq km.

- **The Andes Mountains,** which run over 4500 km down the west side, are the world's longest mountain range.

- **The heart of South America** is the vast Amazon rainforest around the Amazon River and its tributaries.

- **The southeast** is dominated by the huge grasslands of the Gran Chaco, the Pampas and Patagonia.

- **No other continent** reaches so far south. South America extends to within 1000 km of the Antarctic Circle.

- **Three-quarters of South America** is in the tropics. In the high Andes are large zones of cool, temperate climate.

- **Quito, in Ecuador** is called the 'Land of Eternal Spring' because its temperature never drops below 8°C at night, and never climbs above 22°C during the day.

- **The highest volcanic peak** in South America is Aconcagua, 6960 m high.

- **Eastern South America** was joined to western Africa until the Atlantic began to open up 90 million years ago.

▲ *South America's triangular shape gives it the shortest coastline, for its size, of any of the continents.*

- **The Andes** have been built up over the past 60 million years by the collision of the South American plate with both the Nazca plate under the Pacific Ocean and the Caribbean plate. The subduction of the Nazca plate has created the world's highest active volcanoes in the Andes.

# Europe

▲ *Tourism plays an important part in the economy of the countries around the Mediterranean.*

- **Europe** is the smallest continent, with an area of just 10,400,000 sq km. For its size Europe has an immensely long coastline.

- **In the north** are the ancient glaciated mountains of Scandinavia and Scotland, which were once much, much higher.

- **Across the centre** are the lowlands of the North European Plain, stretching from the Urals in Russia to France in the west.

- **Much of southern Europe** has been piled up into young mountain ranges, as Africa drifts north.

- **The highest point** in Europe is Mt Elbrus in the Russian Caucasus, 5642 m high.

- **Northwest Europe** was once joined to Canada. The ancient Caledonian mountains of eastern Canada, Greenland, Scandinavia and Scotland were formed together as a single mountain chain 360–540 million years ago.

- **Mediterranean Europe** has a Mediterranean climate with warm summers and mild winters.

- **NW Europe** is often wet and windy. It has very mild winters because it is bathed by the warm North Atlantic Drift.

▲ *Europe is a small continent but its peninsulas and inlets give it a long coast.*

- **The Russian islands** of Novaya Zimlya are far into the Arctic Circle and are icebound in winter.

- **The largest lake** is Ladoga in Russia, 18,389 sq km.

133

# Asia

- **Asia is the world's largest continent,** stretching from Europe in the west to Japan in the east. It has a total area of 44,680,718 sq km.

- **Asia has huge climate extremes,** from a cold polar climate in the north to a hot tropical one in the south.

- **Verkhoyansk** in Siberia has had temperatures as high as 37°C and as low as –68°C.

- **The Himalayas** are the highest mountains in the world, with 14 peaks over 8000 m high. To the north are vast deserts, broad grasslands and huge coniferous forests. To the south are fertile plains and valleys and tropical jungles.

- **Northern Asia** sits on one giant tectonic plate.

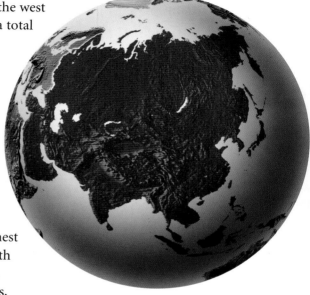

▲ *Asia is a vast continent of wide plains and dark forests in the north, separated from the tropical south by the Himalayas.*

. . . **FASCINATING FACT** . . .
Lake Baikal is the deepest lake – 1743 m – and it holds 20 percent of the world's fresh water.

- **India** is on a separate plate that crashed into the north Asia plate 50 million years ago. It is piling up the Himalayas as it ploughs on northwards.

- **Asia's longest river** is China's Yangtze, 5520 km long.

- **Asia's** highest mountain is the world's highest – Mt Everest, or Sagarmatha, in Nepal at 8848 m.

- **The Caspian Sea** between Azerbaijan and Kazakhstan is the world's largest lake, covering 378,400 sq km.

▲ *Lake Baikal in Siberia, Russia, is about 25 million years old. It contains about one-fifth of all the world's fresh water. The water is carried there by 336 rivers that flow into it. Lake Baikal has the world's only freshwater seals, and among its many unique animals is a fish that bears live young.*

# Africa

- **Africa is the world's second largest** continent. It stretches from the Mediterranean in the north to the Cape of Good Hope in the south. It has a total area of 30,131,536 sq km.

- **Africa is the world's warmest** continent, lying almost entirely within the tropics or subtropics.

- **Temperatures in the Sahara Desert** are the highest on Earth, often soaring over 50°C.

- **The Sahara** in the north of Africa, and the Kalahari in the south, are the world's largest deserts. Most of the continent in between is savannah (grassland) and bush. In the west and centre are lush rainforests.

▶ Africa is a vast, warm, fairly flat continent covered in savannah, desert and tropical forest.

▲ *In the savannah (grassland) trees and bushes are scarce and new grass only grows when the rainy season comes.*

- **Much of Africa** consists of vast plains and plateaux, broken in places by mountains such as the Atlas range in the northwest and the Ruwenzori in the centre.
- **The Great Rift Valley** runs 7200 km from the Red Sea. It is a huge gash in the Earth's surface opened up by the pulling apart of two giant tectonic plates.
- **Africa's largest lake** is Victoria, 69,484 sq km.
- **Africa's highest mountain** is Kilimanjaro, 5895 m high.
- **The world's** biggest sand dune is 430 m high – Erg Tifernine in Algeria.

. . . **FASCINATING FACT** . . .
The river Nile is the world's longest river, measuring 6738 km long.

# Australasia

▲ *The Great Barrier Reef is home to over 1500 species of fish.*

- **Australasia** is a vast region that includes islands spread over much of the Pacific Ocean. The land area is 8,508,238 sq km. However the total sea area is much, much bigger.

- **Australia** is the only country in the world which is also a continent in its own right.

- **The largest island** is New Guinea which has a total area of 787,878 sq km.

- **Fraser Island,** off Queensland, Australia, is the world's largest sand island with a sand dune 120 km long.

- **Australasia** is mostly tropical, with temperatures averaging 30°C in the north of Australia, and slightly lower on the islands where the ocean keeps the land cool.

- **New Zealand** is only a few thousand kilometres from the Antarctic Circle at its southern tip. As a result of occupying this position New Zealand has only mild summers and cold winters.

- **Australasia's highest peak** is Mt Wilhelm on Papua New Guinea, 4300 m high.

- **The Great Barrier Reef** is the world's largest living thing, 2027 km long. It is the only structure built by animals that is visible from space.

- **Australia** was the first continent to break off from Pangaea about 200 million years ago, and so has developed its own unique wildlife.

- **Australia sits** on the Indian – Australian plate, which is moving very slowly north away from Antarctica. New Zealand sits astride the boundary with the Pacific plate.

▲ *Apart from the landmass of Australia, much of Australasia is open water.*

**139**

# Antartica

- **Antarctica** is the fifth largest continent, larger than Europe and Australia, but 98 percent of it is under ice.

- **The Antarctic population** is made up mostly of scientists, pilots and other specialists there to do research in the unique polar environment.

- **About 3000 people** live in Antarctica in the summer, but less than 500 stay all through the bitter winter.

- **The biggest community** in Antarctica is McMurdo which is home to up to 1200 people in summer and has cafés, a cinema, a church and a nuclear power station.

- **People and supplies** reach McMurdo either on ice-breaker ships that smash through the sea ice, or by air.

- **McMurdo settlement** was built around the hut the British polar explorer Captain Scott put up on his 1902 expedition to the South Pole.

- **The Amundsen–Scott** base is located directly underneath the South Pole.

- **Antarctica** has valuable mineral resources including copper and chrome ores.
- **There is coal** beneath the Transarctic Mountains, and oil under the Ross Sea.
- **Under the Antarctic Treaty** of 1961, 27 countries agreed a ban on mining to keep the Antarctic unspoiled. They allow only scientific research.

▼ *Emperor penguins are among the few large creatures that can survive the bitter Antarctic winter. They breed on the ice cap itself.*

# Population

- **The world's population** climbed above 6 billion in 1999.
- **Over a quarter** of a million babies are born every day around the world.
- **World population** is growing at a rate of about 1.22 percent per year.
- **At the current rate** world population will hit 7.5 billion by 2020.
- **Between 1950 and 1990,** the world's population doubled from about 2.5 billion to 5 billion, adding 2.5 billion people in 40 years.

▲ *China will continue to control the growth of its population in the 21st century. Its goal is to keep the number below 1.4 billion until 2010.*

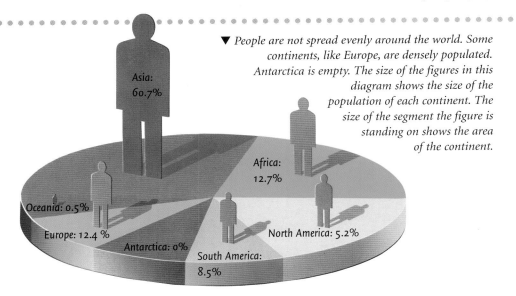

▼ *People are not spread evenly around the world. Some continents, like Europe, are densely populated. Antarctica is empty. The size of the figures in this diagram shows the size of the population of each continent. The size of the segment the figure is standing on shows the area of the continent.*

- **The 1990s** added a billion people. The next decade will add 800 million. This adds 1.8 billion in 20 years.

- **Asia has about 60 per cent** of the world's population. China alone has 1.3 billion people and India has 1 billion.

- **The average number of babies** born to each woman varies from 1.11 in Bulgaria to 7.11 in Somalia.

- **Latvia has 100 women** to every 8 men; Qatar has 184 men to every 100 women.

- **In the developed world** people are living longer. In Japan people expect to live 80 years on average. In Mozambique, people only expect to live 36.6 years.

# NATURAL WORLD

**Why are some plants carnivorous?**

**How do feathers help birds to fly?**

**Which creature has the biggest eyes?**

The answers to these and many other questions can be found in this amazing section. *Natural World* is split into two parts, each dealing with different aspects of plant and animal life. The first part takes a close look at the world of plants.

The second part takes a tour of the animal kingdom. Hundreds of key facts cover all aspects of animal life including migration, habitats and communication. Throughout, stunning colour images illustrate the amazing beauty of the natural world.

# Parts of a plant

- **The first plants** to appear on land were simple plants such as liverworts, ferns and horsetails. They grow from tiny cells called spores.

- **Today, most plants** grow not from spores but from seeds. Unlike primitive plants, seed-making plants have stems, leaves and often roots and flowers.

- **The stem of a plant** supports the leaves and flowers. It also carries water, minerals and food up and down between the plant's leaves and roots.

- **A terminal bud** forms the tip of each stem. The plant grows taller here.

- **Lateral buds** grow further back down the stem at places called nodes.

- **Some lateral buds** develop into new branches. Others develop into leaves or flowers.

- **The leaves** are the plant's green surfaces for catching sunlight. They use the sun's energy for joining water with carbon dioxide from the air to make the sugar the plant needs to grow.

- **The roots** are the parts of the plant that grow down into soil or water. They anchor the plant in the ground and soak up all the water and minerals it needs to grow.

- **The flowers** are the plant's reproductive organs. In gymnosperms – conifers, cycads and gingkos – the flowers are often small and hidden. In angiosperms (flowering plants) they are usually much more obvious.

> **FASCINATING FACT**
> The world's longest plant is the
> rattan vine which can snake
> 150 m through tropical tree tops.

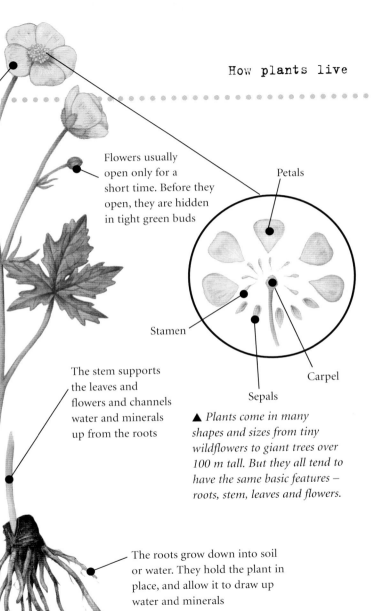

All plants that grow from seeds have flowers, although not all are as bright and colourful as these

Flowers usually open only for a short time. Before they open, they are hidden in tight green buds

Petals

Stamen

Carpel

Sepals

The stem supports the leaves and flowers and channels water and minerals up from the roots

The leaves are the powerhouses of the plant, using sunlight to make sugar, the plant's fuel

The roots grow down into soil or water. They hold the plant in place, and allow it to draw up water and minerals

▲ *Plants come in many shapes and sizes from tiny wildflowers to giant trees over 100 m tall. But they all tend to have the same basic features – roots, stem, leaves and flowers.*

**147**

# Roots

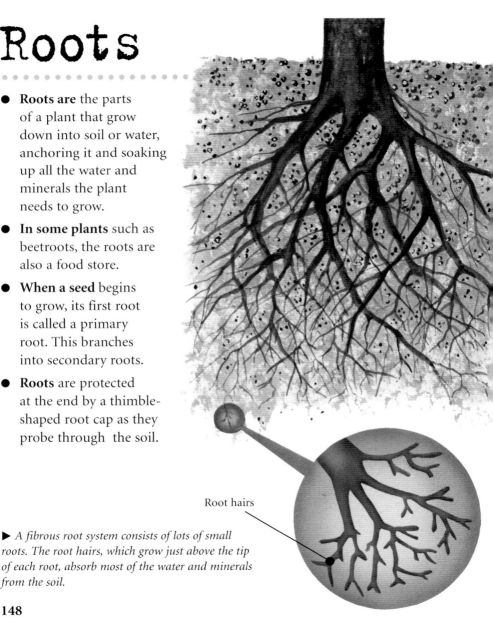

- **Roots are** the parts of a plant that grow down into soil or water, anchoring it and soaking up all the water and minerals the plant needs to grow.

- **In some plants** such as beetroots, the roots are also a food store.

- **When a seed** begins to grow, its first root is called a primary root. This branches into secondary roots.

- **Roots** are protected at the end by a thimble-shaped root cap as they probe through the soil.

Root hairs

▶ *A fibrous root system consists of lots of small roots. The root hairs, which grow just above the tip of each root, absorb most of the water and minerals from the soil.*

- **On every root** there are tiny root hairs that help it to take up water and minerals.

- **Some plants,** such as carrots, have a single large root, called a taproot, with just a few fine roots branching off.

- **Some plants,** such as grass, have lots of small roots, called fibrous roots, branching off in all directions.

- **Some kinds of orchid** that live on trees have 'aerial' roots that cling to the branches.

- **Mistletoe** has roots that penetrate its host tree.

▶ *The fleshy root of the beetroot is delicious when boiled or pickled.*

**...FASCINATING FACT...**
The roots of the South African wild fig tree can grow 120 m down into the ground.

# Leaves

- **Leaves** are a plant's powerhouse, using sunlight to join water and carbon dioxide to make sugar, the plant's fuel.

- **Leaves are** broad and flat to catch maximum sunlight.

- **Leaves** are joined to the stem by a stalk called a petiole.

- **The flat part** of the leaf is called the blade.

- **The leaf blade** is like a sandwich with two layers of cells holding a thick filling of green cells.

▲ *If you hold a leaf blade up to the light, you can clearly see the pattern of its veins.*

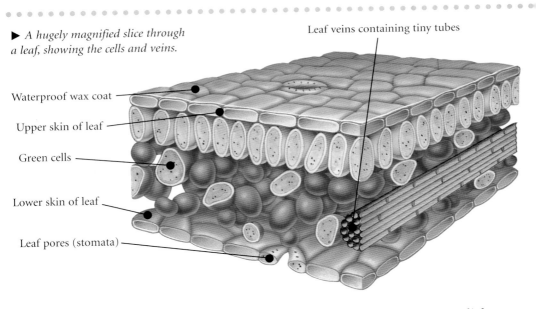

▶ *A hugely magnified slice through a leaf, showing the cells and veins.*

Leaf veins containing tiny tubes

Waterproof wax coat

Upper skin of leaf

Green cells

Lower skin of leaf

Leaf pores (stomata)

- **The green** comes from the chemical chlorophyll. It is this that catches sunlight to make sugar in photosynthesis.

- **Chlorophyll** is held in tiny bags in each cell called chloroplasts.

- **A network** of branching veins (tubes) supplies the leaf with water. It also transports the sugar made there to the rest of the plant.

- **Air containing** carbon dioxide is drawn into the leaf through pores on the underside called stomata. Stomata also let out water in a process called transpiration.

- **To cut down water loss** in dry places, leaves may be rolled-up, long and needle-like, or covered in hairs or wax. Climbing plants, such as peas, have leaf tips that coil into stalks called tendrils to help the plant cling.

151

# Photosynthesis

- **Plants use** sunlight to chemically join carbon dioxide gas from the air with water to make sugary food. The process is called photosynthesis.

- **Photosynthesis** occurs in leaves in two special kinds of cell – palisade and spongy cells.

- **Inside the palisade** and spongy cells are tiny packages called chloroplasts. A chloroplast is like a little bag with a double skin or membrane. Each is filled with a jelly-like substance called the stroma in which float various structures, such as lamellae. The jelly contains a chemical called chlorophyll which makes leaves green.

- **The leaf** draws in air containing the gas carbon dioxide through pores called stomata. It also draws water up from the ground through the stem and veins.

- **When the sun** is shining, the chlorophyll soaks up its energy and uses it to split water into hydrogen and oxygen. The hydrogen released from the water combines with the carbon dioxide to make sugar; the oxygen goes out through the stomata.

- **Sugar is transported** around the plant to where it is needed. Some sugar is burned up at once, leaving behind carbon dioxide and water. This process is called respiration.

- **Some sugar is combined** into large molecules called starches, which are easy for the plant to store. The plant breaks these starches down into sugars again whenever they are needed as fuel.

- **Starch** from plants is the main nutrient we get when we eat food such as bread, rice and potatoes. When we eat fruits, cakes or anything else sweet, the sweetness comes from sugar made by photosynthesis.

- **Together** all the world's plants produce about 150 billion tonnes of sugar each year by photosynthesis.

The oxygen in the air on which we depend for
life was all made by plants during photosynthesis.

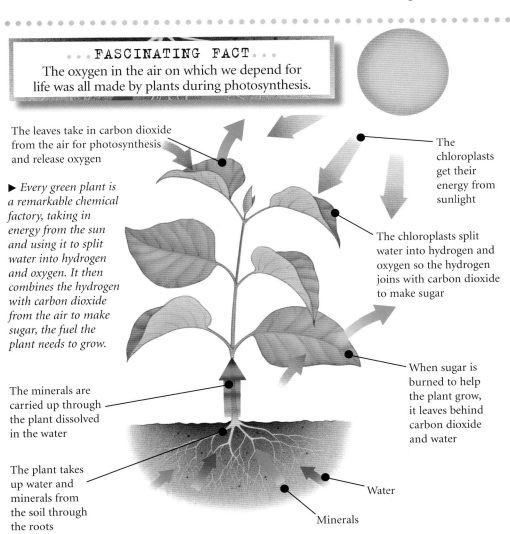

The leaves take in carbon dioxide
from the air for photosynthesis
and release oxygen

▶ *Every green plant is
a remarkable chemical
factory, taking in
energy from the sun
and using it to split
water into hydrogen
and oxygen. It then
combines the hydrogen
with carbon dioxide
from the air to make
sugar, the fuel the
plant needs to grow.*

The minerals are
carried up through
the plant dissolved
in the water

The plant takes
up water and
minerals from
the soil through
the roots

The
chloroplasts
get their
energy from
sunlight

The chloroplasts split
water into hydrogen and
oxygen so the hydrogen
joins with carbon dioxide
to make sugar

When sugar is
burned to help
the plant grow,
it leaves behind
carbon dioxide
and water

Water

Minerals

**153**

# Flower facts

- **The world's tallest** flower is the 2.5 m *titan arum* which grows in the tropical jungles of Sumatra.

- **The *titan arum*** is shaped so that flies are trapped in a chamber at the bottom.

- **The world's biggest flower** is rafflesia, which grows in the jungles of Borneo and Sumatra, Indonesia. It is 1 m in diameter and weighs up to 11 kg.

- **Rafflesia** is a parasite and has no leaves, root or stems.

- **Rafflesia and the *titan arum*** both smell like rotting meat in order to attract the insects that pollinate them.

- **The world's smallest flower** is the Wolffia duckweed of Australia. This is a floating water plant less than 0.6 mm across. It can only be seen clearly when viewed under a magnifying glass.

◀ *The Indonesian name for the* titan arum *is 'Bunga Bangkai', meaning 'corpse flower', due to its repulsive stench.*

- **The biggest flowerhead** is the *puya raimondii* bromeliad of Bolivia which can be up to 2.5 m across and 10 m tall and have 8000 individual blooms.

- **The *Puya raimondii*** takes 150 years to grow its first flower, then dies.

- **Two Australian orchids** actually bloom underground. No-one quite knows how they pollinate.

- **Stapelia flowers** not only smell like rotting meat to attract the flies that pollinate them – they look like it too (pinky-brown and wrinkled).

▼ *Rafflesia was 'discovered' by British explorer John Arnold in 1818. He named the flower after the famous British colonialist Stamford Raffles.*

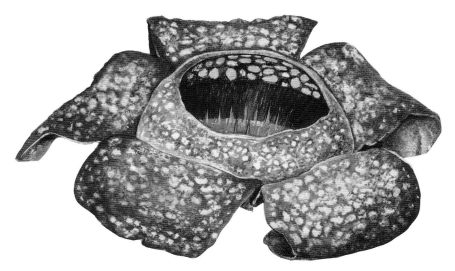

# Pollination

◀ *Butterflies, such as this Monarch, feed mainly on nectar and other plant juices, helping plant pollination in the process.*

- **For seeds** to develop, pollen from a flower's male anther must get to a female stigma.

- **Some flowers are** self-pollinating and the pollen moves from an anther to a stigma on the same plant.

- **In cross-pollinating** flowers, the pollen from the anthers must be carried to a stigma on a different plant of the same kind.

- **Some pollen** is carried by the wind.

- **Most pollen** is carried on the bodies of insects such as bees or by birds or bats that visit the flower.

▶ *Many flowers rely on attracting bees to carry their pollen.*

- **Insect-pollinated flowers** are often brightly coloured and sweet-smelling to attract bees and butterflies.

- **Bees and butterflies** are also drawn by the flower's sweet juice or nectar. As they sip the nectar, they may brush pollen on to the stigma, or take some on their bodies from the anthers to the stigma of other flowers.

- **Bees and butterflies** are drawn to blue, yellow and pink flowers. White flowers draw night-flying moths.

- **Many flowers** have honey guides – markings to guide the bees in. These are often invisible to us and can only be seen in ultraviolet light, which bees and some other insects can see.

- **The cuckoopint** smells like cow-dung to attract the flies that carry its pollen.

**157**

# Fruit

- **Scientists** say a fruit is the ovary of a plant after the eggs are pollinated and grow into seeds. Corn grains, cucumbers, bean pods and acorns are fruit as well as apples and so on.

- **Some fruits,** such as oranges, are soft and juicy. The hard pips are the seeds.

- **With some fruits** such as hazelnuts and almonds, the flesh turns to a hard dry shell.

- **Fleshy fruits** are either berries like oranges which are all flesh, aggregate fruits like blackberries which are made from lots of berries from a single flower, or multiple fruits like pineapples which are single fruits made from an entire multiple flowerhead.

- **Legumes** such as peas and beans are soft, dry fruits held in a case known as a pod.

- **Berries** and other juicy fruits are called 'true fruits' because they are made from the ovary of the flower alone.

▶ Almonds grow in a thin, smooth shell. The almond tree produces two different kinds of fruit – sweet, which is edible, and bitter, which is not.

▼ *There are three kinds of cherries – sweet, sour and 'dukes', which are a sweet-sour cross. We eat mainly sweet cherries like these.*

- **Apples and pears** are called 'false fruits' because they include parts other than the flower's ovary.

- **In an apple** only the core is the ovary.

- **Drupes** are fruit like plums, mangoes and cherries with no pips but just a hard stone in the centre containing the seeds. Aggregate fruits like raspberries are clusters of drupes.

- **Walnuts and dogwood** are actually drupes like cherries.

**159**

# Spores and seeds

◄ *The giant redwood grows in California and is one of the tallest trees in the world. It grows from a tiny seed to over 100 m tall.*

◄ *New sycamore trees grow from their tiny winged seeds (left). Mushrooms (below right) grow from spores.*

● **Seed plants** are plants that grow from seeds of varying size and shape.

● **Seeds** have a tiny baby plant inside called an embryo from which the plant grows plus a supply of stored food and a protective coating.

● **Spores contain** special cells which grow into new organisms. Green plants like ferns and mosses and fungi such as mushrooms all produce spores.

● **All 250,000 flowering plants** produce 'enclosed' seeds. These are seeds that grow inside sacs called ovaries, which turn into a fruit around the seed.

● **The 800 or so** conifers, cycads and gingkos produce 'naked' seeds, which means there is no fruit around them.

● **Seeds** only develop when a plant is fertilized by pollen.

● **The largest seeds** are those of the double coconut or coco-de-mer of the Seychelles, which can sometimes weigh up to 20 kg.

● **30,000 orchid seeds** weigh barely 1 gm.

● **The world's biggest tree,** the giant redwood, grows from tiny seeds that are less than 2 mm long.

● **Coconut trees** produce only a few big seeds; orchids produce millions, but only a few grow into plants.

**161**

# Broad-leaved woodlands

- **Forests** of broad-leaved, deciduous trees grow in temperate regions where there are warm, wet summers and cold winters – in places like North America, western Europe and eastern Asia.

- **Broad-leaved deciduous** woods grow where temperatures average above 10°C for over six months a year, and the average annual rainfall is over 400 mm.

- **If there are** 100 to 200 days a year warm enough for growth, the main trees in broad-leaved deciduous forests are oaks, elms, birches, maples, beeches, aspens, chestnuts and lindens (basswood).

- **In the tropics** where there is plenty of rainfall, broad-leaved evergreens form tropical rainforests.

- **In moist western Europe,** beech trees dominate woods on well-drained, shallow soils, especially chalkland; oak trees prefer deep clay soils. Alders grow in waterlogged places.

- **In drier eastern Europe,** beeches are replaced by durmast oak and hornbeam and in Russia by lindens.

▲ *Broad-leaved trees form shady paths in summer but are light in winter when the trees are bare.*

- **In American woods,** beech and linden are rarer than in Europe, but oaks, hickories and maples are more common.

- **In the Appalachians** buckeye and tulip trees dominate.

- **There is a wide range** of shrubs under the trees including dogwood, holly, magnolia, as well as woodland flowers.

▼ *Plenty of light can filter down through deciduous trees so that all kinds of bushes and flowers grow in the woods, often blooming in spring while the leaves are still thin.*

. . . FASCINATING FACT . . .
Very few woods in Europe are entirely natural; most are 'secondary' woods, growing on land once cleared for farms.

# Tropical rainforest

- **Rainforests** are warm and wet, with over 2000 mm of rain a year and average temperatures over 20°C. This is why they are the world's richest plant habitats.

- **Flowering plants** (angiosperms) originated in tropical rainforests. Eleven of the 13 oldest families live here.

- **Most rainforest trees** are broad-leaved and evergreen.

- **Trees** of the Amazon rainforest include rosewood, Brazil nut and rubber, plus myrtle, laurel and palms. Trees in the African rainforest include mahogany, ebony, limba, wenge, agba, iroko and sapele.

- **Many rainforest plants** have big, bright flowers to attract birds and insects in the gloom. Flowers pollinated by birds are often red, those by night-flying moths white or pink and those by day-flying insects yellow or orange.

- **The gloom** means many plants need big seeds to store enough food while they grow. So they grow fragrant fruits that attract animals to eat them and spread the seed in their body waste. Fruit bats are drawn to mangoes.

- **Many trees** grow flowers on their trunks to make them easy for animals to reach. This is called cauliflory.

- **Rainforest trees** are covered with epiphytes – plants whose roots never reach the soil but take water from the air.

- **Many plants are parasitic.** This means they feed on other plants. Parasites include mistletoes and rafflesia.

> **...FASCINATING FACT...**
> One 23-hectare area of Malaysian rainforest has 375 species of tree with trunks thicker than 91 cm.

▶ *Most tropical rainforests have several layers. Towering above the main forest are isolated emergent trees up to 60 m tall. Below these, 30–50 m above the ground, is a dense canopy of leaves and branches at the top of tall, straight trees. In the gloom beneath is the understorey where young emergents, small conical trees and a huge range of shrubs grow. Clinging lianas wind their way up through the trees and epiphytes grow high on tree branches and trunks where they are able to reach daylight.*

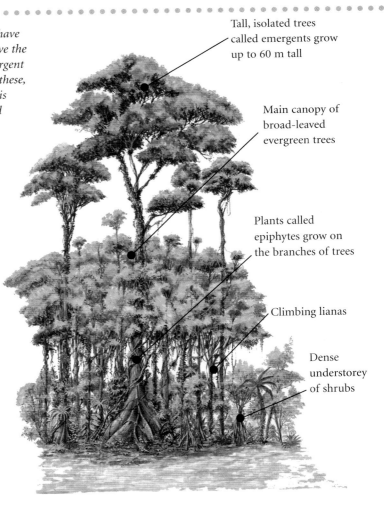

Tall, isolated trees called emergents grow up to 60 m tall

Main canopy of broad-leaved evergreen trees

Plants called epiphytes grow on the branches of trees

Climbing lianas

Dense understorey of shrubs

**165**

# Desert plants

- **Some plants** find water in the dry desert with very long roots. The mesquite has roots that can go down as much as 50 m deep.

- **Most desert plants** have tough waxy leaves to cut down on water loss. They also have very few leaves; cacti have no leaves at all.

- **Pebble plants** avoid the desert heat by growing partly underground.

▲ *Surprisingly, many plants are able to survive the dryness of deserts, including cacti and sagebushes.*

- **Window plants** grow almost entirely underground. A long cigar shape pokes into the ground, with just a small green window on the surface to catch sunlight.

- **Some mosses and lichens** get water by soaking up dew.

- **Resurrection trees** get their name because their leaves look shrivelled, brown and dead most of the time – then suddenly turn green when it rains.

- **The rose of Jericho** is a resurrection plant that forms a dry ball that lasts for years and opens only when damp.

- **Daisies** are found in most deserts.

- **Cacti and ice plants** can store water for many months in special storage organs.

▲ *All cacti produce flowers*
*which bloom only for a few days*
*before they lose water and die.*

**167**

# Marine plants

- **Plants in the sea** can only live in the sunlit surface waters of the ocean, called the photic zone.

- **The photic zone** goes down about 100 m.

- **Phytoplankton** are minute, floating, plant-like organisms made from just a single cell.

- **Almost any marine plant** which is big enough to be seen with the naked eye is called seaweed.

- **Seaweeds** are anchored by 'holdfasts' that look like roots but are really suckers for holding on to rocks.

- **Seaweeds** are red, green or brown algae. Red algae are small and fern-like and grow 30–60 m down in tropical seas. Brown algae like giant kelp are big and grow down to about 20 m, mostly in cold water.

▲ *Seaweeds don't have roots, stems, leaves or flowers, but they are plants and make their food from sunlight.*

▲ *Kelp is kept afloat by air bladders, and is often used as shelter by lobsters and fish.*

● **Some seaweeds** such as the bladderwrack have gas pockets to help their fronds (leaves) float.

● **The fastest growing** plant in the sea is the giant kelp, which can grow 1 m in a single day. Giant kelp can grow up to 60 m long.

● **The Sargasso Sea** is a vast area of sea covering 5.2 million sq ki east of the West Indies. Gulfweed floats so densely here that it looks like green meadows.

● **The Sargasso Sea** was discovered by Christopher Columbus in 1492.

**169**

# Wildflowers

- **All flowers** were originally wild. Garden flowers have been bred over the centuries to be very different from their wild originals.
- **Wildflowers** are flowers that have developed naturally.
- **Most wildflowers** are smaller and more delicate than their garden cousins.
- **Each** kind of place has its own special range of wildflowers, although many wildflowers have now been spread to different places by humans.
- **Heathlands** may have purple blooms of heathers, prickly yellow gorse and scarlet pimpernel.

▼ *There are now very few meadows with rich displays of wildflowers like this.*

- **In meadow grass** flowers like buttercups, daisies, clover, forget-me-nots and ragged robin often grow.

- **In deciduous woodlands** flowers like bluebells, primroses, daffodils and celandines grow.

- **By the sea** among the rocks, sea campion and pink thrift may bloom, while up on the cliffs, there may be birdsfoot trefoil among the grasses.

- **As humans** take over larger and larger areas of the world, and as farmers use more and more weedkillers on the land, many wildflowers are becoming very rare. Some are so rare that they are protected by law.

- **The lady's slipper** orchid grows only in one secret place in Yorkshire, in the north of England.

▶ *The rare lady's slipper orchid is also known as the moccasin flower. Its enlarged labellum (lip) makes it resemble a slipper or moccasin.*

**171**

# Parts of a tree

- **Trees** have one tall, thick, woody stem called a trunk which is at least 10 cm thick, allowing the tree to stand up by itself.

> ...**FASCINATING FACT**...
> The fastest-growing tree is the tropical pea tree *Albizia falcata* which can grow 10 m a year.

- **The branches** and leaves together are called the crown. The trunk supports the crown and holds it up to the sun.

- **The trunks of conifers** typically grow right to the top of the tree. The lower branches are longer because they have been growing longest. The upper branches are short because they are new. So the tree has a conical shape.

- **Trees with wide flat leaves** are called broad-leaved trees. They usually have crowns with a rounded shape.

- **The trunk and branches** have five layers from the centre out – heartwood, sapwood, cambium, phloem and bark.

- **If a tree** is sawn across, you can see the annual growth rings that show how the tree has grown each year. The edge of each ring marks where growth ceased in winter. Counting the rings gives the age of the tree.

- **Heartwood** is the dark, dead wood in the centre of the trunk. Sapwood is pale living wood, where tiny pipes called xylem carry sap from the roots to the leaves.

- **The cambium** is the thin layer where the sapwood is actually growing; the phloem is the thin food-conducting layer.

- **The bark** is the tree's protective skin made of hard dead tissue. Bark takes many different forms and often cracks as the tree grows, but it is always made from cork.

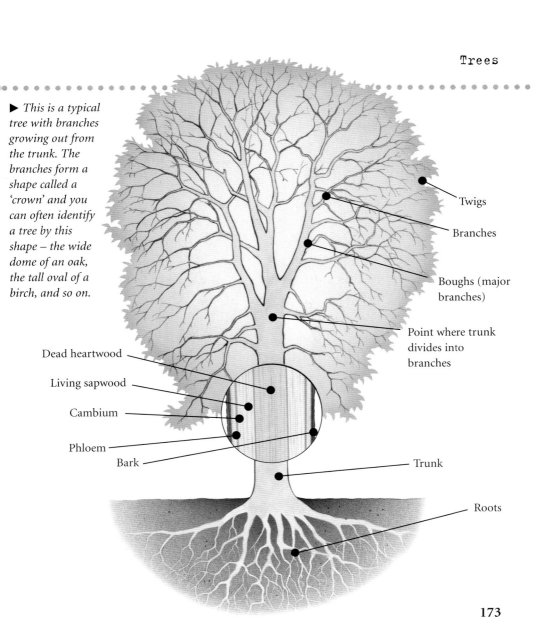

▶ *This is a typical tree with branches growing out from the trunk. The branches form a shape called a 'crown' and you can often identify a tree by this shape – the wide dome of an oak, the tall oval of a birch, and so on.*

Twigs

Branches

Boughs (major branches)

Point where trunk divides into branches

Dead heartwood

Living sapwood

Cambium

Phloem

Bark

Trunk

Roots

173

# Conifers

- **Conifers** are trees with needle-like, typically evergreen leaves that make their seeds not in flowers but in cones.

- **With gingkos and cycads** they make up the group of plants called gymnosperms, all of which make their seeds in cones.

- **The world's tallest tree,** the redwood, is a conifer.

- **The world's most massive tree,** the giant sequoia, is a conifer.

- **One of the world's oldest trees** is the bristlecone pine of California and Nevada, almost 5000 years old.

▶ *The knarled bristlecone pine appears dead, but can survive with just a few of its branches and roots left.*

- **The world's smallest trees** are probably conifers including natural bonsai cypresses and shore pines which reach barely 20 cm when fully grown.

- **Many conifers** are cone-shaped, which helps them shed snow from their branches in winter.

- **The needle-like shape** and waxy coating of the leaves helps the conifer to save water.

- **The needles of some pines** can grow up to 30 cm long. But the biggest needles ever were those of the extinct Cordaites, over 1 m long and 15 cm wide.

- **Conifers** grow over most of the world, but the biggest conifer forests are in places with cold winters, such as north Siberia, northern North America and on mountain slopes almost everywhere.

▲ Most conifers are instantly recognizable from their conical shapes, their evergreen, needle-like leaves and their dark brown cones.

175

# Tree leaves

- **Trees** can be divided into two groups according to their leaves – broad-leaved trees and conifers with needle-like leaves.

- **The leaves** of broad-leaved trees are all wide and flat to catch the sun, but they vary widely in shape.

- **You can identify** trees by their leaves. Features to look for are not only the overall shape, but also the number of leaflets on the same stalk, whether leaflets are paired or offset and if there are teeth round the edges of the leaves.

- **Trees such as birches** and poplars have small triangular or 'deltoid' leaves; aspens and alders have round leaves.

- **Limes** and Indian bean trees have heart-shaped or 'cordate' leaves.

- **Maples** and sycamores have leaves shaped a bit like hands, which is why they are called 'palmate'.

- **Ash and walnut trees** both have lots of leaflets on the same stalk, which gives them a feathery or 'pinnate' look.

Hand-shaped leaf of a horse chestnut

Lobed leaves of the English oak

- **Oaks and whitebeams** have leaves indented with lobes round the edge.

- **Many shrubs**, like magnolias and buddleias, and trees like willows, cherries, sweet chestnuts and cork oaks, have long narrow leaves.

- **Elms, beeches**, pears, alders and many others all have oval leaves.

Long, narrow willow leaves

Pinnate or feather-shaped walnut leaves

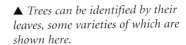
▲ *Trees can be identified by their leaves, some varieties of which are shown here.*

**177**

# Seeds and nuts

- **Seeds are the tiny** hard capsules from which most new plants grow.

- **Seeds** develop from the plant's egg once it is fertilized by pollen.

- **Each seed** contains the new plant in embryo form plus a store of food to feed it until it grows leaves.

- **The seed** is wrapped in a hard shell known as a testa.

- **Some fruit** contain many seeds. Nuts are fruit with a single seed in which the outside has gone hard.

▶ *Neither Brazil nuts nor coconuts are true nuts. Coconuts (right) are the stones of drupes, while Brazil nuts (left) are just large seeds.*

- **Acorns and hazelnuts** are true nuts.

- **Cola drinks** get their name from the African kola nut, but there are no nuts in them. The flavour is artificial.

- **Some nuts**, such as almonds and walnuts, are not true nuts but the hard stones of drupes (fruit like plums).

- **Brazil nuts** and shelled peanuts are not true nuts but just large seeds.

- **Nuts are** a concentrated, nutritious food – about 50 percent fat and 10–20 percent protein. Peanuts contain more food energy than sugar and more protein, minerals and vitamins than liver.

▶ *Almonds come from trees native to southwest Asia but are now grown all over the world.*

179

# Evergreen trees

- **An evergreen** is a plant that keeps its leaves in winter.

- **Many tropical broad-leaved trees** are evergreen.

- **In cool temperate regions** and the Arctic, most evergreen trees are conifers such as pines and firs. They have needle-like leaves.

- **Old needles** do turn yellow and drop, but they are replaced by new needles (unless the tree is unhealthy).

- **Evergreens** may suffer from sunscald – too much sun – in dry, sunny spots, especially in early spring.

▲ *In cool northern climates where the summers are brief, conifers stay evergreen to make the most of the available sunshine.*

- **Five coniferous groups,** including larches and cypresses, are not evergreen.

- **Many evergreens** were sacred to ancient cultures. The laurel or bay was sacred to the Greek god Apollo and was used by the Romans as a symbol of high achievement.

- **Yews are grown** in many European churchyards – perhaps because the trees were planted on the sites by pagans in the days before Christianity. But the bark of the yew tree and its seeds are poisonous.

- **The sakaki** is sacred to the Japanese Shinto religion, and entire trees are uprooted to appear in processions.

◄ *The leaves of the conifer may be scale-like, as they are here, or needle-like. The scale-like leaves cling to the stem.*

**181**

# Pine trees

- **Pine trees** are evergreen conifers with long needle-like leaves. They grow mostly in sandy or rocky soils in cool places.

- **Pine trees** belong to the largest family of conifers.

- **There are 90–100 species of pine** – most of them coming originally from northern Eurasia and North America.

- **Pines grow** fast and straight, reaching their full height in less than 20 years – which is why they provide 75 percent of the world's timber.

- **Some pines** produce a liquid called resin which is used to make substances such as turpentine, paint and soap.

- **Soft or white pines**, such as sugar pines and piñons, have soft wood. They grow needles in bundles of five and have little resin.

▼ *Like all conifers, Corsican pines produce cones. The cones look very different from flowers but serve the same purpose – making the seeds from which new trees grow.*

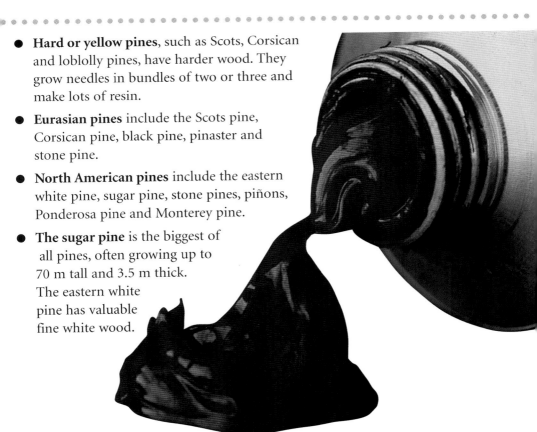

- **Hard or yellow pines**, such as Scots, Corsican and loblolly pines, have harder wood. They grow needles in bundles of two or three and make lots of resin.

- **Eurasian pines** include the Scots pine, Corsican pine, black pine, pinaster and stone pine.

- **North American pines** include the eastern white pine, sugar pine, stone pines, piñons, Ponderosa pine and Monterey pine.

- **The sugar pine** is the biggest of all pines, often growing up to 70 m tall and 3.5 m thick. The eastern white pine has valuable fine white wood.

▲ *Resin comes from several varieties of pine tree. It is used in the preparation of paints, varnishes and glues.*

**183**

# Deciduous trees

- **Deciduous trees** lose their leaves once a year.

- **In cool places,** deciduous trees lose their leaves in autumn to cut their need for water in winter when water may be frozen.

- **In the tropics** deciduous trees lose their leaves at the start of the dry season.

- **Leaves fall** because a layer of cork grows across the leaf stalk, gradually cutting off its water supply.

- **Eventually the leaf** is only hanging on by its veins, and is easily blown off by the wind.

- **Leaves go brown** and other colours in autumn because their green chlorophyll breaks down, letting other pigments shine through instead.

- **Among the most spectacular** autumn colours are those of the sweet gum tree, which was brought to Europe from Mexico c.1570.

- **The main deciduous trees** found in cool climates are oaks, beeches, birches, chestnuts, aspens, elms, maples and lindens.

- **Most deciduous trees** are broad-leaved, but five conifer groups including larches are deciduous.

- **Some tropical evergreen trees** are deciduous in regions where there is a marked dry season.

▶ *In autumn, the leaves of deciduous trees turn glorious colours.*

# Tree facts

- **The biggest tree** ever known was the Lindsey Creek Tree, a massive redwood which blew over in 1905. It weighed over 3300 tonnes.

- **The tallest living tree** is the 112-m high Mendocino redwood tree, which is growing in Montgomery State Reserve, California, United States.

- **The tallest tree** ever known was a Eucalyptus on Watts River, Victoria, Australia, which was measured at over 150 m in 1872.

- **The great banyan** tree in the Indian Botanical Garden, Calcutta has a canopy covering 1.2 hectares.

▲ *The banyan tree or Indian fig tree has wide-spreading branches that send down hundreds of hanging roots. These take hold of the soil and act as supports for the branches.*

- **Banyan trees** grow trunk-like roots from their branches.

- **A European chestnut** known as the Tree of the Hundred Horses on Mt Etna in Sicily had a girth (the distance round the trunk) of 57.9 m during the 1790s.

▲ *General Sherman in California is the biggest living tree. It is a giant sequoia over 83 m tall and with a trunk 11 m across.*

- **A Moctezuma baldcypress** near Oaxaca in Mexico has a trunk of over 12 m across.

- **The world's oldest plant** is the King's Holly in southwestern Tasmania, thought to be 43,000 years old.

- **The ombu tree** of Argentina is the world's toughest tree, able to survive axes, fire, storms and insect attacks.

...**FASCINATING FACT**...
The 'Eternal God' redwood tree in Prairie Creek, California is 12,000 years old.

187

# Algae

- **Algae** are simple organisms that live in oceans, lakes, rivers and damp mud.

- **Some algae** live inside small transparent animals.

- **Algae vary** from single-celled microscopic organisms to huge fronds of seaweed (brown algae) over 60 m long.

- **The smallest** float freely, but others, such as seaweeds, need a place to grow like a plant.

- **Algae** are so varied and often live very differently from plants, so scientists put them not in the plant kingdom but in a separate kingdom called the Proctista, along with slime moulds.

- **The most ancient** algae are called blue-green algae or cyanobacteria and are put in the same kingdom as bacteria. They appeared on the Earth 3 billion years ago.

- **Some algae** can multiply very quickly in polluted lakes and rivers. The thick layers can often upset the water's natural balance and deprive it of oxygen.

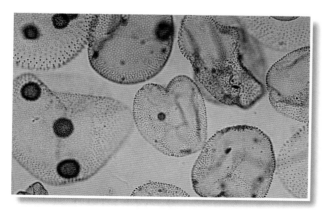

◀ *Volvox are green algae that live in colonies about the size of a pinhead, containing as many as 60,000 cells.*

▲ *Algae may be tiny but they are a vital food source for creatures from shrimps to whales.*

- **Green algae** are found mostly in freshwater. The green is the chlorophyll that enables plants to get their energy from sunlight.

- **Green algae** called Spirogyra form long threads.

- **Red or brown algae** are found in warm seas. Their chlorophyll is masked by other pigments.

**189**

# Fungi

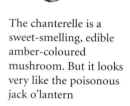

- **Fungi** are a huge group of 50,000 species. They include mushrooms, toadstools, mould, mildew and yeast.

- **Fungi** are not plants, because they have no chlorophyll to make their food. So scientists put them in a group or kingdom of their own.

- **Because fungi** cannot make their own food, they must live off other plants and animals – sometimes as partners, sometimes as parasites.

- **Parasitic fungi** feed off living organisms; fungi that live off dead plants and animals are called saprophytic.

- **Fungi** feed by releasing chemicals called enzymes to break down chemicals in their host. The fungi then use the chemicals as food.

- **Cheeses** like Camembert, Rocquefort, Stilton and Danish Blue get their distinctive flavours from chemicals made by moulds added to them to help them ripen. The blue streaks in some cheeses are actually moulds.

The chanterelle is a sweet-smelling, edible amber-coloured mushroom. But it looks very like the poisonous jack o'lantern

▶ *These are some of the tens of thousands of different fungi, which are found growing everywhere, from on rotting tree stumps to inside your body.*

Fly agaric is a toadstool – that is, a poisonous mushroom. It is easy to recognize from its spotted red cap

The destroying angel is the most poisonous of all fungi, and usually kills anyone who eats one

Many mould fungi are the source of life-saving antibiotic drugs such as penicillin.

Fungi can grow in all kinds of shapes, earning them names like this orange peel fungi

- **Fungi are made** of countless cotton-like threads called hyphae which absorb the chemicals they feed on. Hyphae are usually spread out in a tangled mass. But they can bundle together to form fruiting bodies like mushrooms.

- **Some fungi** grow by spreading their hyphae in a mat or mycelium; others scatter their spores. Those that grow from spores go through the same two stages as mosses.

- **Truffles** are fungi that grow near oak and hazel roots. They are prized for their flavour and sniffed out by dogs or pigs. The best come from Perigord in France.

The field mushroom, grown wild or cultivated, is the mushroom most widely eaten

Honey mushrooms belong to the Armillaria genus of fungi, which includes the world's largest and oldest living organisms

Puffballs have big round fruiting bodies that dry out and puff out their spores in all directions when burst

The water-measure earthstar grows in soil or on rotting wood in grassy areas or woods

**191**

# Mushrooms

- **Mushrooms** are umbrella-shaped fungi, many of which are edible.

- **Mushrooms** feed off either living or decaying plants.

- **Poisonous mushrooms** are called toadstools.

- **The umbrella-shaped** part of the mushroom is called the fruiting body. Under the surface is a mass of fine stalk threads called the mycelium.

- **The threads** making up the mycelium are called hyphae (said 'hi-fi'). These absorb food.

- **The fruiting body** grows overnight after rain and lasts just a few days. The mycelium may survive underground for many years.

- **The fruiting body** is covered by a protective cap. On the underside of this cap are lots of thin sheets called gills. These gills are covered in spores.

- **A mushroom's** gills can produce 16 billion spores in its brief lifetime.

- **The biggest mushrooms** have caps up to 50 cm across and grow up to 40 cm tall.

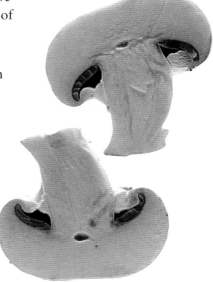

▶ *The ubiquitous button mushroom forms part of many international dishes, from Italian risotto to the classic English fry-up.*

192

● **Fairy rings** are rings of bright green grass once said to have been made by fairies dancing. They are actually made by a mushroom as its hyphae spread outwards. Chemicals they release make grass grow greener. Gradually the mycelium at the centre dies while outer edges grow and the ring gets bigger.

◀ *Like other fungi, mushrooms cannot make their own food and feed off hosts such as trees.*

**193**

# Garden flowers

- **All garden flowers** are descended from plants that were once wild, but they have been bred over the centuries to produce flowers quite unlike their wild relatives.

- **Garden flowers** like tea roses, created by cross-breeding two different species, are called hybrids.

- **Garden flowers** tend to have much bigger blooms and last for longer than their wild cousins.

- **By hybridization** gardeners have created colours that are impossible naturally, such as black roses.

- **Ornamentals** are flowers cultivated just for show.

▲ *Gardeners try to mix flowers that bloom at different times so the garden is always full of colour.*

- **Botanical gardens** such as those at Kew, London, display collections of flowers from many parts of the world.

- **18th-century botanist** Carl Linnaeus made a clock by planting flowers that bloomed at different times of day.

- **The earliest flowerbeds** were the borders of flower tufts Ancient Persians grew along pathways.

- **A herbaceous border** is a traditional flowerbed planted with herbaceous perennial flowers like delphiniums, chrysanthemums and primroses. It flowers year after year.

◀ *Most gardens now have a mix of trees and shrubs, mixed beds of herbaceous flowers and early-flowering bulbs such as crocuses.*

195

# The first crops

- **The first crops** were probably root crops like turnips. Grains and green vegetables were probably first grown as crops later.

- **Einkorn and emmer** wheat and wild barley may have been cultivated by Natufians (stone-age people) around about 7000BC at Ali Kosh on the border of Iran and Iraq.

▲ *Pumpkins are grown on bushes or on vines like these throughout Europe and North America.*

► *Flax was the most important vegetable fibre in Europe before cotton. It is still used to make linen.*

- **Pumpkins** and beans were cultivated in Mexico as long ago as c.7000BC.

- **People** in the Amazon have grown manioc to make a flat bread called cazabi for thousands of years.

- **Corn** was probably first grown about 9000 years ago from the teosinte plant of the Mexican highlands.

- **Russian botanist** N I Vavilov worked out that wheat and rye came from the wild grasses of central Asia, millet and barley from highland China and rice from India.

- **Millet** was grown in China from c.4500BC.

- **In northern Europe** the first grains were those now called fat hen, gold of pleasure and curl-topped lady's thumb.

- **Sumerian** farmers in the Middle East c.3000BC grew barley along with other produce such as wheat, flax, dates, apples, plums and grapes.

...**FASCINATING FACT**...
Beans, bottle gourds and water chestnuts were grown at Spirit Cave in Thailand 11,000 years ago.

# Cereals

- **Cereals** such as wheat, maize, rice, barley, sorghum, oats, rye and millet are the world's major sources of food.

- **Cereals are grasses** and we eat their seeds or grain.

- **The leaves and stalks** are usually left to rot into animal feed called silage.

- **Some grains** such as rice are simply cooked and eaten. Most are milled and processed into foods such as flour, oils and syrups.

- **In the developed world** – that is, places like North America and Europe – wheat is the most important food crop. But for half the world's population, including most people in Southeast Asia and China, rice is the staple food.

- **Many grains** are used to make alcoholic drinks such as whisky. A fermentation process turns the starch in the grains to alcohol. Special processing of barley creates a food called malt, which is used by brewers to make beer and lager.

- **Oats** have a higher food value than any other grain.

- **Rye** makes heavy, black bread. The bread is heavy because rye does not contain much gluten which yeast needs to make bread rise.

- **Russia** grows more oats and rye than any other country.

- **Millet** produces tiny seeds and is grown widely in dry regions of Africa and Asia. It was the main crop all over Europe, Asia and Africa in ancient and medieval times.

▶ *Harvesting wheat and using it to make flour is a surprisingly complex process. The process is still done with simple tools in some parts of the world. But in the developed world, the entire process is largely mechanized.*

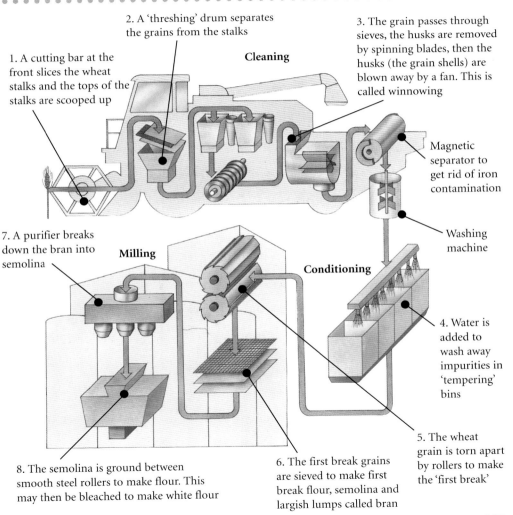

1. A cutting bar at the front slices the wheat stalks and the tops of the stalks are scooped up

2. A 'threshing' drum separates the grains from the stalks

**Cleaning**

3. The grain passes through sieves, the husks are removed by spinning blades, then the husks (the grain shells) are blown away by a fan. This is called winnowing

Magnetic separator to get rid of iron contamination

Washing machine

7. A purifier breaks down the bran into semolina

**Milling**

**Conditioning**

4. Water is added to wash away impurities in 'tempering' bins

5. The wheat grain is torn apart by rollers to make the 'first break'

8. The semolina is ground between smooth steel rollers to make flour. This may then be bleached to make white flour

6. The first break grains are sieved to make first break flour, semolina and largish lumps called bran

**199**

# Green vegetables

- **Green vegetables** are the edible green parts of plants, including the leaves of plants such as cabbages and lettuces, and the soft stems of plants like asparagus.

- **Cabbages** are a large group of green vegetables called the brassicas.

- **Cabbages were** originally developed from the sea cabbage (Brassica oleracea) which grew wild near sea coasts around Europe.

- **Kale and collard** are types of cabbage with loose, open leaves.

- **Common and savoy** cabbages are cabbages with leaves folded into a tight ball. Brussels sprouts are cabbages with lots of compact heads.

- **Cauliflower and broccoli** are cabbages with thick flowers. Kohlrabi is a cabbage with a  bulbous stem.

▶ *The edible young stems of the asparagus are called spears. If the spears are not harvested they grow into tall, feathery plants.*

- **The leaves of green vegetables** are rich in many essential vitamins including vitamin A, vitamin E and folic acid (one of the B vitamins).

- **Spinach** looks a little like kale, but it is actually a member of the goosefoot family, rich in vitamins A and C, and also in iron. The discovery of the iron content made spinach into the superfood of the cartoon hero Popeye, who would eat it to give himself extra strength.

- **Asparagus** belongs to the lily family. Garden asparagus has been prized since Roman times.

- **In Argenteuil** in France, asparagus is grown underground to keep it white. White asparagus is especially tender and has the best flavour.

▲ *Fresh spinach can be steamed or boiled, or used in salads, soups and pies. Sometimes it is sold frozen or tinned.*

◄ *Lettuces are among the most popular green salad vegetables, used in everything from the famous 'Caesar salads' to garnishes with fast food.*

**201**

# Root vegetables

▲ *Turnip roots are most commonly cooked in stews and casseroles, or used as animal feed.*

- **Vegetables** are basically any parts of a plant, except for the fruit, that are eaten, cooked or raw.

- **Root vegetables** are parts of a plant that grow underground in the soil.

- **Turnips, rutabaga,** beets, carrots, parsnips and sweet potatoes are the actual roots of the plant.

- **Potatoes and cassava** are tubers or storage stems.

- **Potatoes** were grown in South America at least 1800 years ago. They were brought to Europe by the Spanish in the 16th century.

- **Poor Irish** farmers came to depend on the potato, and when blight ruined the crop in the 1840s, many starved.

- **Yams are tropical roots** similar to sweet potatoes. They are an important food in West Africa. A single yam can weigh 45 kg or more.

- **Mangel-wurzels** are beet plants grown mainly to feed to farm animals.

- **Tapioca** is a starchy food made from cassava. It makes a popular pudding.

- **Carrots came** originally from Afghanistan, but were spread around the Mediterranean 4000 years ago. They reached China by the 13th century AD.

*▼▶ Potatoes and carrots are important root vegetables. Carrot is a source of vitamin A, potatoes are sources of many vitamins, such as C.*

# Herbs

- **Herbs** are small plants used as medicines or to flavour food.

- **Most herbs** are perennial and have soft stems which die back in winter.

- **With some herbs** such as rosemary, only the leaves are used. With others, such as garlic, the bulb is used. Fennel is used for its seeds as well as its bulb and leaves. Coriander is used for its leaves and seeds.

- **Basil** gets its name from the Greek *basilikon* or 'kingly', because it was so highly valued around the Mediterranean for its strong flavour. In the Middle Ages, judges and officials used to carry it in posies so as to ward off unpleasant smells.

- **Rosemary** is a coastal plant and gets its name from the Latin *ros marinus*, meaning 'sea dew'. People who study herbs – herbalists – once thought it improved memory.

- **Bay leaves** are the leaves of an evergreen laurel tree. They were used to make crowns for athletes, heroes and poets in Ancient Rome. It is said that a bay tree planted by your house protects it from lightning.

- **Oregano** or marjoram is a Mediterranean herb used in Italian cooking. The plant gave its name to the American state of Oregon where it is now commonly used.

- **Sage** is a herb thought by herbalists of old to have special healing qualities. Its scientific name *Salvia* comes from the Latin word *salvere*, 'to save'.

- **St John's wort** is a perennial herb with yellow flowers which was said to have healing qualities given by St John the Baptist. The red juice of its leaves represented his blood. Now many people use it to treat depression.

▼ *These are some of the more common herbs used in cooking, either fresh or dried. The flavour comes from what are called 'essential oils' in the leaves. Parsley, thyme and a bay leaf may be tied up in a piece of muslin cloth to make what is called a bouquet garni. This is hung in soups and stews while cooking to give them extra flavour, but is not actually eaten.*

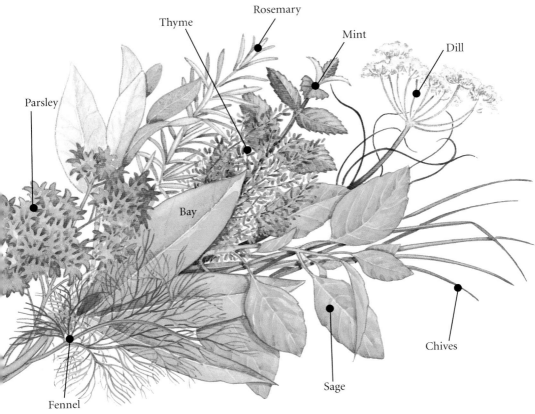

Rosemary

Thyme

Mint

Dill

Parsley

Bay

Fennel

Sage

Chives

**205**

# Medicinal plants

● **Prehistoric neanderthal people** probably used plants as medicines at least 50,000 years ago.

● **Until quite recently** herbaceous plants were our main source of medicines. Plants used as medicines were listed in books called herbals.

● **An ancient Chinese** list of 1892 herbal remedies drawn up over 3000 years ago is still used today.

● **The famous illustrated herbal** of Greek physician Dioscorides was made in the 1st century BC.

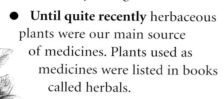

▲ Henbane is a pungent, poisonous herb. It produces a drug called hyoscyamine, used to dilate the pupils of the eyes.

▶ The bitter-tasting Centaury herb was once used to combat fevers and treat digestive disorders.

...FASCINATING FACT...

Vincristine is a drug made from the Madagascar periwinkle that helps children fight cancer.

- **The most famous English** herbalist was Nicholas Culpeper, who wrote *A Physical Directory* in 1649.

- **Most medicines**, except antibiotics, come from flowering plants or were first found in flowering plants.

- **Powerful painkilling** drugs come from the seeds of the opium poppy.

- *Digitalis* is a heart drug that came from foxgloves. It is poisonous if taken in large doses.

- **Garlic** is thought to protect the body against heart disease – and vampires!

▶ *The bark of the willow tree was originally used to make aspirin, the painkiller most widely used today.*

# Evolution

- **Charles Darwin's** Theory of Evolution, first published in 1859, showed how all species of plant and animal adapt and develop over millions of years.

- **Darwin's theory** depended on the fact that no two living things are alike.

- **Some animals** start life with characteristics that give them a better chance of surviving to pass the characteristics on to their offspring.

- **Other animals' characteristics** mean that they are less likely to survive.

- **Over many generations** and thousands of years, better-adapted animals and plants survive and flourish, while others die out or find a new home.

- **Fossil discoveries** since Darwin's time have supported his theory, and lines of evolution can be traced for thousands of species.

- **Fossils** also show that evolution is not always as slow and steady as Darwin thought. Some scientists believe change comes in rapid bursts, separated by long slow periods when little changes. Other scientists believe that bursts of rapid change interrupt periods of long steady change.

▼ *One of the horse's earliest ancestors,* Hyracotherium, *appeared about 45 million years ago. It was a small woodland creature which browsed on leaves. When the woods began to disappear and grasslands became more widespread, it paid to be faster to escape predators. The modern horse,* Equus, *is the latest result of this evolutionary adaptation.*

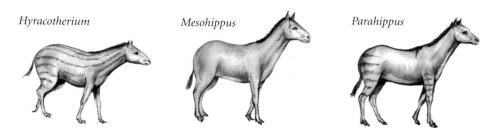

*Hyracotherium*          *Mesohippus*          *Parahippus*

- **For the first 3 billion years** of Earth's history, the only life forms were microscopic, single-celled, marine (sea) organisms such as bacteria and amoeba. Sponges and jellyfish, the first multi-celled creatures, appeared by 700 million years ago.

- **About 600 million years ago**, evolution speeded up dramatically in what is called the Precambrian explosion. Thousands of different organisms appeared within a very short space of time, including the first proper animals with bones and shells.

- **After the Precambrian**, life evolved rapidly. Fish developed, then insects and then, about 380 million years ago, amphibians, which were the first large creatures to crawl on land. About 340 million years ago, reptiles evolved – the first large creatures to live entirely on land.

- **Dinosaurs** developed from these early reptiles about 220 million years ago and dominated the Earth for 160 million years. Birds also evolved from the reptiles, and cynodonts furry, mammal-like creatures.

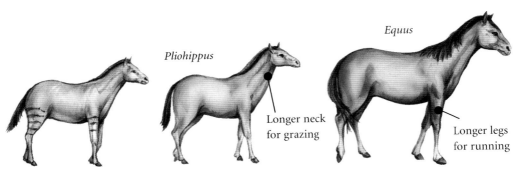

*Equus*

*Pliohippus*

Longer neck
for grazing

Longer legs
for running

**209**

# Life on the seashore

- **Seashores** contain a huge variety of creatures which can adapt to the constant change from wet to dry as the tide rolls in and out.

- **Crabs, shellfish** and other creatures of rocky shores have tough shells to protect them from pounding waves and the sun's drying heat.

- **Anemones, starfish** and shellfish such as barnacles have powerful suckers for holding on to rocks.

- **Limpets** are the best rock clingers and can only be prised off if caught by surprise.

- **Anemones** may live on a hermit crab's shell, feeding on its leftovers but protecting it with their stinging tentacles.

- **Rock pools** are water left behind among the rocks as the tide goes out.

- **Rock pool creatures** include shrimps, hermit crabs, anemones and fish such as blennies and gobies.

- **Sandy shores** are home to burrowing creatures such as crabs, razor clams, lugworms, sea cucumbers and burrowing anemones.

- **Sandhoppers** are tiny shelled creatures that live along the tide line, feeding on seaweed.

- **Beadlet anemones** look like blobs of jelly on rocks when the tide is out. But when the water returns, they open a ring of flower-like tentacles to feed.

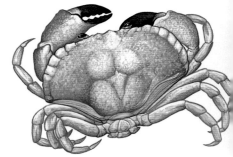

▶ *The edible crab, like all crabs, has five pairs of legs, the front pair with pincers.*

▼ *Crabs, lugworms, sandhoppers, shellfish and many other creatures live on seashores. Many birds come to feed on them.*

# Life in the oceans

- **Oceans** cover 70 percent of the Earth and they are the largest single animal habitat.

- **Scientists divide the ocean** into two main environments – the pelagic (which is the water itself), and the benthic (which is the seabed).

- **Most benthic animals** live in shallow waters around the continents. They include worms, clams, crabs and lobsters, as well as bottom-feeding fish.

- **Scientists call the sunny surface waters** the euphotic zone. This extends down 150 m and it is where billions of plankton (microscopic animals and plants) live.

- **Green plant plankton** (algae) in the oceans produce 30 percent of the world's vegetable matter each year.

- **Animal plankton** include shrimps and jellyfish.

- **The surface waters** are also home to squid, fish and mammals such as whales.

- **Below the surface zone,** down to about 2000 m, is the twilight bathyal zone. Here there is too little light for plants to grow, but many hunting fish and squid live.

- **Below 2000 m** is the dark abyssal zone, where only weird fish like gulper eels and anglerfish live.

- **The Sargasso** is a vast area in the west Atlantic where seaweed grows thick. It is a rich home for barnacles and other sea creatures.

▶ *The tassel-finned anglerfish is hardly larger than your thumb. The fleshy tassels on its chin resemble seaweed.*

▼ *Many kinds of fish and other sea creatures live in the sunlit zone near the surface of the oceans.*

# Life in rivers and lakes

- **Rivers, lakes** and other freshwater habitats are home to all sorts of fish, including bream and trout.

- **Fast-flowing streams** are preferred by fish such as trout and grayling. Slow-flowing rivers and lakes are home to tench, rudd and carp.

- **Some fish feed** on floating plant matter, while others take insects from the surface of the water.

- **Common bream and barbel** hunt on the riverbed, eating insect larvae, worms and molluscs.

- **Perch and pike** are predators of lakes and slow-flowing rivers.

- **Pike** are the sharks of the river – deadly hunters that lurk among weeds waiting for fish, or even rats and birds. Pike can weigh up to 30 kg.

▶ *Upland lakes like these are home to many fish, including char, powan and bullhead. Fish such as brown trout swim in the streams that tumble down into the lake.*

- **Mammals of rivers and lakes** include voles, water rats and otters.
- **Birds of rivers and lakes** include birds that dive for fish (such as kingfishers), small wading birds (such as redshanks, avocets and curlews), large wading birds (such as herons, storks and flamingos), and waterfowl (such as ducks, swans and geese.
- **Insects** include dragonflies and water boatmen.
- **Amphibians** include frogs and newts.

▶ *The grayling looks like a small trout, about 45 cm long, but with a larger sail-shaped back or dorsal fin. Like most members of the salmon family it has little, sharp teeth.*

215

# Life on the grasslands

- **Grasslands** form in temperate (moderate temperature) regions where there is too little rainfall for forests, but enough to allow grass to grow.

- **Temperate grasslands** include the prairies of North America, the pampas of South America, the veld of South Africa, and the vast steppes of Eurasia.

- **There is little cover** on grasslands, so many grassland animals have very good eyesight and large ears to detect predators from afar.

- **Some grassland animals escape** from predators by speed. These include jack rabbits, deer, pronghorn antelopes, wild asses and flightless birds like emus.

- **Some animals,** such as mice and prairie dogs, escape by hiding underground in burrows.

- **Some birds hide** by building their nests in bushes. These include meadowlarks, quails and blackbirds.

- **The main predators** are dogs like the coyote and fox.

- **The North American prairies** have a small wild cat called the bobcat.

- **Prairie dogs** live in huge underground colonies called towns. One contained 400 million animals and covered over 60,000 square kilometres.

- **When they meet,** prairie dogs kiss each other to find out whether they are from the same group.

▼ *Coyotes eat a vast range of prey from beetles to deer as well as fruits.*

▲*Until they were wiped out by European settlers, vast herds of bison (buffalo) roamed the North American prairies.*

# Life in woodlands

▲ *On a walk through a deciduous wood, you may be lucky enough to catch a glimpse of a shy young red deer as it crosses a clearing.*

- **Woodlands** in temperate zones between the tropics and the poles are home to many creatures.

- **Deciduous trees** lose their leaves in autumn. Evergreens keep theirs through cold winters.

- **In the leaf litter** under the trees live tiny creatures such as worms, millipedes, and ants and other insects.

- **Spiders, shrews, salamanders and mice** feed on the small creatures living in the leaf litter.

- **Some birds**, such as woodcocks, nest on the woodland floor and have mottled plumage to hide themselves.

- **Birds such as owls**, nuthatches, treecreepers, tits, woodpeckers and warblers live on and in trees, as well as insects such as beetles, moths and butterflies, and small mammals such as squirrels and raccoons.

- **Other woodland mammals** include badgers, chipmunks, opossums, stoats, weasels, polecats, pine martens and foxes.

- **Beavers, frogs, muskrats and otters** live near woodland streams.

- **The few large woodland mammals** include bears, deer, wolves and wild boar. Many of these have become rare because woods have been cleared away.

- **In winter,** many birds of deciduous woods migrate south, while small mammals like dormice hibernate.

▶ *The long flight feathers of an owl's wings are tipped with down which muffles the noise of the wing beats. Silent flying allows the owl a much better chance of catching prey.*

**219**

# Life in tropical rainforests

- **Tropical rainforests** are the richest and most diverse of all animal habitats.

- **Most animals** in tropical rainforests live in the canopy (treetops), and are either agile climbers or can fly.

- **Canopy animals** include flying creatures such as bats, birds and insects, and climbers such as monkeys, sloths, lizards and snakes.

- **Many rainforest creatures** can glide through the treetops – these include gliding geckos and other lizards, flying squirrels and even flying frogs.

▶ *Year-round rainfall and warm temperatures make rainforests incredibly lush, with a rich variety of plant life.*

▶ *Like the other 41 species in the bird of paradise group, the king bird lives in rainforests. In courtship the male vibrates his wings for display.*

- **Some tree frogs** live in the cups of rainwater held by plants growing high up in trees.

- **Antelopes, deer, hogs, tapir** and many different kinds of rodent roam the forest floor, hunting for seeds, roots, leaves and fruit.

- **Beside rivers** in Southeast Asian rainforests, there may be rhinoceroses, crocodiles and even elephants.

- **Millions of insect species** live in rainforests, including butterflies, moths, bees, termites and ants. There are also many spiders.

- **Rainforest butterflies and moths** are often big or vividly coloured, including the shimmering blue morpho of Brazil and the birdwing butterflies.

- **Rainforest birds** can be vividly coloured too, and include parrots, toucans and birds of paradise.

**221**

# Life in tropical grasslands

▲ *With their long necks, giraffes can feed on the high branches of the thorn trees that dot the savannah grasslands of Africa.*

- **Tropical grasslands** are home to vast herds of grazing animals such as antelope and buffalo – and to the lions, cheetahs and other big cats that prey on them.

- **There are few places to hide** on the grasslands, so most grassland animals are fast runners with long legs.

- **Pronghorn** can manage 67 km/h for 16 km.

- **There are more than 60 species** of antelope on the grasslands of Africa and southern Asia.

- **A century ago in South Africa,** herds of small antelopes called springboks could be as large as 10 million strong and hundreds of kilometres long.

222

▼ *The white rhino can weigh over 3.5 tonnes. The 'white' does not refer to the colour, which is pale grey. It means 'wide' from the broad snout.*

● **The springbok** gets its name from its habit of springing 3 m straight up in the air.

● **Grazing animals** are divided into perrisodactyls and artiodactyls, according to how many toes they have.

● **Artiodactyls** have an even number of toes. They include camels buffaloes, deer, antelope and cattle.

● **Perrisodactyls** have an odd number of toes on each foot. They include horses, rhinos and tapirs.

...FASCINATING FACT...
Cheetahs are the fastest runners in the world, reaching 110 km/h in short bursts.

223

# Life in the desert

- **In the Sahara desert,** a large antelope called the addax survives without waterholes because it gets all its water from its food.

- **Many small animals** cope with the desert heat by resting in burrows or sheltering under stones during the day. They come out to feed only at night.

- **Desert animals** include many insects, spiders, scorpions, lizards and snakes.

- **The dwarf puff adder** hides from the sun by burying itself in the sand until only its eyes show.

- **The fennec fox** and the antelope jack rabbit both lose heat through their ears. This way they keep cool.

- **The kangaroo rats** of California's Death Valley save water by eating their own droppings.

- **The Mojave squirrel** survives through long droughts by sleeping five or six days a week.

- **Swarms of desert locusts** can cover an area as big as 5000 sq km.

- **Sand grouse** fly hundreds of kilometres every night to reach watering holes.

◀ *The fennec fox lives in the Sahara Desert region where it feeds mainly on ants, termites and other tiny prey.*

224

▼ *Deserts like this are among the world's toughest environments for animals to survive.*

...FASCINATING FACT...
The African fringe-toed lizard dances to keep
cool, lifting each foot in turn off the hot sand.

# Life in the mountains

- **Mountains** are cold, windy places where only certain animals can survive – including agile hunters such as pumas and snow leopards, and nimble grazers such as mountain goats, yaks, ibex and chamois.

- **The world's highest-living** mammal is the yak, a type of wild cattle, which can survive more than 6000 m up in the Himalayas of Tibet.

- **Mountain goats** have hooves with sharp edges that dig into cracks in the rock, and hollow soles that act like suction pads.

◄ *Sheep like these dall sheep are well equipped for life in the mountains, with their thick woolly coats and ninmble feet.*

- **In winter,** the mountain goat's pelage (coat) turns white, making it hard to spot against the snow.
- **The Himalayan snowcock** nests higher than almost any other bird – often above 4000 m in the Himalayas.
- **The Alpine chough** has been seen flying at 8200 m up on Everest.
- **Lammergeiers** are the vultures of the African and southern European mountains. They break tough bones by dropping them from a great height onto stones and then eating the marrow.
- **The Andean condor** of the South American Andes is a gigantic scavenger that can carry off deer and sheep. It is said to dive from the skies like a fighter plane.
- **The puma,** or mountain lion, can jump well over 5 m up on to a rock ledge – that is like you jumping into an upstairs window.
- **The snow leopard** of the Himalayan mountains is now one of the rarest of all the big cats – it has been hunted almost to extinction for its beautiful fur coat.

▶ *The puma ranges from southern canada through North and central America to Patagonia in South America. It has a muscular build and uses the stalk-and-pounce method to catch prey.*

# Life in cold regions

- **The world's coldest places** are at the Poles in the Arctic and Antarctic, and high up mountains.

- **Only small animals** such as ice worms and insects can stand the extreme polar cold all year round.

- **Insects** such as springtails can live in temperatures as low as -38°C in Antarctica because their body fluids contain substances that do not freeze easily.

- **Birds** such as penguins, snow petrels and skuas live in Antarctica, as well as the leopard seals that eat penguins.

- **Polar seas** are home to whales, fish and shrimp-like krill.

- **Fish of cold seas** have body fluids that act like car anti-freeze to stop them freezing.

- **Mammals such as polar bears**, sea lions and walruses are so well insulated against the cold with their fur and fat that they can live on the Arctic ice for most of the year.

- **Many animals** live on the icy tundra land in the far north of America and Asia. They include caribou, Arctic foxes and hares, and birds such as ptarmigans and snowy owls.

- **Arctic foxes and hares**, ermines and ptarmigans turn white in winter to camouflage them against the snow.

◀ *The leopard seal is so-called because of its spotted grey coat. Its diet includes fish, squid and other seals. It lives on the pack ice around Antarctica.*

▼ *Other animals are the only substantial food in the Arctic wastes, so polar bears have to be carnivorous.*

....FASCINATING FACT....
Ptarmigans can survive through the bitter
Arctic winter by eating twigs.

229

# Baby animals

- **All baby mammals** except monotremes, are born from their mother's body, but most other creatures hatch from eggs.

- **Most creatures** hatch long after their parents have disappeared. Birds and mammals, however, usually look after their young.

- **Most birds** feed their hungry nestlings until they are big enough to find food for themselves.

- **Some small birds** may make 10,000 trips to the nest to feed their young.

- **Cuckoos** lay their egg in the nest of another, smaller bird. The foster parents hatch it and look after it as it grows. It then pushes its smaller, foster brothers and sisters out of the nest.

▶ *Lion cubs are looked after by several females until they are big enough to fend for themselves. Like many babies they have big paws, head and ears compared to the size of their bodies.*

- **Mammals nurse** their young (they feed them on the mother's milk).The nursing period varies. It tends to be just a few weeks in small animals like mice, but several years in large animals like elephants.

- **Many animals** play when they are young. Playing helps them develop co-ordination and strength, and practise tasks they will have to do for real as adults.

- **When they are young**, baby opossums cling all over their mother as she moves around.

- **Some baby animals**, including baby shrews and elephants, go around in a long line behind the mother, clinging to the tail of the brother or sister in front.

▶ *A baby elephant is fed by its mother for two years. By the time it is fully grown, it will be eating about 150 kg of food each day – the weight of two people!*

**231**

# Communication

- **Crows** use at least 300 different croaks to communicate with each other. However, crows from one area cannot understand crows from another one.

- **When two howler monkey troops** meet, the males scream at each other until one troop gives way.

- **The male orang-utan** burps to warn other males to keep away.

- **Dogs** communicate through barks, yelps, whines, growls and howls.

- **Many insects communicate** through the smell of chemicals called pheromones, which are released from special glands.

- **Tropical tree ant species** use ten different pheromones, combining them with different movements to send 50 different kinds of message.

◀ Orang-utans are shy and seldom seen. However, they may be heard occasionally – making burping noises to scare off other males!

▶ *Lone wolves often howl at dusk or in the night to signal their ownership of a particular territory and to warn off rival wolves.*

- **A gorilla** named Coco was trained so that she could use over 1000 different signs to communicate, each sign meaning different words. She called her pet cat 'Soft good cat cat', and herself 'Fine animal gorilla'.

- **Female glow worms** communicate with males by making a series of flashes.

- **Many birds** are mimics and can imitate a whole variety of different sounds, including the human voice and machines like telephones.

```
...FASCINATING FACT...
Using sign language, Coco the gorilla
took an IQ test and got a score of 95.
```

# Migration

- **Migration** is when animals move from one place to another to avoid the cold or to find food and water.

- **Some migrations** are daily, some are seasonal, and some are permanent.

- **Starlings** migrate every day from the country to their roosts in the towns and cities.

- **Many birds, whales seals and bats** migrate closer to the tropics in the autumn to escape the winter cold.

- **One knot** (a kind of small bird) took just 8 days to fly 5600 km, from Britain to West Africa.

- **Barheaded geese** migrate right over the top of the Himalayan mountains, flying as high as 8000 m.

▲ *No other creature migrates so far every year as the Arctic tern. It breeds in the short Arctic summer, then flies halfway around the world to spend another summer in Antarctica.*

- **Migrating birds** are often brilliant navigators. Bristle-thighed curlews find their way from Alaska to tiny islands in the Pacific 9000 km away.

- **Shearwaters,** sparrows and homing pigeons are able to fly home when released by scientists in strange places, thousands of kilometres away.

- **The Arctic tern** is the greatest migrator, flying 30,000 km from the Arctic to the Antarctic and back again each year.

- **Monarch butterflies** migrate 4000 km every year, from North America to small clumps of trees in Mexico. Remarkably, the migrating butterflies have never made the journey before.

▲ *In summer, moose spend most of the time alone. In winter they gather and trample areas of snow (called yards) to help each other get at the grass beneath.*

235

# What are insects?

*◀ Insects were the first creatures to live on land – nearly a quarter of a billion years before the first dinosaurs – and the first to fly.*

- **Insects** may be tiny, but there are more of them than all the other animals put together – over 1 million known species.

- **They range** from tiny flies to huge beetles, and they are found everywhere there is land.

- **Insects** have six legs and a body divided into three sections – which is why they are called insects ('in sections'). The sections are the head, thorax and abdomen.

- **An insect's body** is encased in such a tough shell (its exoskeleton) that there is no need for bones.

- **Insects grow** by getting rid of their old exoskeleton and replacing it with a bigger one. This is called moulting.

- **Insects change** dramatically as they grow. Butterflies, moths, and beetles undergo metamorphosis. Grasshoppers and mayflies begin as wingless nymphs, then gradually grow wings with each moult. Silverfish and springtails simply get bigger with each moult.

- **Insects' eyes** are called compound because they are made up of many lenses – from six (worker ants) to more than 30,000 (dragonflies).

- **Insects have** two antennae (feelers) on their heads.

- **Insects** do not have lungs. Instead, they breathe through holes in their sides called spiracles, linked to their body through tubes called tracheae.

- **The world's longest insect** is the giant stick insect of Indonesia, which can grow to 33 cm long.

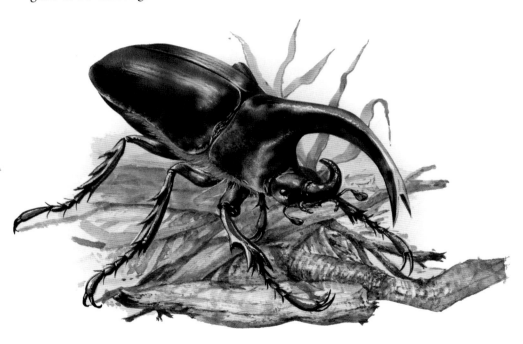

▲ *The rhinoceros beetle shown here can push an object 850 times its own weight, which is equivalent to a person pushing a 50-tonne army tank!*

237

# Butterflies

- **Butterflies** are insects with four large wings that feed either on the nectar of flowers or on fruit.

- **Together with moths,** butterflies make up the scientific order Lepidoptera – meaning 'scaly wings'. There are more than 165,000 species of Lepidoptera – 20,000 butterflies and 145,000 moths.

- **Many butterflies** are brightly coloured and fly by day. They have slim, hairless bodies and club-shaped antennae (feelers).

- **The biggest butterfly** is the Queen Alexandra's birdwing of New Guinea, with 25 cm-wide wings. The smallest is the Western pygmy blue.

▲ *Every species of butterfly has its own wing pattern, just like humans have their own fingerprint.*

- **Butterflies can only fly** if their wing muscles are warm. To warm up, they bask in the sun so their wings soak up energy like solar panels.

- **The monarch butterfly** is such a strong flier it can cross the Atlantic Ocean.

- **The shimmering blue wings** of the South American morpho butterfly are very beautiful. In the 19th century, millions of them were made into brooches.

- **Most female butterflies** live only a few days, so they have to mate and lay eggs quickly. Most males court them with elaborate flying displays.

- **Butterflies** taste with their tarsi (feet). Females 'stamp' on leaves to see if they are ripe enough for egg laying.

- **Every butterfly's caterpillar** has its own chosen food plants – different from the flowers the adult feeds on.

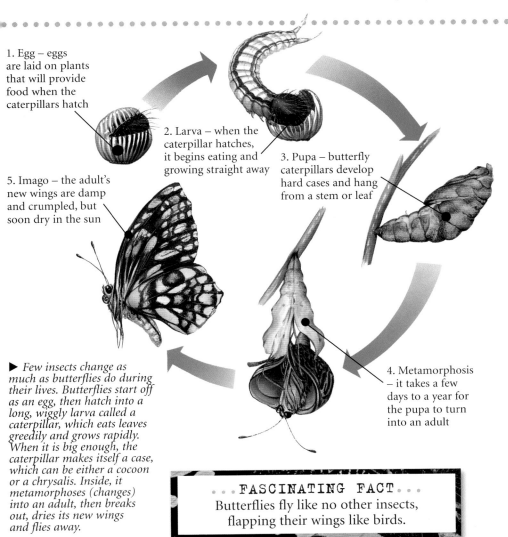

1. Egg – eggs are laid on plants that will provide food when the caterpillars hatch

2. Larva – when the caterpillar hatches, it begins eating and growing straight away

3. Pupa – butterfly caterpillars develop hard cases and hang from a stem or leaf

4. Metamorphosis – it takes a few days to a year for the pupa to turn into an adult

5. Imago – the adult's new wings are damp and crumpled, but soon dry in the sun

▶ *Few insects change as much as butterflies do during their lives. Butterflies start off as an egg, then hatch into a long, wiggly larva called a caterpillar, which eats leaves greedily and grows rapidly. When it is big enough, the caterpillar makes itself a case, which can be either a cocoon or a chrysalis. Inside, it metamorphoses (changes) into an adult, then breaks out, dries its new wings and flies away.*

...FASCINATING FACT...
Butterflies fly like no other insects,
flapping their wings like birds.

239

# Ants and termites

- **Ants are a vast group** of insects related to bees and wasps. Most ants have a tiny waist and are wingless.

- **Ants are the main insects** in tropical forests, living in colonies of anything from 20 to millions.

- **Ant colonies** are all female. Most species have one or several queens which lay the eggs. Hundreds of soldier ants guard the queen, while smaller workers build the nest and care for the young.

- **Males** only enter the nest to mate with young queens, then die.

- **Wood ants** squirt acid from their abdomen to kill enemies.

- **Army ants** march in huge swarms, eating most small creatures they meet.

- **Groups of army ants** cut any large prey they catch into pieces which they carry back to the nest. Army ants can carry 50 times their own weight.

- **Ants** known as slavemakers raid the nests of other ants and steal their young to raise as slaves.

- **Termite colonies** are even more complex than ant ones. They have a large king and queen who mate, as well as soldiers to guard them and workers to do all the work.

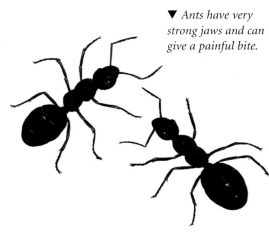

▼ *Ants have very strong jaws and can give a painful bite.*

- **Termite nests** are mounds built like cities with many chambers – including a garden used for growing fungus. Many are air-conditioned with special chimneys.

▶ *African termites use mud and saliva to build amazing nests more than 12 m high, housing over 5 million termites. Termites (Isoptera) belong to a separate insect group from ants, bees and wasps (Hymenoptera).*

# Spiders

▶ Like all arachnids, spiders have eight legs, plus two 'arms' called pedipalps and a pair of fangs called chelicerae. They also have eight simple eyes.

- **Spiders** are small scurrying creatures which, unlike insects, have eight legs – not six, and bodies with two parts – not three.

- **Spiders** belong to a group of 70,000 creatures called arachnids, which also includes scorpions, mites and ticks.

- **Spiders** live in nooks and crannies almost everywhere in the world, especially where there is plenty of vegetation to feed tiny creatures.

- **Spiders are hunters** and most of them feed mainly on insects. Despite their name, bird-eating spiders rarely eat birds, preferring lizards and small rodents such as mice.

- **Spiders have eight eyes,** but most have poor eyesight and hunt by feeling vibrations with their legs.

- **Many spiders** catch their prey by weaving silken nets called webs. Some webs are simple tubes in holes. Others, called orb webs, are elaborate and round. Spiders' webs are sticky to trap insects.

- **The Australian trapdoor** spider ambushes its prey from a burrow with a camouflaged entrance flap.

- **Most spiders** have a poisonous bite which they use to stun or kill their prey. Tarantulas and sun spiders crush their victims with their powerful jaws.

- **The bite of black widow** and red-back funnel web spiders is so poisonous that it can kill humans.

▶ *All spiders produce silk. Some turn this silk into inticate webs, first for catching prey and then for trussing them up.*

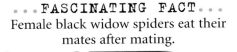

...FASCINATING FACT...
Female black widow spiders eat their
mates after mating.

# What is a fish?

- **Fish** are mostly slim, streamlined animals that live in water. Many are covered in tiny shiny plates called scales. Most have bony skeletons and a backbone.

- **There are well over 21,000 species** of fish, ranging from the 8 mm-long pygmy goby to the 12 m-long whale shark.

- **Fish** are cold-blooded.

- **Fish breathe** through gills – rows of feathery brushes inside each side of the fish's head.

- **To get oxygen**, fish gulp water in through their mouths and draw it over their gills.

- **Fish** have fins for swimming, not limbs.

▲ *The arapaima lives in the swampy parts of tropical south America. It can breathe in the normal fish way using its gills or gulp down air. It can grow to a vast 3 m in length and weigh up to 200 kg.*

- **Most fish** have a pectoral fin behind each gill and two pelvic fins below to the rear, as well as a dorsal fin on top of their body, an anal fin beneath, and a caudal (tail) fin.

- **Fish let gas in** and out of their swim bladders to float at particular depths.

- **Some fish** communicate by making sounds with their swim bladder. Catfish use them like bagpipes.

244

▼ *Angling (catching fish) is a popular pastime all around the world. The fish is hooked as it bites the lure or bait.*

...FASCINATING FACT...
The drum fish makes a drumming sound
with its swim bladder.

245

# Sharks

- **Sharks** are the most fearsome predatory fish of the seas. There are 375 species, living mostly in warm seas.

- **Sharks** have a skeleton made of rubbery cartilage – most other kinds of fish have bony skeletons.

- **The world's biggest fish** is the whale shark, which can grow to well over 12 m long. Unlike other sharks, the whale shark and the basking shark (at 9 m long) mostly eat plankton and are completely harmless.

- **A shark's main weapons** are its teeth – they are powerful enough to bite through plate steel.

▼ *A shark's torpedo-shaped body makes it a very fast swimmer.*

> ...FASCINATING FACT...
> Great white sharks are the biggest meat-eating
> sharks, growing to over 7 m long.

- **Sharks** put so much strain on their teeth that they always have three or four spare rows of teeth in reserve.

- **Nurse sharks** grow a new set of teeth every 8 days.

- **Up to 20** people die from recorded shark attacks each year.

- **The killing machine** of the shark world is the great white shark, responsible for most attacks on humans.

- **Hammerhead sharks** can also be dangerous. They have T-shaped heads, with eyes and nostrils at the end of the T.

▶ *The super-streamlined blue shark lives in warm seas and is 3.7 m in length. It has very long side fins and eats surface fish like herring and mackerel.*

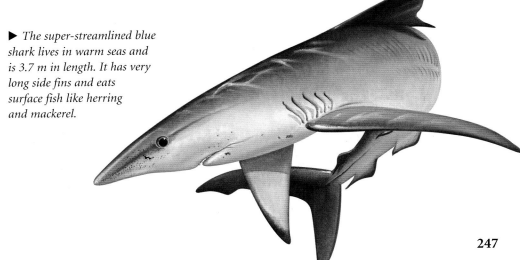

# Ocean fish

- **Nearly 75 percent** of all fish live in the seas and oceans.

- **The biggest, fastest swimming fish,** such as swordfish and marlin, live near the surface of the open ocean, far from land. They often migrate vast distances to spawn (lay their eggs) or find food.

- **Many smaller fish** live deeper down, including seabed-dwellers like eels and flatfish (such as plaice, turbot and flounders).

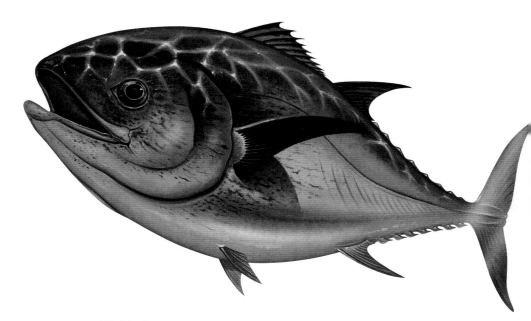

▲ *The bluefin tuna can grow to a massive 4 m in length and 700 kg in weight. It lives in all seas and oceans but moves around with the seasons.*

◀ *Flying fish beat their tails so fast they are able to 'fly' away from predators.*

- **Flatfish** start life as normal-shaped fish. As they grow older, one eye slowly slides around the head to join the other. The pattern of scales also changes so that one side is the top and one side is the bottom.

- **Plaice** lie on the seabed on their left side, while turbot lie on their right side. Some flounders lie on their left and some on their right.

- **The upper side** of a flatfish is usually camouflaged to help it blend in with the seabed.

- **In the temperate waters** of the Atlantic there are rich fishing grounds for fish such as herring.

- **The swordfish** can swim at up to 80 km/h. It uses its long spike to stab squid.

- **The bluefin tuna** can grow to as long as 3 m and weigh more than 500 kg. It is also a fast swimmer – one crossed the Atlantic in 199 days.

> **. . . FASCINATING FACT . . .**
> Flying fish can glide over the sea for 400 m
> and soar up to 6 m above the waves.

249

# Strange deep-sea creatures

- **Deep-sea anglerfish** live deep down in the ocean where it is pitch black. They lure prey into their mouths using a special fishing-rod-like fin spine with a light at its tip.

- **Anglerfish** cannot find each other easily in the dark, so when a male meets a female he stays with her until mating time.

- **Hatchet fish** have giant eyeballs that point upwards so they see prey from below as silhouettes against the surface.

▼ *The viperfish looks fearsome and is one of the larger predators of the ocean depths. Yet it is only 30 cm long. The general lack of food in the deep means animals are mostly small.*

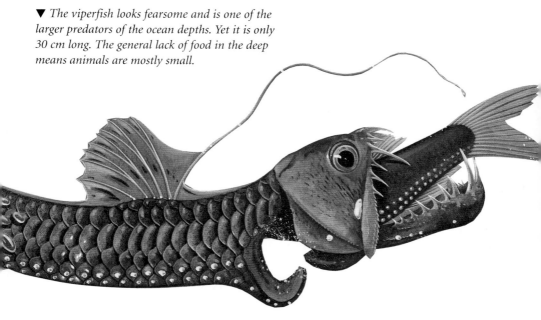

- **Viperfish** shine in the dark, thousands of metres down, and look like a jet airliner at night, with rows of lights along their bodies.

- **Siphonophores** are colonies of tiny creatures that live in the deep oceans. They string themselves together in lines 20 m long and glow – so they look like fairy lights.

- **The cirrate octopod** looks like a jelly because its skin is 95 percent water – the water cannot be crushed by the intense pressure of the deep oceans where it lives.

▲ *The porcupine fish inflates like a spiny balloon.*

- **The weedy seadragon** of Australia is a seahorse, but it looks just like a piece of flapping seaweed.

- **The sleeper shark** lives in the freezing depths of the North Atlantic and Arctic Oceans. This shark is 6.5 m long, but very slow and sluggish.

- **Flashlight fish** have light organs made by billions of bacteria which shine like headlights. The fish can suddenly block off these lights and change direction in the dark to confuse predators.

- **In the Arab-Israeli War** of 1967 a shoal of flashlight fish was mistaken for enemy frogmen and blown right out of the water.

**251**

# Whales

- **Whales,** dolphins and porpoises are large mammals called cetaceans that live mostly in the seas and oceans. Dolphins and porpoises are small whales.

- **Like all mammals**, whales have lungs – this means they have to come to the surface to breathe every 10 minutes or so, although they can stay down for up to 40 minutes. A sperm whale can hold its breath for 2 hours.

- **Whales breathe** through blowholes on top of their head. When a whale breathes out, it spouts out water vapour and mucus. When it breathes in, it sucks in about 2000 litres of air within about 2 seconds.

- **Like land mammals,** whales nurse their babies with their own milk. Whale milk is so rich that babies grow incredibly fast. Blue whale babies are over 7 m long when they are born and gain an extra 100 kg or so a day for about 7 months.

▶ *Killer whales or orcas are big deep-sea predators, growing to as long as 9 m and weighing up to 10 tonnes. They feed on fish, seals, penguins and dolphins.*

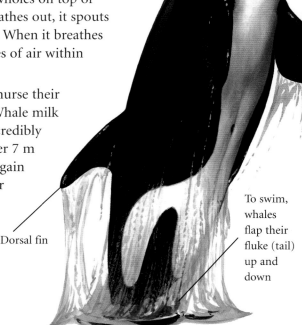

Dorsal fin

To swim, whales flap their fluke (tail) up and down

▶ *Humpback whales live together in groups called pods and keep in touch with their own 'dialect' of noises.*

- **Toothed whales,** such as the sperm whale and the orca or killer whale, have teeth and prey on large fish and seals. The six groups of toothed whale are sperm whales, beaked whales, belugas and narwhals, dolphins, porpoises, and river dolphins.

- **Baleen whales,** such as the humpback and blue, have a comb of thin plates called baleen in place of teeth. They feed by straining small, shrimp-like creatures called krill through their baleen. There are five baleen whale groups, including right whales, grey whales and rorquals. Rorquals have grooves on their throats and include humpback, minke and blue whales.

- **The blue whale** is the largest creature that ever lived. Blue whales grow to be over 30 m long and weigh more than 150 tonnes. In summer, they eat over 4 tonnes of krill every day – that is 4 million krill.

- **Whales keep in touch** with sounds called phonations. Large baleen whales make sounds which are too low for humans to hear, but they can be heard by other whales at least 80 km away.

- **Most baleen whales** live alone or in small groups, but toothed whales – especially dolphins – often swim together in groups called pods or schools.

> **. . . FASCINATING FACT . . .**
> Male humpbacks make elaborate 'songs' lasting
> 20 minutes or more – perhaps to woo females.

**253**

# Dolphins

◄ *The Atlantic humpbacked dolphin inhabits mainly shallower waters, but is also known to swim close to fishing boats where it can feed on the rich shoals.*

- **Groups of common dolphins**, travelling and feeding together, may number up to 2000 individuals.

- **Orcas**, or killer whales, are actually the largest species of dolphin, though they feed on other dolphin species.

- **There are five species** of freshwater dolphin living in Asian and South American rivers. Most catch fish by sound rather than sight.

- **Dolphins** have been known to aid humans by keeping them afloat and driving off attacking sharks.

- **Spinner dolphins** are named for the acrobatic leaps they perform, spinning up to seven times in mid air.

- **The Atlantic hump-backed dolphin** helps fishermen in West Africa by driving shoals of mullet into their nets.

- **In Mexico's Baja California**, bottle-nosed dolphins chase fish up onto the shore, then roll up onto the beach, completely out of the water, to grab them.

- **Military observers** once recorded a group of dolphins swimming at 64 km/h in the bow wave of a warship.

- **The striped dolphin**, seen in ancient Greek paintings, leaps up to 7 m to perform somersaults and spins.

- **The Yangtse dolphin**, or baiji, is one of the world's rarest mammals – probably less than 300 survive.

▼ *Many dolphin species 'spy-hop'. holding their heads out of the water as they check on their surroundings for predators and potential food.*

# Reptiles and amphibians

- **Reptiles** are scaly-skinned animals which live in many different habitats mainly in warm regions. They include crocodiles, lizards, snakes and tortoises.

- **Reptiles are cold-blooded,** but this does not mean that their blood is cold. A reptile's body cannot keep its blood warm, and it has to control its temperature by moving between hot and cool places.

- **Reptiles bask in the sun** to gain energy to hunt, and are often less active at cooler times of year.

◀ *Like all reptiles, crocodiles rely on basking in the sun to gain energy for hunting. At night, or when it is cold, they usually sleep.*

*◄ Newts are amphibians. The long, finlike crest on the back of this great crested newt becomes taller and more colourful in spring when the male attracts a female for mating. This large newt measures 17 cm.*

- **Reptiles bask in the sun** to gain energy to hunt, and are often less active at cooler times of year.

- **A reptile's skin** looks slimy, but it is quite dry. It keeps in moisture so well that reptiles can survive in deserts. The skin often turns darker to absorb the sun's heat.

- **Although reptiles grow** for most of their lives, their skin does not, so they must slough (shed) it every now and then.

- **Amphibians** are animals that live both on land and in water. They include frogs, toads, newts and salamanders.

- **Most reptiles** lay their eggs on land, but amphibians hatch out in water as tadpoles, from huge clutches of eggs called spawn.

- **Like fish,** tadpoles have gills to breathe in water, but they soon metamorphose (change), growing legs and lungs.

- **Amphibians** never stray far from water.

> ...FASCINATING FACT...
> Reptiles were the first large creatures to live
> entirely on land, over 350 million years ago.

# Dinosaurs

- **Dinosaurs** were reptiles that dominated life on land from about 220 million to 65 million years ago, when all of them mysteriously became extinct.

- **Although modern reptiles** walk with bent legs splayed out, dinosaurs had straight legs under their bodies – this meant they could run fast or grow heavy.

- **Some dinosaurs** ran on their back two legs, as birds do. Others had four sturdy legs like an elephant's.

- **Dinosaurs** are split into two groups according to their hip bones – saurischians had reptile-like hips and ornithischians had birdlike hips.

▶ Stegosaurus *had a tiny skull relative to its body size, and a brain the size of a walnut. It had rows of plates along its back with four long spines at the end of its tail.*

*◄ Dinosaur means 'terrible lizard', and they came in all shapes and sizes. This is a plant-eating sauropod called* Diplodocus.

- **Saurischians** were either swift, two-legged predators called theropods, or hefty four-legged herbivores called sauropods.

- **Theropods** had acute eyesight, fearsome claws and sharp teeth. They included *Tyrannosaurus rex*, one of the biggest hunting animals to ever live on land – over 15 m long, 5 m tall and weighing more than 7 tonnes.

- **Sauropods** had massive bodies, long tails, and long, snake-like necks.

- **The sauropod *Brachiosaurus*** was over 23 m long, weighed 80 tonnes and towered 12 m into the air. It was one of the biggest creature ever to live on land.

- **Most dinosaurs** are known from fossilized bones, but fossilized eggs, footprints and droppings have also been found. In 1913, mummified hadrosaur skin was discovered.

- **Some scientists** think the dinosaurs died out after a huge meteor struck Earth off Mexico, creating a cloud that blocked the sun's light and heat.

# Lizards

- **Lizards** are a group of 3800 scaly-skinned reptiles, varying from a few centimetres long to the 3 m-long Komodo dragon.

- **Lizards cannot** control their own body heat, and so rely on sunshine for warmth. This is why they live in warm climates and bask in the sun for hours each day.

- **Lizards move** in many ways – running, scampering and slithering. Some can glide. Unlike mammals, their limbs stick out sideways rather than downwards.

- **Most lizards** lay eggs, although a few give birth to live young. Unlike birds or mammals, a mother lizard does not nurture (look after) her young.

- **Most lizards** are meat-eaters, feeding on insects and other small creatures.

▶ *Lizards have four legs and a long tail. In most lizards, the back legs are much stronger than the front, and are used to drive the animal forwards in a kind of writhing motion.*

► *Geckos are small lizards that are mainly active at night. Their toes are are covered in hairy pads, which help them to stick to rough surfaces. Some geckos can even walk upside down.*

● **The glass lizard** has no legs. Its tail may break off and lie wriggling as a decoy if it is attacked. The lizard later grows another one.

● **The Australian frilled lizard** has a ruff around its neck. To put off attackers, it can spread out its ruff to make itself look three or four times bigger.

● **Horned lizards** can squirt a jet of blood from their eyes almost as far as 1 m to put off attackers.

● **The Komodo dragon** of Sumatra is the biggest lizard, weighing up to 150 kg or more. It can catch deer and pigs and swallow them whole.

...FASCINATING FACT...
The Basilisk lizard is also known as the Jesus
Christ lizard because it can walk on water.

# What are birds?

◀ *One of Europe's smallest birds, the wren is found in many habitats from open moor to dense marsh. It holds its tail almost upright and builds a domed nest among tree roots.*

- **Not all birds** can fly, but they all have feathers.

- **Feathers** are light, but they are linked by hooks called barbs to make them strong enough for flight.

- **Wrens** have 1000 feathers, while swans have 20,000.

- **Birds have four kinds** of wing feather – large primaries, smaller secondaries, coverts and contours.

- **Every kind of bird** has its own formation pattern and colour of feathers, called its plumage.

- **Instead of a teeth,** birds have a hard beak or bill.

- **Unlike humans,** birds do not give birth to babies. Instead they lay eggs, usually sitting on them to keep them warm until they hatch.

- **Birds fly in two ways** – by gliding with their wings held still, or by flapping their wings up and down.

- **Gliding is less effort** than flapping, and birds that stay in the air a long time tend to be superb gliders – including birds of prey, swifts, gulls and gannets.

- **Albatrosses and petrels** have long narrow wings that help them sail upwards on rising air currents.

▼ *Most birds flap their wings to fly. Even birds that spend much of their time gliding have to flap their wings to take off and land.*

...FASCINATING FACT...
Birds may be descended from dinosaurs and
took to the air 150 million years ago.

# Early birds

- **The earliest known bird** is *Archaeopteryx*, which lived 155–150 million years ago. It had feathers like a modern bird but teeth like a reptile.

- **Ichthyornis** was a seabird with long, toothed jaws. It lived alongside dinosaurs in the Late Cretaceous Period.

- **Although it could fly**, *Archaeopteryx* could not take off from the ground, and probably had to climb a tree before launching itself into the air.

- **Scientists believe** that birds evolved from lightly built dinosaurs such as *Compsognathus*, which ran on two legs.

- **The dodo** stood 1 m tall and lived on the island of Mauritius. It became extinct in the 17th century.

◄ Archaeopteryx *had a wingspan of about 50 cm. Its name means 'ancient wing'.*

- ***Aepyornis*** (also known as the 'elephant bird'), a 3-m tall ostrich ancestor from Madagascar, probably became extinct in the 17th century.

- **The eggs** of *Aepyornis* may have weighed as much as 10 kg – more than 9 times the weight of an ostrich egg today.

- **The tallest bird ever** was the moa (*Dinornis*) of New Zealand. It was a towering 3.5 m tall.

- **The great auk** first lived 2 million years ago. It became extinct in the mid 19th century after being overhunted for its fat, which was burned in oil lamps.

- **An early member** of the vulture family, *Argentavix* of South America had an amazing 7.3 m wingspan.

▶ *Like today's seabirds,* Ichthyornis *probably fed on fish which it caught in its long toothed jaws.*

265

# Beaks and feet

- **No bird** has more than four toes, but some have three and the ostrich has only two.

- **Four-toed birds** have different arrangements of toes: in swifts, all four point forwards; in most perching birds, three point forwards and one backwards; and in parrots, two point forwards and two backwards.

- **A beak** is made up of a bird's projecting jaw bones, covered in a hard horny material.

- **The hyacinth macaw** has one of the most powerful beaks of any bird, strong enough to crack brazil nuts.

- **Webbed feet** make all waterbirds very efficient paddlers.

- **The Australian pelican** has the largest beak of any bird, at up to 50 cm long.

- **Nightjars** have the shortest beaks, at 8–10 mm long.

◀ *The sword-billed hummingbird has an extremely long beak and a long tongue for extracting nectar from flowers.*

- **A bird stands** on the tips of its toes – the backward bending joint halfway down its leg is the ankle joint.

- **A bird's beak** is extremely sensitive to touch. Birds that probe in the ground for food have extra sensory organs at the beak tip.

▲ *The crossbill is so-called because the upper and lower portions of its beak cross over one another.*

▼ *Below is the foot of a bird of prey. Its long, curving talons make deadly weapons.*

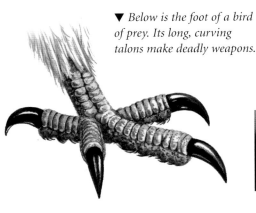

. . . **FASCINATING FACT** . . .
A baby bird has a spike called an 'egg-tooth' on its beak for breaking its way out of its egg.

# Birds' eggs and nests

*◄ After they lay their eggs, most birds sit on them to keep their eggs warm until they are ready to hatch. This is called incubating the eggs.*

- **All birds** begin life as eggs. Each species' egg is a slightly different colour.

- **The plover's egg** is pear-shaped. The owl's is round.

- **Hornbills** lay just one egg a year. Partridges lay up to 20 eggs. Hens and some ducks can lay around 350 a year.

- **Most birds build nests** to lay their eggs in – usually bowl-shaped and made from twigs, grasses and leaves.

- **The biggest nest** is that of the Australian mallee fowl, which builds a mound of soil 5 m across, with egg-chambers filled with rotting vegetation to keep it warm.

- **The weaverbirds** of Africa and Asia are very sociable. Some work together to weave huge, hanging nests out of straw, with scores of chambers. Each chamber is for a pair of birds and has its own entrance.

- **Ovenbirds** of Central and South America get their name because their nests look like the clay ovens made by local people. Some ovenbirds' nests can be as much as 3 m high.

- **Flamingos** nest on lakes, building mud nests that look like upturned sandcastles poking out of the water. They lay one or two eggs on top.

- **The great treeswift** lays its single egg in a nest the size of an eggcup.

▼ *The bittern, famous for its bull-like booming call, feeds on animals living in reed beds. This is where it makes its nest.*

.·.·FASCINATING FACT·.·.
Great auks' eggs are pointed at one end to stop them rolling off their cliff-edge nests.

269

# What are mammals?

- **Humans** feel close to mammals because they, too, are mammals, with hairy bodies, a large brain and special mammary glands for feeding their young with milk.

- **There are about 4500 species** of mammals in the world (and at least 1 million insect species!).

- **All mammals** except the duckbilled platypus and spiny anteater give birth to live young.

- **Mammals** evolved from reptiles, but are warm blooded.

- **The two main mammal groups** are the marsupials (whose young develop in the mother's pouch) and placentals.

- **All mammals have three little bones** in their ears that transfer sound vibrations to the inner ear from the eardrum.

▲ *Some mammals are very vulnerable because of human influences such as hunting or loss of habitat. The tiger is in the 'critically endangered' category on the Red List of Threatened Species.*

- **Mammals** have a variety of teeth shapes: chisels for gnawing, long fangs for fighting and killing prey, sharp-edged slicers and flat-topped crushers.
- **The platypus and spiny anteater** are egg-laying mammals called monotremes.
- **Mammals have a palate** that enables them to breathe through their noses while chewing.
- **Mammals** give a level of maternal care beyond that of other animals.

▼ *Young mammals mature more slowly than other animal young, so they are looked after for longer.*

# Mammals' senses

- **Cheetahs have a band of light-sensitive nerve cells** across their retinas that give clear vision ahead and to the sides.

- **Desert mammals** such as the long-eared kit fox find sharp hearing more useful than a keen sense of smell in the dry air.

- **Polar bears** can smell seals up to 60 km away across the ice.

- **Cats have glands** between their toes that leave an identifying scent when they scratch trees.

- **Blue whales** and fin whales communicate by means of the loudest sounds produced by any living creature (up to 188 dB).

▼ *Large cats have eyes on the front of their heads rather than at the sides, helping them to focus on their prey as they hunt.*

▲ *Whales and dolphins communicate with each other using echolocation.*

● **Baby wood-mice** emit ultrasonic distress calls in their first 10 days to summon their mother.

● **Many nocturnal mammals** have reflective areas in their eyes that help night vision.

● **Migrating whales** can sense the Earth's magnetic field, due to particles of the mineral magnetite in their bodies.

● **The exceptionally large ears** of fennec foxes can detect the sound of termites chewing beneath the ground.

● **Skunks** use a powerful scent weapon to deter their enemies.

273

# Heat regulation

◀ *The coat of a bighorn sheep comprises a double layer of hairs to protect it from harsh winds and snow.*

- **Fruit bats** are susceptible to heat stroke, so to keep themselves cool, some lick themselves all over and fan cool air at their bodies with their wings.

- **The oryx** has special blood vessels in its nose to keep its blood temperature low in the desert heat.

- **Large-eared desert species** such as fennec foxes use their ears as radiators to get rid of body heat.

- **The desert bighorn sheep** draws air over a thickly veined area of its throat to cool its blood.

- **Wallowing in mud** keeps pigs cool and protects their skin from the sun.

- **A hippo's skin** exudes a red, lacquer-like substance to protect it from sunburn.

- **During hot spells**, kangaroos lick their wrists a lot, so that the evaporation of the saliva causes cooling.

- **Indian zebu cattle** have more sweat glands than western cattle, and can maintain a lower body temperature, making them common in warm countries, such as China, Africa and South America.

- **The eland's temperature** can rise several degrees without causing sweating, allowing it to conserve 5 litres of water daily.

- **After feeding their young**, mother bats often leave them in the heat of the cave and perch near the cooler entrance.

▼ *Hippopotamuses spend much of their time submerged in water as their skin quickly dries out and cracks in the hot African sun.*

# Camouflage

- **Stripes** benefit both predators and prey by breaking up the body shape, for example in tigers and zebras.

- **The simplest camouflage** makes an animal a similar colour to its surroundings, such as the white of a polar bear in snow.

- **Some whales** and dolphins are dark on top and light underneath, camouflaging them against the dark of deep water or the light of the sky.

- **Some camouflage** mimics the broken shapes of light shining through trees, as in the dappled markings of giraffes.

▶ *The pattern of a giraffe's coat (which remains the same all through life) varies according to area and is an important camouflage tool.*

- **The young of many mammal species**, such as lions and pigs, have early camouflage markings that disappear as the animals grow older.

- **The coats of Arctic foxes** and hares change from dark in summer to white in winter.

- **Bold markings**, such as the contrasting shapes of the oryx, camouflage by breaking up body outline.

- **The bobcat's spots** camouflage it in rocks, while the similar-shaped plain lynx merges with its forest home.

▲ *The orca's light underparts make it less visible against the water's surface in daytime.*

- **The elephant's huge grey form** disappears as it stands still in the shadows.

> ...FASCINATING FACT...
> Not all camouflage is visual –
> some mammals roll in dung to disguise
> their own scents.

# Parental care in mammals

- **Many mammals carry their young** around with them. Some bats even go hunting with a youngster aboard.

- **Mother whales** have to nudge and encourage newly born young up to the surface to take their first breath, often aided by 'aunts' from the same pod.

- **In wild dog packs**, several females may take turns to suckle and guard all the young in the group.

- **Sperm whale** offspring may suckle for up to 15 years.

- **Elephant young** are born after 22 months. Several of the herd cows help the new baby to stand.

- **Mother cheetahs** teach their young how to hunt by bringing small live prey back for them to practice on.

◀ *The baby baboon depends on its mother for food and transport, but is also protected from danger by certain males in the group.*

▲ *Elephants live in family groups of females and their young, led by a dominant female.*

- **A big cat female** carries her young by holding the entire head in her mouth, in a gap behind her teeth.

- **Young kangaroos** leave the pouch at 5–11 months, but continue to stick their head in to suckle for 6 months.

- **Many cats,** large and small, start to train their young by allowing them to attack their twitching tails.

> **...FASCINATING FACT...**
> Baby gorillas may only climb on the silver-back while they still have a white rump tuft.

# Kangaroos and koalas

- **Kangaroos** are big Australian mammals that hop around on their hind (back) legs.

- **A kangaroo's tail** can be over 1.5 m long. It is used for balance when hopping, and to hold the kangaroo up when walking.

- **Red kangaroos** can hop at 55 km/h for short distances.

- **Red kangaroos** can leap 9 m forwards in one huge bound.

▲ *Koalas drink very little water, and their name comes from an Aboriginal word for 'no drink'.*

- **There are two kinds of kangaroo** – red kangaroos and grey kangaroos. Red kangaroos live in the dry grasslands of central Australia. Grey kangaroos live in the southeast, in woods and grassland.

- **Kangaroos are marsupials** – animals whose babies are born before they are ready to survive in the outside word and so live for a while protected in a pouch on their mother's belly.

- **Koalas** may look like teddy bears, but they are actually marsupials and are not related to bears.

- **Like kangaroos,** koalas are marsupials. A koala baby spends 6 months in its mother's pouch and another 6 months riding on her back.

- **Koalas** spend 18 hours a day sleeping. The rest of the time they feed on the leaves of eucalyptus trees.

- **Other Australian marsupials** include the wombat, several kinds of wallaby (which look like small kangaroos) and bandicoots (which looks like rats).

▼ *When they are first born, kangaroos are naked and look like tiny jellybabies – just a few centimetres long, with two tiny arms. Straight away they have to haul themselves up through the fur on their mother's belly and into her pouch. Here the baby kangaroo (called a joey) lives and grows for 6–8 months, sucking on teats inside the pouch.*
*Only when it is quite large and covered in fur will it pop out*
*of the pouch to live by itself.*

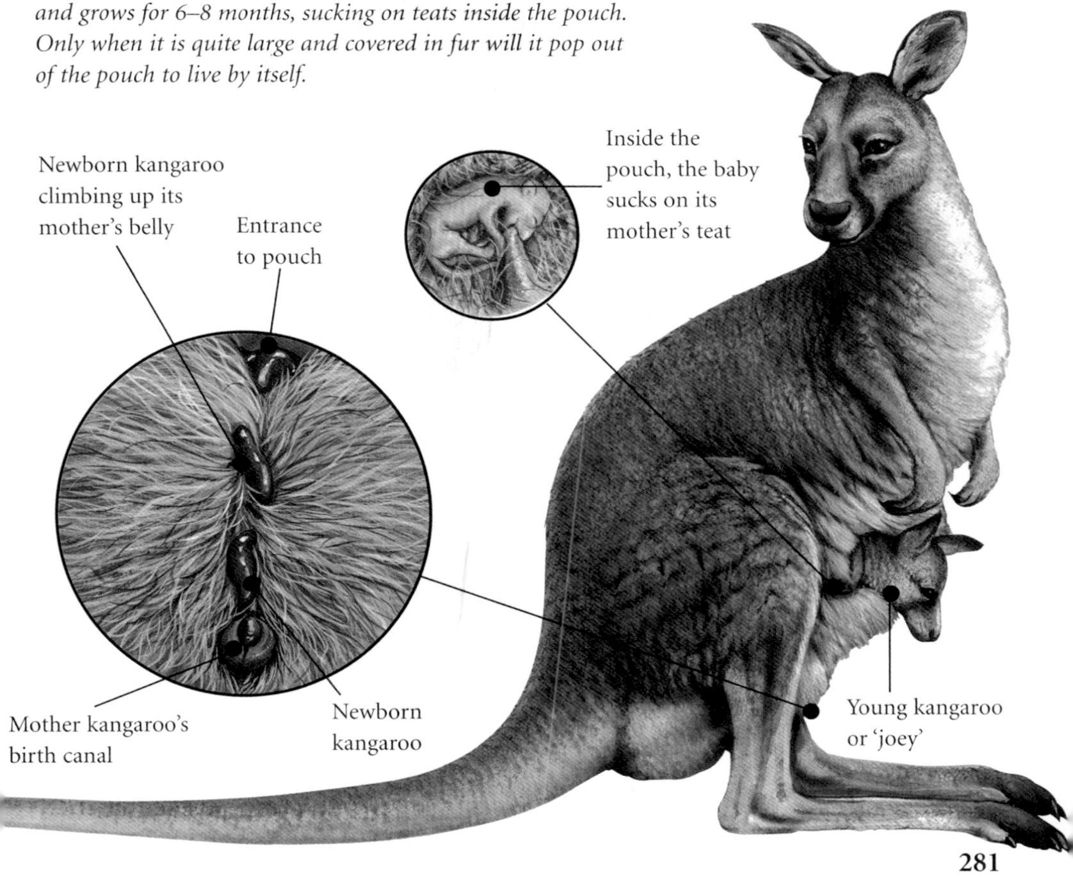

Newborn kangaroo
climbing up its
mother's belly

Entrance
to pouch

Inside the
pouch, the baby
sucks on its
mother's teat

Mother kangaroo's
birth canal

Newborn
kangaroo

Young kangaroo
or 'joey'

# Bats

- **Bats** are the only flying mammals. Their wings are made of leathery skin.

- **Most types of bats sleep** during the day, hanging upside down in caves, attics and other dark places. They come out at night to hunt.

- **Bats find things** in the dark by giving out a series of high-pitched clicks – the bats tell where they are and locate (find) prey from the echoes (sounds that bounce back to them). This is called echolocation.

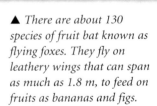

- **Bats are not blind** – their eyesight is as good as that of most humans.

- **There are 900 species** of bat, living on all continents except Antarctica.

- **Most bats feed** on insects, but fruit bats feed on fruit.

▲ *There are about 130 species of fruit bat known as flying foxes. They fly on leathery wings that can span as much as 1.8 m, to feed on fruits as bananas and figs.*

- **Many tropical flowers** rely on fruit bats to spread their pollen.

- **A frog-eating bat** can tell edible frogs from poisonous ones by the mating call of the frog.

- **The vampire bats** of tropical Latin America feed on blood, sucking it from animals such as cattle and horses. A colony of 100 vampire bats can feed from the blood of 25 cows or 14,000 chickens in one night.

- **False vampire bats** are bats that do not suck on blood, but feed on other small creatures such as bats and rats. The greater false vampire bat of Southeast Asia is one of the biggest of all bats.

▶ *Bats spend their lives in darkness, finding their way with sounds so high-pitched only a young child can hear them.*

# Polar bears

◀ *Apart from pregnant females, which spend the winter in dens where they give birth, polar bears are active all through the winter months, often travelling great distances in search of food.*

● **The polar bear** is the only bear which is almost exclusively a meat eater, other bears eat plants too.

● **While stalking a seal**, a polar bear will sometimes lie on its chest with its front legs trailing at its sides and its rump in the air, pushing itself forward with its rear legs.

● **Polar bears** can detect the scent of seal pups in dens buried 1 m deep in snow.

● **Lying in ambush** for a seal, a polar bear will sometimes cover its black nose with its paws to remain unseen against the snow and ice.

● **Polar bears** have a number of tiny protrusions and suction pads on the soles of their feet to give them a firm grip on the ice.

● **The most southerly place** that polar bears regularly visit is James Bay in Canada, which is on the same line of latitude as London.

● **Female polar bears** can put on as much as 400 kg in weight in the course of their summer feeding binge on seal cubs.

- **The polar bear** is a powerful swimmer, even though it uses only its front paws as paddles, letting its rear legs trail behind.

- **Beneath its thick white fur**, a polar bear's skin is black. Translucent (semi-transparent)hairs channel heat from the sun to the animal's skin, which absorbs the heat.

▼ *Outside the breeding season, polar bears are normally solitary animals.*

### · · ·FASCINATING FACT· · ·
Female polar bears may go without eating for up to 8 months – existing solely on their body fat.

# Lions

*▶ To other lions, a male lion's shaggy mane makes him look even bigger and stronger, and protects him when fighting. A male lion is born without a mane. It starts growing when he is about three and is fully grown by the time he is five.*

The mane can be blonde, but gets darker with age

- **Lions** (along with tigers) are the biggest members of the cat family, weighing up to 230 kg. Male lions may be 3 m long.

- **Lions used to live** through much of Europe and Asia. Now they are restricted to East and Southern Africa. Around 200 lions also live in the Gir forest in India.

- **Lions usually live** in grassland or scrub, in families called prides.

- **Lions are hunters** and they prey on antelopes, zebras and even young giraffes. The lionesses (females) do most of the hunting.

- **Male lions** are easily recognizable because of their huge manes. There is usually more than one adult male in each pride and they usually eat before the lionesses and cubs.

- **Lions usually catch** something to eat every four days or so. They can eat up to 40 kg in a single meal. Afterwards they rest for 24 hours.

- **The lions in a pride** usually spend about 20 hours a day sleeping and resting, and they walk no farther than 10 km or so a day.

- **Lionesses catch their prey** not by speed, but by stealth and strength. They stalk their prey quietly, creeping close to the ground. Then, when it is about 15 m away, the lionesses make a sudden dash and pull the victim down with their strong forepaws.

- **Lionesses usually hunt** at dusk or dawn, but they have very good night vision, and so will often hunt in the dark.

- **Male lion cubs** are driven out of the pride when they are two years old. When a young male is fully grown, he has to fight an older male to join another pride.

> ...FASCINATING FACT...
> A male lion can drag along a 300 kg zebra
> – it would take at least six men to do this.

◀ *Female lions are called lionesses. They are slightly smaller than males but usually do most of the hunting, often in pairs. There are typically five to ten lionesses in each pride, and each one mates with the male when she is about three years old.*

287

# Horses

- **Horses** are big, four-legged, hooved animals, now bred mainly for human use.

- **Male horses** are called stallions, females are mares, babies are foals, and young males are colts.

- **The only wild horse** is the Przewalski of central Asia.

- **The mustangs** (wild horses) of the USA are descended from tame horses.

- **Tame horses** are of three main kinds – light horses for riding (such as Morgans and Arabs), heavy horses for pulling ploughs and wagons (such as Percherons and Suffolk Punches), and ponies (such as Shetlands).

▶ *All horses, wild and tame, may be descended from the prehistoric Merychippus.*

▶ *A domestic horse. The rare Przewalski's horse of the Mongolian steppes is probably similar to the ancestor of today's many domestic horse breeds. Horses are built for grazing on grasses and for galloping at high speed for long distances.*

● **Most racehorses and hunting horses** are thoroughbred (pure) Arab horses descended from just three stallions that lived around 1700 – Darley Arabian, Godolphin Barb and Byerly Turk.

● **Lippizaners** are beautiful white horses, the best-known of which are trained to jump and dance at the Spanish Riding School in Vienna.

● **The shire horse** is probably the largest horse, bred after King Henry VIII had all horses under 1.5 m destroyed.

● **You can tell a horse's age** by counting its teeth – a 1-year-old has six pairs, a 5-year-old has twelve.

● **Quarter horses** are agile horses used by cowhands for cutting out (sorting cows from the herd). They got their name from running quarter-mile races.

# Elephants

- **There are three kinds** of elephant – the African forest elephant (Central and West Africa), the African savanna elephant (East and South Africa) and the Asian elephant, which lives in India and Southeast Asia.

- **African elephants** are the largest land animals, growing as tall as 4 m and weighing more than 6000 kg.

- **Asian elephants** are not as large as African elephants, and have smaller ears and tusks. They also have one 'finger' on the tip of their trunk, while African elephants have two.

- **The scientific word** for an elephant's trunk is a proboscis. It is used like a hand to put food into the elephant's mouth, or to suck up water to squirt into its mouth or over its body to keep cool.

▶ *When the leader of the herd senses danger, she lifts her trunk and sniffs the air – then warns the others by using her trunk to give a loud blast called a trumpet. If an intruder comes too close, she will roll down her trunk, throw back her ears, lower her head and charge at up to 50 km/h.*

▼ *In dry areas, herds may travel vast distances to find food, with the bigger elephants protecting the little ones between their legs.*

- **Elephants** are very intelligent animals, with the biggest brain of all land animals. They also have very good memories.

- **Female elephants,** called cows, live with their calves and younger bulls (males) in herds of 20 to 30 animals. Older bulls usually live alone.

- **Once a year,** bull elephants go into a state called musth (said 'must'), when male hormones make them very wild and dangerous.

- **Elephants** usually live for about 70 years.

- **When an elephant dies,** its companions seem to mourn and cry.

...FASCINATING FACT...
Elephants use their trunks like snorkels
when crossing deep rivers.

291

# Farm animals

- **Cattle** are descended from a creature called the wild auroch, which was tamed 9000 years ago. There are now over 200 breeds of domestic cow.
- **Female cows** reared for milk, butter and cheese production are called dairy cows. They give birth to a calf each year, and after it is born they provide milk twice a day.
- **A typical dairy cow** gives 16 litres of milk a day, or almost 6000 litres a year.
- **Male cattle** are reared mainly for their meat, called beef. Beef breeds are usually heftier than dairy ones.

▼ *Female cattle are called cows, and males are called bulls. The young are calves. Female calves are also called heifers.*

▶ *Domesticated over 4000 years ago and at first used for religious sacrifices, the chicken now is probably the most numerous bird in the world.*

- **Sheep were first domesticated** over 10,000 years ago. There are now more than 700 million sheep in the world, and 800 different breeds.

- **Hairy sheep** are kept for their milk and meat (lamb and mutton). Woolly sheep are kept for their wool.

- **Hens** lay one or two eggs a day – about 350 a year.

- **To keep hens laying,** their eggs must be taken from them every day. Otherwise the hens will try to nest so they can hatch them.

- **Turkeys** may have got their name from the mistaken idea that they came from Turkey.

...FASCINATING FACT...
When a cow chews the cud, the cud is food regurgitated from one of its four stomachs.

# Pets

- **There are over 500 breeds** of domestic dog. All are descended from the wolves first tamed 12,000 years ago to help humans hunt. Dogs have kept some wolf-like traits such as guarding territory and hiding bones.

- **Many pet dogs** were originally working dogs. Collies were sheepdogs. Terriers, setters, pointers and retrievers get their names from their roles as hunting dogs.

- **The heaviest dog breed** is the St Bernard, which weighs over 90 kg. The lightest is the miniature Yorkshire terrier, which weighs under 500 g.

- **Cocker spaniels** were named because they were used by hunters to flush out woodcocks in the 14th century.

- **Chihuahuas** were named after a place in Mexico – the Aztecs thought them sacred.

- **The first domestic cats** were wild African bushcats tamed by the Ancient Egyptians to catch mice 3500 years ago.

- **Like their wild ancestors**, domestic cats are deadly hunters – agile, with sharp eyes and claws – and often catch mice and birds.

▶ *The domestic cat, of which there are over 30 breeds, is a small member of the cat family measuring 75 cm with tail.*

- **Cats spend** a great deal of time sleeping in short naps, but can be awake and ready for action in an instant.

- **Tabby cats** get their name from Attab in Baghdad (now in Iraq), where striped silk was made in the Middle Ages.

- **A female cat** is called a queen. A group of cats is called a clowder. A female dog is a bitch. A group of dogs is a kennel.

- **All pet golden hamsters** are descended from a single litter which was discovered in Syria in 1930.

▶ *Powerfully built and strong-jawed, pit bull terriers were first bred from bulldogs and terriers as fighting dogs, by miners in the 18th century.*

# SCIENCE

**How fast is the speed of light?**

**Where is the hottest place on Earth?**

**What is the largest internal organ of the body?**

The answers to these and many other questions can be found in this amazing section. *Science* is split into two parts. The first part deals with core subjects such as matter, chemicals and materials through to electricity, energy, force and motion.

The second part takes a closer look at human biology. As well as covering main body systems, there are hundreds of facts on subjects such as mind, senses and health.

# Elements

- **Elements** are the basic chemicals of the Universe. Each element is made from only one kind of atom, with a certain number of sub atomic particles and its own unique character.

- **More than 115** elements have so far been identified.

- **Each element** is listed in the periodic table.

- **At least 20** of the most recently identified elements were created entirely by scientists and do not exist naturally.

- **All the most recently discovered elements** have very large, heavy atoms.

- **The lightest atom** is hydrogen.

- **The densest naturally occurring element** is osmium.

- **When different elements combine** they make chemical compounds.

- **New elements** get their name from their atomic number. So the new element with atomic number 116 is called ununhexium. *Un* is the Latin word for one; *hex* is Latin for six.

▲ *Very few elements occur naturally by themselves. Most occur in combination with others in compounds. Gold is one of the few elements found as a pure 'native' element.*

▶ *Silver is a chemical element. It is a soft, white metal which is used for jewellery and also in dentistry, medicine, photography and electronics.*

▲ As the demand for aluminium grows each year with more and more uses being found for it, so recycling becomes ever more important.

▲ Aluminium is used to make drink cans since it is a light weight metal that does not rust and resists wear from weather or chemicals.

FASCINATING FACT
Scientists in Berkeley, California, have made three atoms of a new element 118 or, ununoctium, which is probably a colourless gas.

299

# Atoms

- **Atoms are** tiny particles which build together to make every substance. An atom is the tiniest bit of any pure substance or chemical element.

- **You could fit** two billion atoms on the full stop after this sentence.

- **The number of atoms** in the Universe is about 10 followed by 80 zeros.

- **Atoms are mostly** empty space dotted with a few even tinier particles called subatomic particles.

- **In the centre** of each atom is a dense core, or nucleus, made from two kinds of particle: protons and neutrons. Protons have a positive electrical charge, and neutrons none. Both protons and neutrons are made from different combinations of quarks.

- **If an atom** were the size of a sports arena, its nucleus would be just the size of a pea.

- **Around the nucleus** whizz even tinier, negatively-charged particles called electrons.

- **Atoms can be split** but they are usually held together by three forces – the electrical attraction between positive protons and negative electrons, and the strong and weak 'nuclear' forces that hold the nucleus together.

- **Every element** is made from atoms with a certain number of protons in the nucleus. An iron atom has 26 protons, gold has 79. The number of protons is the atomic number.

- **Atoms with the same number** of protons but a different number of neutrons are called isotopes.

▶ *The nucleus of an atom is made up of two kinds of particle: protons (red) and neutrons (green). Protons have a positive electric charge while neutrons have none. Tiny electrons (blue) whizz around the nucleus.*

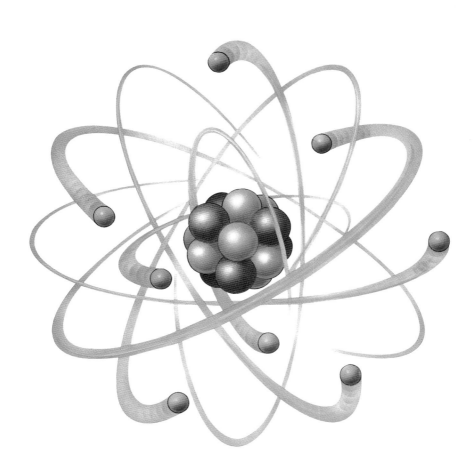

# Electrons

- **Electrons** are by far the smallest of the three main, stable parts of every atom; the other two parts are protons and neutrons. In a normal atom there are the same number of electrons as protons.

- **Electrons** are 1836 times as small as protons and have a mass of just $9.109 \times 10^{-31}$ kg. $10^{-31}$ means there are 30 zeros after the decimal point. So they weigh almost nothing.

- **Electrons were discovered** by English physicist Joseph John Thomson in 1897 as he studied the glow in a cathode-ray tube. This was the first time anyone realized that the atom is not just one solid ball.

▼ *Each atom has a different number of electrons. Its chemical character depends on the number of electrons in its outer shell. Atoms with only one electron in their outer shell, such as lithium, sodium and potassium, have many properties in common. The electron shell structures for five common atoms are shown here.*

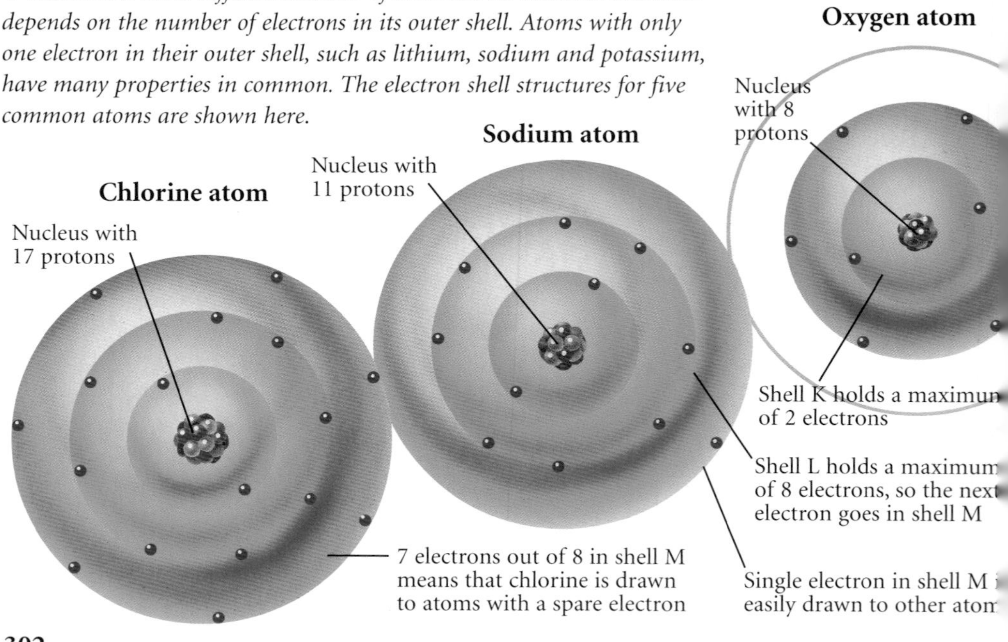

**Oxygen atom**

Nucleus with 8 protons

**Sodium atom**

Nucleus with 11 protons

**Chlorine atom**

Nucleus with 17 protons

Shell K holds a maximum of 2 electrons

Shell L holds a maximum of 8 electrons, so the next electron goes in shell M

7 electrons out of 8 in shell M means that chlorine is drawn to atoms with a spare electron

Single electron in shell M is easily drawn to other atom

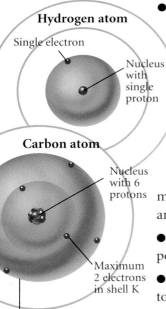

**Hydrogen atom**

Single electron

Nucleus with single proton

**Carbon atom**

Nucleus with 6 protons

Maximum 2 electrons in shell K

Shell L holds 4 electrons out of a possible 8. So carbon has four vacancies to form complex compounds with other elements

Shell L holds 6 electrons out of a possible 8. So oxygen has 2 'missing' electrons and is very reactive

● **Electrons are** packets of energy. They can be thought of either as a tiny vibration or wave, or as a ball-like particle. They travel as waves and arrive as particles.

   ● **You can never be sure** just where an electron is. It is better to think of an electron circling the nucleus not as a planet circling the Sun but as a cloud wrapped around it. Electron clouds near the nucleus are round, but those farther out are other shapes.

● **Electrons** have a negative electrical charge. This means they are attracted to positive electrical charges and pushed away by negative charges.

● **Electrons cling** to the nucleus because protons have a positive charge equal to the electron's negative charge.

● **Electrons have so much energy** that they whizz round too fast to fall into the nucleus. Instead they circle the nucleus in shells (layers) at different distances, or energy levels, depending on how much energy they have. The more energetic an electron, the farther from the nucleus it is. There is room for only one other electron at each energy level, and it must be spinning in the opposite way. This is called Pauli's exclusion principle.

● **Electrons are** stacked around the nucleus in shells. Each shell is labelled with a letter and can hold up to a particular number of electrons. Shell K can hold up to 2, L 8, M 18, N 32, O about 50, and P about 72.

**303**

# Molecules

- **A molecule** is two or more atoms bonded together. It is normally the smallest bit of a substance that exists independently.

- **Hydrogen atoms** exist only in pairs, or joined with atoms of other elements. A linked pair of hydrogen atoms is a hydrogen molecule.

- **The atoms in a molecule** are held together by chemical bonds.

- **The shape of a molecule** depends on the arrangement of bonds that hold its atoms together.

Carbon dioxide
($CO_2$)

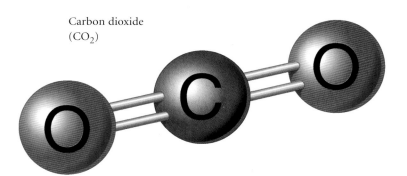

◄ *A carbon dioxide molecule consists of one carbon atom and two oxygen atoms, and has the chemical formula $CO_2$.*

- **Ammonia molecules** are pyramid shaped; some protein molecules are long spirals.

- **Compounds** only exist as molecules. If the atoms in the molecule of a compound were separated, the compound would cease to exist.

- **Chemical formulas** show the atoms in a molecule.

- **The formula for ammonia,** a kind of gas, is $NH_3$ – one nitrogen atom and three hydrogen.

- **The mass of a molecule** is called the molecular mass. It is worked out by adding the mass of all the atoms in it.

◄ *A crystal such as this is built from billions of identical molecules.*

```
....FASCINATING FACT....
If the DNA molecule in every human
body cell were as thick as a hair, it would
be eight km long.
```

# Chemical compounds

- **Compounds** are substances that are made when the atoms of two or more different elements join together.

- **The properties of a compound** are usually very different from those of the elements which it is made of.

- **Compounds** are different from mixtures because the elements are joined together chemically. They can only be separated by a chemical reaction.

- **Every molecule** of a compound is exactly the same combination of atoms.

- **The scientific name** of a compound is usually a combination of the elements involved, although it might have a different common name.

- **Table salt** is the chemical compound sodium chloride. Each molecule has one sodium and one chlorine atom.

- **The chemical formula** of a compound summarizes which atoms a molecule is made of. The chemical formula for water is $H_2O$ because each water molecule has two hydrogen (H) atoms and one oxygen (O) atom.

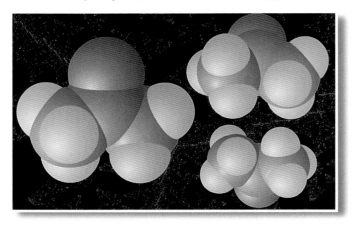

◀ *The molecules of a compound are identical combinations of atoms.*

▲ *Table salt, or sodium chloride, forms when sodium hydroxide neutralizes hydrocloric acid.*

- **There only 100 or so elements** but they can combine in different ways to form many millions of compounds.

- **The same combination of elements,** such as carbon and hydrogen, can form many different compounds.

- **Compounds** are either organic, which means they contain carbon atoms, or inorganic.

# Solids, liquids and gases

- **Most substances** can exist in three states – solid, liquid or gas. These are the states of matter.

- **Substances** change from one state to another at particular temperatures and pressures.

- **As temperature rises,** solids melt to become liquids. As it rises further, liquids evaporate to become gases.

- **The temperature** at which a solid melts is its melting point.

- **The maximum temperature** a liquid can reach before turning to gas is called its boiling point.

- **Every solid has strength** and a definite shape as its molecules are firmly bonded in a rigid structure.

- **A liquid has a fixed volume** and flows to take up the shape of any solid container into which it is poured.

- **A liquid flows** because although bonds hold molecules together, they are loose enough to move over each other, rather like dry sand.

- **A gas** such as air does not have any shape, strength or fixed volume. This is because its molecules are moving too quickly for any bonds to hold them together.

- **When a gas cools,** its molecules slow down until bonds form between them to create drops of liquid. This process is called condensation.

▲ *The grains of sand in this egg timer act like a liquid, taking on the shape of the glass as they flow from top to bottom.*

▲ *A giant iceberg floats on the sea. Although ice is lighter than water and looks so different, chemically it is exactly the same.*

# Air

- **The air** is a mixture of gases, dust and moisture.

- **The gas nitrogen** makes up 78.08 percent of the air. Nitrogen is largely unreactive, but it sometimes reacts with oxygen to form oxides of nitrogen.

- **Nitrogen** is continually recycled by the bacteria that consume plant and animal waste.

- **Oxygen** makes up 20.94 percent of the air. Animals breathe in oxygen. Plants give it out as they take their energy from sunlight in photosynthesis.

- **Carbon dioxide** makes up 0.03 percent of the air. Carbon dioxide is continually recycled as it is breathed out by animals and taken in by plants in photosynthesis.

- **The air contains** other, inert (unreactive) gases: 0.93 percent is argon; 0.0018 percent is neon; 0.0005 percent is helium.

- **There are tiny traces** of krypton and xenon which are also inert.

- **Ozone makes up** 0.00006 percent of the air. It is created when sunlight breaks up oxygen.

- **Hydrogen makes up** 0.00005 percent of the air. This gas is continually drifting off into space.

▶ *People often think that air is largely made up of oxygen. In fact, only 21 percent of air is oxygen, while 78 percent of it is nitrogen.*

...**FASCINATING FACT**...
Air is a unique mixture that exists on Earth and nowhere else in the Solar System.

▶ *Air is the mixture of gases that surrounds the Earth and is contained in the atmosphere. Clouds form when large masses of moist air rise and cool.*

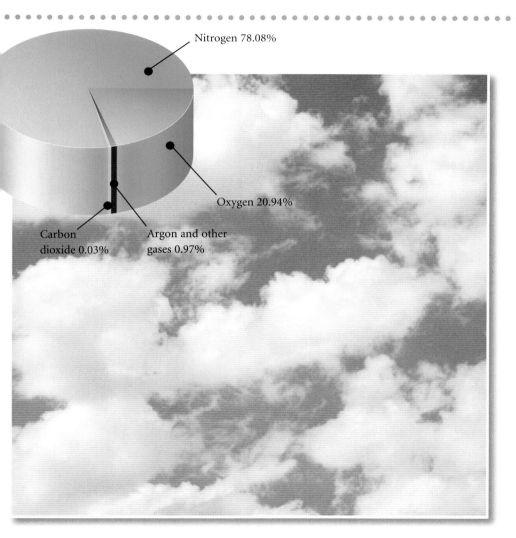

Nitrogen 78.08%

Oxygen 20.94%

Carbon
dioxide 0.03%

Argon and other
gases 0.97%

# Carbon

▶ *The extraordinary hardness of diamonds comes from the incredibly strong tetrahedron (pyramid shape) that carbon atoms form.*

- **Pure carbon** occurs in four forms: diamond, graphite, amorphous carbon and fullerenes.

- **Fullerenes** are made mostly artificially, but all four forms of carbon can be made artificially.

- **Diamond** is the world's hardest natural substance.

- **Natural diamonds** were created deep in the Earth billions of years ago. They were formed by huge pressures as the Earth's crust moved, and then brought nearer the surface by volcanic activity.

- **Graphite** is the soft black carbon used in pencils. It is soft because it is made from sheets of atoms that slide over each other.

- **Amorphous carbon** is the black soot left behind when candles and other objects burn.

▲ *The pencil is the most widely used writing instrument in the world. Astronauts use pencils in space because they are not affected by gravity or pressure.*

- **Fullerenes** are big molecules made of 60 or more carbon atoms linked together in a tight cylinder or ball. The first was made in 1985.

- **Fullerenes** are named after the architect Buckminster Fuller who designed a geodesic (Earth-shaped) dome.

- **Carbon forms** over one million compounds which are the basis of organic chemistry. It does not react chemically at room temperature. Carbon has the chemical formula C and the atomic number 6. Neither diamond nor graphite will melt at normal pressures.

▲ *Diamonds are crystals made up almost entirely of carbon. They occur in various shapes and sizes, and were formed under great heat and pressure.*

. . .**FASCINATING FACT**. . .
All living things are based on carbon, yet it makes up just 0.032 percent of the Earth's crust.

# Water

- **Water is the only substance** that is solid, liquid and gas within the natural range of Earth temperatures. It melts at 0°C and boils at 100°C.

- **Water is at its densest** at 4°C.

- **Ice is much less dense** than water, which is why ice forms on the surface of ponds and why icebergs float.

- **Water is one of the few substances** that expands as it freezes, which is why pipes burst during cold winter weather.

- **Water has a unique capacity** for making mild solutions with other substances.

- **Water is a compound** made of two hydrogen atoms and one oxygen atom. It has the chemical formula $H_2O$.

- **A water molecule** is shaped like a flattened V, with the two hydrogen atoms on each tip.

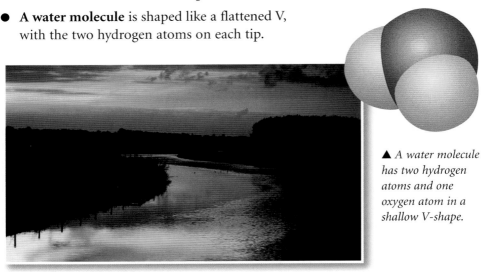

▲ *A water molecule has two hydrogen atoms and one oxygen atom in a shallow V-shape.*

▲ *Water is found in liquid form in many places, such as rivers, and as a gas in the atmosphere.*

314

- **A water molecule** is said to be polar because the oxygen end is more negatively charged electrically.

- **Similar substances** such as ammonia ($NH_3$) are gases to below 0°C.

- **Water stays liquid** until 100°C because pairs of its polar molecules make strong bonds, as the positively charged end of one molecule is drawn to the negatively charged end of another.

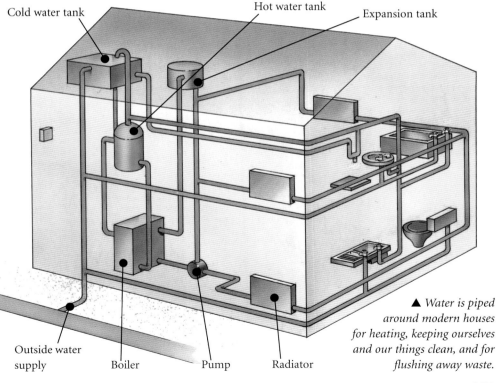

Cold water tank

Hot water tank

Expansion tank

▲ *Water is piped around modern houses for heating, keeping ourselves and our things clean, and for flushing away waste.*

Outside water supply

Boiler

Pump

Radiator

**315**

# Iron and steel

- **Iron** is the most common element in the world. It makes up 35 percent of the Earth, but most of it is in the Earth's core.

- **Iron is never found** in its pure form in the Earth's crust. Instead it is found in iron ores, which must be heated in a blast furnace to extract the iron.

- **The chemical symbol** for iron is Fe from *ferrum*, the Latin word for iron. Iron compounds are called either ferrous or ferric.

- **Iron has** an atomic number of 26 and an atomic weight of 55.85.

- **Iron melts** at 1535°C and boils at 3000°C. It conducts heat and electricity quite well and dissolves in water very slowly. Iron is easily magnetized. It also loses its magnetism easily, but steel can be permanently magnetic.

- Iron combines readily with oxygen to form iron oxide, especially in the presence of moisture. This is rusting.

◀ *Pouring molten iron into a steelmaking furnace in a steel mill. The temperature of the liquid metal is about 1500°C.*

▶ *A solid-state laser can cut through carbon steel like butter even though steel is incredibly tough.*

- **Cast iron** is iron with 2 to 4 percent carbon and 1 to 3 percent silicon. It is suitable for pouring into sand moulds. Wrought iron is almost pure iron with carbon removed to make it easy to bend and shape for railings and gates.

- **Iron is made into steel** by adding traces of carbon for making cars, railway lines, knives and much more. Alloy steels are made by adding traces of metals such as tungsten (for tools) and chromium (for ball bearings).

- **60 percent of steel** is made by the basic oxygen process in which oxygen is blasted over molten iron to burn out impurities.

- **Special alloy steels** such as chromium steels can be made from scrap iron (which is low in impurities) in an electric arc furnace.

317

# Light

- **Light is a form of energy.** It is one of the forms of energy sent out by atoms when they become excited.

- **Light is just one** of the forms of electromagnetic radiation. It is the only form we can see.

- **Although we are surrounded** by light during the day, very few things give out light. The Sun and other stars and electric lights are light sources, but we see most things only because they reflect light. If something does not send out or reflect light, we cannot see it.

▶ *This straw is not a light source, so we see it by reflected light. As the light rays reflected from the straw leave the water, they are bent, or refracted, as they emerge from the water and speed up. So the straw looks broken even though it remains intact.*

- **Light beams** are made of billions of tiny packets of energy called photons. Together, the photons behave like waves on a pond. But the waves are tiny – 2000 would fit on a pinhead.

- **Light travels** in straight lines. The direction can be changed when light bounces off something or passes through it, but it is always straight. The straight path of light is called a ray.

- **When the path of a light ray** is blocked altogether, it forms a shadow. Most shadows have two regions – the umbra and penumbra. The umbra is the dark part where light rays are blocked altogether. The penumbra is the lighter rim where some rays reach.

- **When light rays** hit something, they bounce off, are soaked up or pass through. Anything that lets light through, such as glass, is transparent. If it mixes the light on the way through, as does frosted glass, it is translucent. If it stops light altogether, it is opaque.

- **When light strikes a surface,** some or all of it is reflected. Most surfaces scatter light in all directions, and all you see is the surface. But mirrors and other shiny surfaces reflect light in exactly the same pattern in which it arrived, so you see a mirror image.

- **When light passes** into transparent things such as water, rays are bent, or refracted. This happens because light travels more slowly in glass or water, and the rays swing round like the wheels of a car running onto sand.

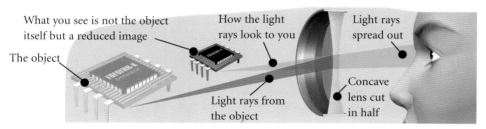

What you see is not the object itself but a reduced image

The object

How the light rays look to you

Light rays from the object

Light rays spread out

Concave lens cut in half

▲ *Glass lenses are shaped to refract light rays in particular ways. Concave lenses are dish-shaped lenses – thin in the middle and fat at the edges. As light rays pass through a concave lens they are bent outwards, so they spread out. The result is that when you see an object through a concave lens, it looks smaller than it really is.*

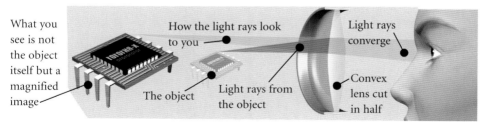

What you see is not the object itself but a magnified image

How the light rays look to you

The object

Light rays from the object

Light rays converge

Convex lens cut in half

▲ *Convex lenses bulge outwards. They are fatter in the middle and thin around the edges. As light rays pass through a convex lens they are bent inwards, so they come together, or converge. When you see an object through a convex lens, it looks magnified.*

**319**

# Colour

- **Colour is the way** our eyes see different wavelengths of light.

- **Red light** has the longest waves – about 700 nanometres, or nm (billionths of a metre).

- **Violet light** has the shortest waves – about 400 nm.

- **Light that is a mixture** of every colour, such as sunlight and the light from torches and ordinary lightbulbs, is called white light.

- **Things are different colours** because molecules in their surface reflect and absorb certain wavelengths of light.

- **Deep-blue printers' inks** and bright-red blood are vividly coloured because both have molecules shaped like four-petalled flowers, with a metal atom at the centre.

- **Iridescence** is the shimmering rainbow colours you see flashing every now and then on a peacock's feathers, a fly's wings, oil on the water's surface or a CD.

◄ *The macaw gets its brilliant colours because pigment molecules in its feathers soak up certain wavelengths of light and reflect others, including reds, yellows and blues, very strongly.*

- **Iridescence** can be caused by the way a surface breaks the light into colours like a prism does.

- **Iridescence** can also be caused by interference when an object has a thin, transparent surface layer. Light waves reflected from the top surface are slightly out of step with waves reflected from the inner surface, and they interfere.

▲ *Iridescence on a CD is a result of light waves reflecting from both the top surface and the inner surface. This causes the spectrum of light which is sometimes visible.*

▲ *The surface skin of water on some spilt oil interferes with the vibrations of light causing it to be split up into the colours of the spectrum.*

**. . . FASCINATING FACT . . .**
As a light source gets hotter, so its colour changes from red to yellow to white to blue.

**321**

# Sound

- **Most sounds** you hear, from the whisper of the wind to the roar of a jet, are simply moving air. When any sound is made it makes the air vibrate, and these vibrations carry the sound to your ears.

- **The vibrations** that carry sound through the air are called sound waves.

- **Sound waves** move by alternately squeezing air molecules together and then stretching them apart like a spring.

- **The parts of the air** that are squeezed are called condensations; the parts of the air that are stretched are called rarefactions.

- **Sound waves** travel faster through liquids and solids than through air because the molecules are more closely packed together in liquids and solids.

- **In a vacuum** such as space there is complete silence because there are no molecules to carry the sound.

▲ *When you sing, talk or shout, you are actually vibrating the vocal cords in your throat. These set up sound waves in the air you push up from your lungs.*

- **Sound travels** at about 344 m per second in air at 20°C.

- **Sound travels** faster in warm air, reaching 386 m per second at 100°C.

- **Sound travels** at 1500 m per second in pure water and at about 6000 m per second in solid steel.

- **Sound travels a million times** slower than light, which is why you hear thunder well after you see a flash of lightning, even though they both happen at the same time.

▶ *This fishing boat is using sonar to find out the depth of an object. It bounces sound waves off the object and measures how long they take to be reflected back to the boat.*

# Magnetism

- **Magnetism** is the invisible force between materials such as iron and nickel. Magnetism attracts or repels.

- **A magnetic field** is the area around a magnet inside which its magnetic force can be detected.

- **An electric current** creates its own magnetic field.

- **A magnet** has two poles: a north pole and a south pole.

- **Like (similar) poles** (e.g. two north poles) repel each other; unlike poles attract each other.

- **The Earth** has a magnetic field that is created by electric currents inside its iron core. The magnetic north pole is close to the geographic North Pole.

- **If left to swivel freely,** a magnet will turn so that its north pole points to the Earth's magnetic north pole.

- **The strength of a magnet** is measured in teslas. The Earth's magnetic field is 0.00005 teslas.

- **All magnetic materials** are made up of tiny groups of atoms called domains. Each one is like a mini-magnet with north and south poles. When material is magnetized, millions of domains line up.

...FASCINATING FACT...
One of the world's strongest magnets is at the Lawrence Berkeley National Laboratory, California, USA. Its field is 250,000 times stronger than the Earth's.

▶ *Some animals seem to detect the Earth's magnetic field and use it to help them find their way when they migrate. Birds which have this built-in compass include swallows, geese and pigeons.*

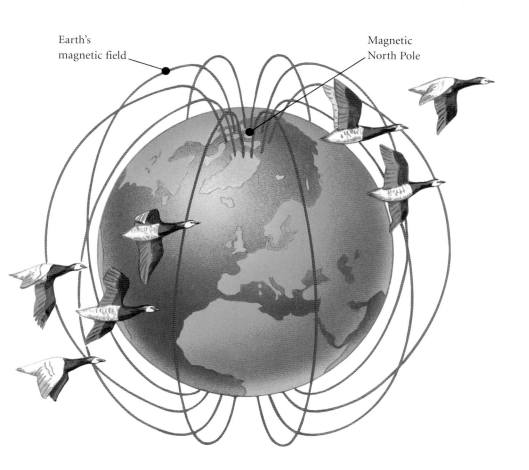

Earth's magnetic field

Magnetic North Pole

# Electricity

- **Electricity** is the energy that makes everything from toasters to televisions work. It is also linked to magnetism. Together, as electromagnetism, they are one of the four fundamental forces holding the Universe together.

- **Electricity** is made by tiny bits of atoms called electrons. Electrons have an electrical charge which is a force that either pulls bits of atoms together or pushes them apart.

- **Some particles** (bit of atoms) have a negative electrical charge; others have a positive charge.

- **Particles** with the same charge push each other away. Particles with the opposite charge pull together.

▲ *Try making your own static electricity. Comb your hair quickly, if possible on a cold, dry day, and watch how it stands up.*

- **Electrons** have a negative electrical charge.

- **There are the same number** of positive and negative particles in most atoms so the charges usually balance out.

- **Electricity** is created when electrons move, building up negative charge in one place, or carrying it along.

- **Static electricity** is when the negative charge stays in one place. Current electricity is when the charge moves.

- **Electric charge** is measured with an electroscope.

- **Materials** that let electrons (and electrical charge) move through them easily, such as copper, are called conductors. Materials that stop electrons passing through, such as rubber, are called insulators.

▲ *Lightning is one of the most dramatic displays of natural electricity.*

# Electronics

- **Electronics** are the basis of many modern technologies, from hi-fi systems to missile control systems.

- **Electronics** are systems that control things by automatically switching tiny electrical circuits on and off.

- **Transistors** are electronic switches. They are made of materials called semiconductors that change their ability to conduct electricity.

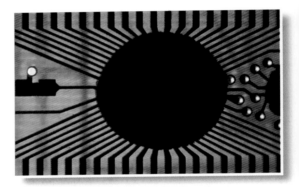

▼ *Microprocessors contain millions of transistors in a package that is no bigger than a human fingernail.*

- **Electronic systems work** by linking many transistors together so that each controls the way the others work.

- **Diodes** are transistors with two connectors. They control an electric current by switching it on or off.

- **Triodes** are transistors with three connectors that amplify the electric current (make it bigger) or reduce it.

- **A silicon chip** is thousands of transistors linked together by thin metal strips in an integrated circuit, on a single crystal of the semi-conductor, silicon.

- **The electronic areas** of a chip are those treated with traces of chemicals such as boron and phosphorus, which alter the conductivity of silicon.

- **Microprocessors** are complete Central Processing Units on a single silicon chip.

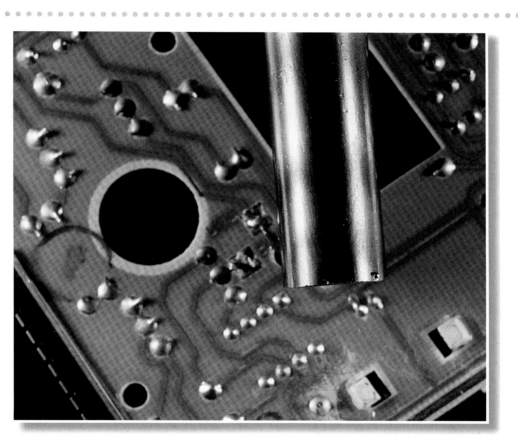

▲ *The components on silicon chips are so minute that photographing them involves using a microscope.*

... FASCINATING FACT ...
Some microprocessors can now handle
billions of bits of data every second.

329

# Telecommunication

- **Telecommunication** is the almost instantaneous transmission of sounds, words, pictures, data and information by electronic means.

- **Every communication system** needs three things: a transmitter, a communications link and a receiver.

- **Transmitters** can be telephones or computers with modems. They change the words, pictures, data or sounds into an electrical signal and send it. Similar receivers pick up the signal and change it back into the right form.

- **Communications links** carry the signal from the transmitter to the receiver in two main ways. Some give a direct link through telephone lines and other cables. Some are carried on radio waves through the air, via satellite or microwave links.

- **Telephone lines** used to be mainly electric cables which carried the signal as pulses of electricity. More and more are now fibre optics, which carry the signal as coded pulses of light.

- **Communications satellites** are satellites orbiting the Earth in space. Telephone calls are beamed up on radio waves to the satellite, which beams them back down to the right part of the world.

- **Microwave links** use very short radio waves to transmit telephone and other signals from one dish to another in a straight line across Earth's surface.

- **Mobile phones** or cellular phones transmit and receive phone calls directly via radio waves. The calls are picked up and sent on from a local aerial.

- **The information superhighway** is the network of high-speed links that might be achieved by combining telephone systems, cable TV and computer networks. TV programmes, films, data, direct video links and the Internet could all enter the home in this way.

● ● ● ● ● ● ● ● ● ● ● ● ● ● ● ● ● ● ● ● ● ● ● ● ● ● ● ● ● ● ● ● ● ● ● ●

▼ *This illustration shows some of the many ways in which telecommunications are carried. At present, TV, radio and phone links are all carried separately, but increasingly they will all be carried the same way. They will be split up only when they arrive at their destination.*

**...FASCINATING FACT...**
Calls across the ocean go one way by satellite and the other by undersea cable to avoid delays.

TV and radio signals are broadcast as pulses of radio waves, sent through cables or bounced off satellites.

Computer data is translated by a modem into signals that can be carried on phone lines.

Signals from individual transmitters are sent on from a telephone exchange or a service provider.

More and more communications are beamed from antenna dishes on the ground to satellites in space.

Telephones can link to the phone network by a direct cable link. Mobile phones link through to local relay towers by radio waves.

# Television

- **Television relies** on the photoelectric effect – the emission of electrons by a substance when struck by photons of light. Light-sensitive photocells in cameras work like this.

- **TV cameras** have three sets of tubes with photocells (reacting to red, green and blue light) to convert the picture into electrical signals.

- **The sound signal** from microphones is added, and a 'sync pulse' is put in to keep both kinds of signal in time.

- **The combined signal** is turned into radio waves and broadcast.

- **An aerial** picks up the signal and feeds it to your television set.

- **Most TV sets** are based on glass tubes shaped like giant lightbulbs, called cathode-ray tubes. The narrow end contains a cathode, which is a negative electrical terminal. The wide end is the TV screen.

- **The cathode** fires a non-stop stream of electrons at the inside of the TV screen.

◄ *TV cameras convert a scene into electrical signals that can be transmitted via radio waves.*

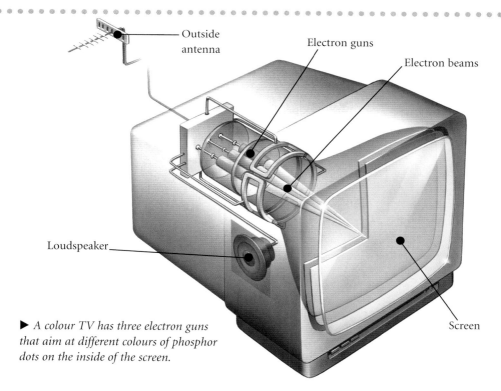

Outside antenna

Electron guns

Electron beams

Loudspeaker

Screen

▶ *A colour TV has three electron guns*
*that aim at different colours of phosphor*
*dots on the inside of the screen.*

- **Wherever electrons** hit the screen, the screen glows as its coating of phosphors heats up.

- **To build up the picture** the electron beam scans quickly back and forth across the screen, making it glow in certain places. This happens so quickly that it looks as if the whole screen is glowing.

- **Colour TVs** have three electron guns: one to make red phosphors glow, another for green and a third for blue.

333

# Computers

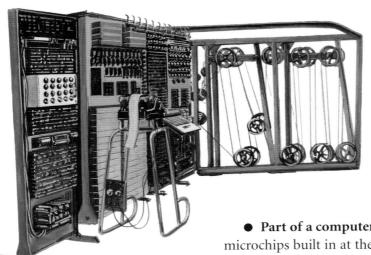

◀ *Created in the 1940s, the Colossus computer successfully cracked the German Enigma war codes.*

- **Part of a computer's** memory is microchips built in at the factory and known as ROM, or read-only memory. ROM carries the basic working instructions.

- **RAM** (random-access memory) consists of microchips that receive new data and instructions when needed.

- **Data can also** be stored as magnetic patterns on a removable floppy disk, or on the laser-guided bumps on a CD (compact disc) or DVD (digital versatile disk).

- **At the heart** of every computer is a powerful microchip called the central processing unit, or CPU.

- **The CPU** performs logical and mathematical operations on data, within the guidelines set by the computer's ROM. It carries out programmes by sending data to the right place in the RAM.

**334**

◄ *Computers are developing so rapidly that models from the 1990s already look dated.*

- **Computers** store information in bits (binary digits), either as 0 or 1.
- **The bits 0 and 1** are equivalent to the OFF and ON of electric current flow. Eight bits make a byte.
- **A kilobyte** is 1000 bytes; a megabyte (MB) is 1,000,000 bytes; a gigabyte (GB) is 1,000,000,000 bytes; a terabyte (TB) is 1,000,000,000,000 bytes.
- **A CD can hold** about 600 MB of data – approximately 375,000 pages of ordinary text.

> ....**FASCINATING FACT**....
> The US Library of Congress's 70 million books could be stored in 25 TB of computer capacity.

# The Internet

- **The Internet** is a vast network linking millions of computers around the world.

- **The Internet began** in the 1960s when the US Army developed a network called ARPAnet to link computers.

- **To access the Internet** computer data is translated into a form that can be sent through phone lines with a modem (short for modulator/demodulator).

- **Computers** access the Internet via a local phone to a large computer called the Internet Service Provider (ISP).

- **Each ISP** is connected to a giant computer called a main hub. There are about 100 linked main hubs worldwide.

- **Some links between** hubs are made via phone lines; some are made via satellite.

- **Links between** hubs are called fast-track connections.

▲ *The Internet links computers instantly around the world.*

- **The World Wide Web** is a way of finding your way to the data in sites on all the computers linked to the Internet. The Web makes hyperlinks (fast links) to sites with the word you select.

- **The World Wide Web** was invented in 1989 by Tim Berners-Lee of the CERN laboratories in Switzerland.

▲ *E-mail, sending electronic messages from one computer to another, is used for business and pleasure.*

...FASCINATING FACT...
People can now access the Internet via mobile phones.

337

# Nuclear power

- **Nuclear power** is based on the huge amounts of energy that bind together the nucleus of every atom in the Universe. It is an incredibly concentrated form of energy.

- **Nuclear energy** is released by splitting the nuclei of atoms in a process called nuclear fission. One day scientists hope to release energy by nuclear fusion – by fusing nuclei together as in the Sun.

- **Most nuclear reactors** use uranium-235. These are special atoms, or isotopes, of uranium with 235 protons and neutrons in their nucleus rather than the normal 238.

- **The fuel** usually consists of tiny pellets of uranium dioxide in thin tubes, separated by sheets called spacers.

- **Three kilograms of uranium fuel** provide enough energy for a city of one million people for one day.

- **The earliest reactors,** called N-reactors, were designed to make plutonium for bombs. Magnox reactors make both plutonium and electricity.

- **Pressurized water reactors** (PWRs), originally used in submarines, are now the most common kind. They are built in factories, unlike Advanced Gas Reactors (AGRs).

- **Fast-breeder reactors** actually create more fuel than they burn, but the new fuel is highly radioactive.

- **Every stage of the nuclear process** creates dangerous radioactive waste. The radioactivity may take 80,000 years to fade. All but the most radioactive liquid waste is pumped out to sea. Gaseous waste is vented into the air. Solid waste is mostly stockpiled underground. Scientists debate fiercely about what to do with radioactive waste.

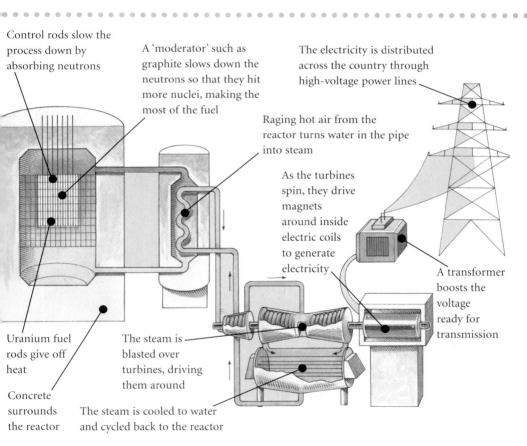

Control rods slow the process down by absorbing neutrons

A 'moderator' such as graphite slows down the neutrons so that they hit more nuclei, making the most of the fuel

The electricity is distributed across the country through high-voltage power lines

Raging hot air from the reactor turns water in the pipe into steam

As the turbines spin, they drive magnets around inside electric coils to generate electricity

A transformer boosts the voltage ready for transmission

Uranium fuel rods give off heat

Concrete surrounds the reactor

The steam is blasted over turbines, driving them around

The steam is cooled to water and cycled back to the reactor

▲ Like coal- and oil-fired power stations, nuclear power stations use steam to drive turbines to generate electricity. The difference is that nuclear power stations obtain the heat by splitting uranium atoms, not by burning coal or oil. When an atom is split, it sends out gamma rays, neutrons and immense heat. In a nuclear bomb this happens in a split second. In a nuclear power plant, control rods soak up some of the neutrons and slow the process down.

**339**

# Temperature

- **Temperature** is how hot or cold something is. The best-known temperature scales are Celsius and Fahrenheit.

- **The Celsius (C) scale** is part of the metric system of measurements and is used everywhere except in the USA. It is named after Swedish astronomer Anders Celsius, who developed it in 1742.

- **Celsius is also** known as centigrade because water boils at 100°C. Cent is the Latin prefix for 100. Water freezes at 0°C.

- **On the Fahrenheit (F) scale** water boils at 212°F. It freezes at 32°F.

- **To convert Celsius** to Fahrenheit, divide by 5, multiply by 9 and add 32.

- **To convert Fahrenheit** to Celsius, subtract 32, divide by 9 and multiply by 5.

- **The Kelvin (K) scale** used by scientists is like the Celsius scale, but it begins at –273.15°C. So 0°C is 273.15K.

- **Cold:** absolute zero is –273.15°C. The coldest temperature ever obtained in a laboratory is –272.99999°C. Helium turns liquid at –269°C. Oxygen turns liquid at –183°C. Gasoline freezes at –150°C. The lowest air temperature ever recorded on Earth is –89.2°C.

◄ *A digital thermometer measures temperature with a thermistor, which is a probe whose electrical resistance varies with the heat.*

- **Hot:** the highest shade temperature recorded on Earth is 58°C. A log fire burns at around 800°C. Molten magma is about 1200°C. Tungsten melts at 3410°C. The surface of the Sun is around 6000°C. The centre of the Earth is over 7000°C. A lightning flash reaches 30,000°C. The centre of a hydrogen bomb reaches four million°C.

- **The blood temperature** of the human body is normally 37°C. A skin temperature above 40°C is very hot, and below 31°C is very cold. Hands feel cold below 20°C and go numb below 12°C. Anything above 45°C that touches your skin hurts, although people have walked on hot coals at 800°C. The knee can tolerate 47°C for 30 seconds.

▲ *Molten iron is poured into a furnace as part of the process of producing steel. The temperature of the liquid metal is about 1500°C.*

**341**

# Heat

- **Heat is the energy** of moving molecules. The faster molecules move, the hotter the substance is.

- **When you hold your hand** over a heater the warmth you feel is the assault of billions of fast-moving air molecules.

- **Heat** is the combined energy of all the moving molecules – temperature is how fast they are moving.

- **The coldest temperature possible** is absolute zero, or –273°C, when molecules stop moving.

- **When you heat a substance** its temperature rises because heat makes its molecules move faster.

- **The same amount** of heat raises the temperature of different substances by different amounts.

▶ *Cooking helps chemical reactions to take place in food, maybe changing its flavour, its texture or consistency.*

▶ *Fire changes the energy in fuel into heat energy. Heat makes the molecules rush about.*

- **The specific heat** of a substance is the energy needed, in joules, to heat it by 1°C.

- **Argon gas** gets hotter quicker than oxygen. The shape of oxygen molecules means they absorb some energy not by moving faster but by spinning faster.

- **Heat always spreads out** from its source. It heats up its surroundings while cooling down itself.

**· · · FASCINATING FACT · · ·**
Heat makes the molecules of a solid vibrate; it makes gas molecules zoom about.

# Energy

- **Energy is the ability** to make things happen or, as scientists say, do work.

- **Energy comes in many forms,** from the chemical energy locked in sugar to the mechanical energy in a speeding train.

- **Energy does its work** either by transfer or conversion.

- **Energy transfer** is the movement of energy from one place to another, such as heat rising above a fire or a ball being thrown.

- **Energy conversion** is when energy changes from one form to another – as when wind turbines generate electric power, for instance.

- **Energy is never lost nor gained;** it simply moves or changes. The total amount of energy in the Universe has stayed the same since the beginning of time.

▼ *Power stations do not create energy. They simply convert it into a convenient form for us to use electricity.*

- **Energy and mass** are actually the same thing. They are like opposite sides of a coin and are interchangeable.

- **Potential energy** is energy stored up ready for action – as in a squeezed spring or stretched piece of elastic.

● **Kinetic energy** is energy that something has because it is moving, such as a rolling ball or a falling stone.

● **Kinetic energy** increases in proportion with the velocity of an object squared. So a car has four times more kinetic energy at 40 km/h than at 20 km/h.

▼ *Found near the Earth's surface and at various depths, coal is an important primary fossil fuel.*

▼ *Wind farms can be constructed in areas where there is a steady wind. About 47 percent of the kinetic energy of the wind can be harnessed.*

345

# Weight and mass

- **Mass** is the amount of matter in an object.

- **Weight** is not the same as mass. Scientists say weight is the force of gravity pulling on an object. Weight varies with the mass of the object and the strength of gravity.

- **Objects weigh more** at sea level, which is nearer the centre of the Earth, than up a mountain.

- **A person on the Moon** weighs one sixth of their weight on Earth because the Moon's gravity is one sixth of the Earth's gravity.

- **Weight varies** with gravity but mass is always the same, so scientists use mass when talking about how heavy something is.

- **The smallest** known mass is that of a photon. Its mass is 5.3 times $10^{-63}$ (62 zeros and a 1 after the decimal point) kg.

- **The mass of the Earth** is $6 \times 10^{24}$ (six trillion trillion) kg. The mass of the Universe may be $10^{51}$ (10 followed by 50 zeros) kg.

- **Density is** the amount of mass in a certain space. It is measured in grams per cubic centimetre ($g/cm^3$).

- **The lightest** solids are silica aerogels made for space science, with a density of 0.005 $g/cm^3$. The lightest gas is hydrogen, at 0.00008989 $g/cm^3$. The density of air is 0.00128 $g/cm^3$.

- **The densest** solid is osmium at 22.59 $g/cm^3$. Lead is 11.37 $g/cm^3$. A neutron star has an incredible density of about one billion trillion $g/cm^3$.

▲ *Brass weights are used in chemical laboratories because brass is dense and does not corrode.*

▲ *The pull of gravity at the Moon's surface is only one sixth as strong as on Earth.*

# Relativity

- **Einstein** was the creator of two theories of relativity which have revolutionized scientists' way of thinking about the Universe: the special theory of relativity (1905) and the general theory (1915).

- **Time is relative** because it depends where you measure it from. Distances and speed are relative too. If you are in a car and another car whizzes past you, for instance, the slower you are travelling, the faster the other car seems to be moving.

- **Einstein showed** in his special theory of relativity that you cannot even measure your speed relative to a beam of light, which is the fastest thing in the Universe. This is because light always passes you at the same speed, no matter where you are or how fast you are going.

- **Einstein** realized that if light always travels at the same speed, there are some strange effects when you are moving very fast (see below).

- **If a rocket** passing you zoomed up to near the speed of light, you would see it shrink.

▶ In normal everyday life, the effects of relativity are so tiny that you can ignore them. However, in a spacecraft travelling very fast they may become quite significant.

◀ A spacecraft travelling almost at the speed of light seems to shrink. Of course, if you were actually on board everything would seem entirely normal. Instead, it would be the world outside that seemed to shrink, since it is travelling almost at the speed of light relative to you.

- **If a rocket** passing you zoomed up to near the speed of light, you'd see the clocks on the rocket running more slowly as time stretched out. If the rocket reached the speed of light, the clocks would stop altogether.

- **If a rocket** passing you zoomed near the speed of light, it would seem to get heavier and heavier. But it would gradually become so heavy, there wouldn't be enough energy in the Universe to speed it up any further.

- **Einstein's general relativity theory** brought in gravity. It showed that gravity works basically by bending space-time. From this theory scientists predicted black holes and wormholes.

▼ *In a spacecraft travelling almost at the speed of light, time runs slower. So astronauts going on a long, very fast journey into space come back a little younger than if they had stayed on the Earth.*

- **In 1919** an eclipse of the Sun allowed Arthur Eddington to observe how the Sun bends light rays, proving Einstein's theory of general relativity.

◄ *In a spacecraft travelling almost at the speed of light, everything becomes heavier. Many scientists believe objects will never be able to accelerate to the speed of light because the faster it goes, the heavier it gets.*

> ....FASCINATING FACT....
> When astronauts went to the Moon, their clock lost a few seconds. The clock was not faulty, but time actually ran slower in the speeding spacecraft.

# The skeleton

- **Your skeleton** is a rigid framework of bones, which provides an anchor for your muscles, supports your skin and other organs, and protects vital organs.

- **An adult's skeleton has 206 bones** joined together by rubbery cartilage. Some people have extra vertebrae (the bones of the backbone, or spine).

- **A baby's skeleton has 300** or more bones, but some of these fuse (join) together as the baby grows.

- **The parts of an adult skeleton** that have fused into one bone include the skull and the pelvis. The pelvis came from fusing the ilium bones, the ischium bones and the pubis. The ischium is the bone that you sit on.

▶ *Your skeleton is the remarkably light, but very tough framework of bones that supports your body. It is made up of more than 200 bones.*

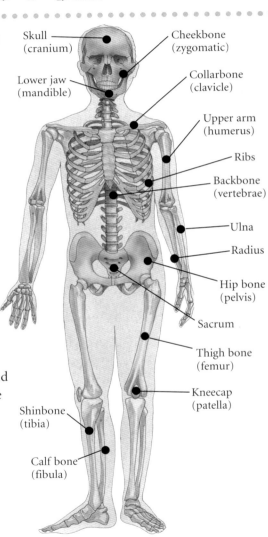

Skull (cranium)
Cheekbone (zygomatic)
Lower jaw (mandible)
Collarbone (clavicle)
Upper arm (humerus)
Ribs
Backbone (vertebrae)
Ulna
Radius
Hip bone (pelvis)
Sacrum
Thigh bone (femur)
Kneecap (patella)
Shinbone (tibia)
Calf bone (fibula)

- **The skeleton** has two main parts – the axial and the appendicular skeleton.

- **The axial skeleton** is the 80 bones of the upper body. It includes the skull, the vertebrae of the backbone, the ribs and the breastbone. The arm and shoulder bones are suspended from it.

- **The appendicular skeleton** is the other 126 bones – the arm and shoulder bones, and the leg and hip bones. It includes the femur (thigh bone), the body's longest bone.

- **The word skeleton** comes from the Ancient Greek word for 'dry'.

- **Most women and girls** have smaller and lighter skeletons than men and boys. But in women and girls, the pelvis is much wider than in men and boys. This is because the opening has to be wide enough for a baby to pass through when it is born.

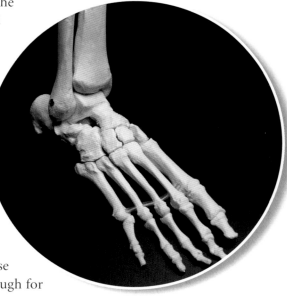

▲ *There are 14 bones in the toes, and 12 in the sole and the ankle, making 26 bones altogether that can be seen in this photograph.*

> ... **FASCINATING FACT** ...
> The tiniest bone in your body is only 3 mm long and is found in your ear.

351

# Bone

- **Bones are so strong** that they can cope with twice the squeezing pressure that granite can, or four times the stretching tension that concrete can.
- **Weight for weight,** bone is at least five times as strong as steel.
- **Bones are so light** they only make up 14 percent of your body's total weight.
- **Bones get their rigidity** from hard deposits of minerals such as calcium and phosphate.

▶ *Bones are strong but very light because, on the inside, they have many holes.*

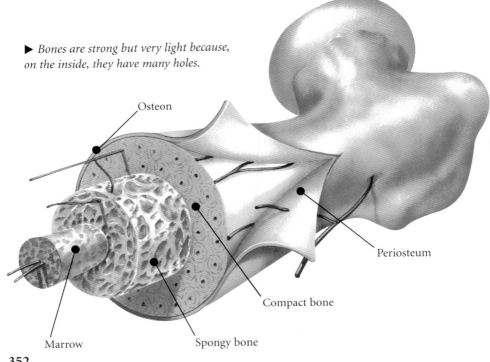

Osteon

Periosteum

Compact bone

Marrow

Spongy bone

- **Bones get their flexibility** from tough, elastic, rope-like fibres of collagen.

- **The hard outside of bones** (called compact bone) is reinforced by strong rods called osteons.

- **The inside of bones** (called spongy bone) is a light honeycomb, made of thin struts or trabeculae, perfectly angled to take stress.

- **The core of some bones,** such as the long bones in an arm or leg, is called bone marrow. It is soft and jelly-like.

- **In some parts of each bone,** there are special cells called osteoblasts which make new bone. In other parts, cells called osteoclasts break up old bone.

- **Bones grow** by getting longer near the end, at a region called the epiphyseal plate.

▲ *Milk contains a mineral called calcium, which is essential for building strong bones. Babies and children need plenty of calcium to help their bones develop properly.*

# Muscles

- **Muscles are special fibres** that contract (tighten) and relax to move different parts of the body.

- **Voluntary muscles** are all the muscles you can control by will or thinking, such as your arm muscles.

- **Involuntary muscles** are the muscles you cannot control at will, but work automatically, such as the muscles that move food through your intestine.

- **Most voluntary muscles** cover the skeleton and are therefore called skeletal muscles. They are also called striated (striped) muscle because there are dark bands on the bundles of fibre that form them.

- **Most involuntary muscles** form sacs or tubes such as the intestine or the blood vessels. They are called smooth muscle because they lack the bands or stripes of voluntary muscles.

- **Most muscles are arranged in pairs,** because although muscles can shorten themselves, they cannot make themselves longer. So the flexor muscle that bends a joint is paired with an extensor muscle to straighten it again.

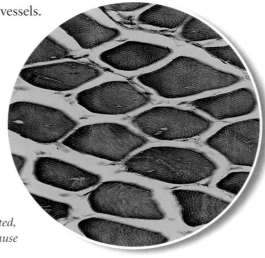

▶ *This microscopic cross-section shows striated, or striped, skeletal muscle. It is so-called because its fibres are made of light and dark stripes.*

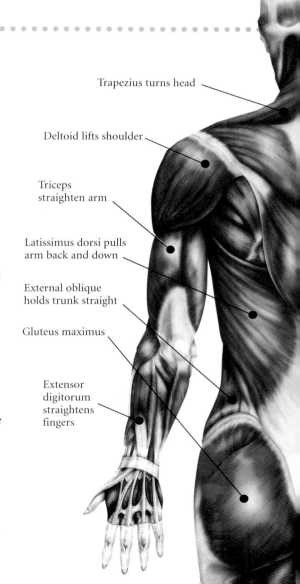

- **The heart muscle** is a unique combination of skeletal and smooth muscle. It has its own built-in contraction rhythm of 70 beats per minute, and special muscle cells that work like nerve cells for transmitting the signals for waves of muscle contraction to sweep through the heart.

- **Your body's longest muscle** is the sartorius on the inner thigh.

- **Your body's widest muscle** is the external oblique which runs around the side of the upper body.

- **Your body's biggest muscle** is the gluteus maximus in your buttocks (bottom).

▶ *You have more than 640 skeletal muscles and they make up over 40 percent of your body's entire weight, covering your skeleton like a bulky blanket. This illustration shows only the main surface muscles of the back, but your body has at least two, and sometimes three, layers of muscle beneath its surface muscles. Most muscles are firmly anchored at both ends and attached to the bones either side of a joint, either directly or by tough fibres called tendons.*

Trapezius turns head

Deltoid lifts shoulder

Triceps straighten arm

Latissimus dorsi pulls arm back and down

External oblique holds trunk straight

Gluteus maximus

Extensor digitorum straightens fingers

# Teeth

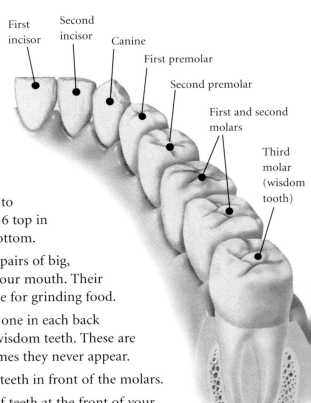

▶ *This shows one side of an adult's lower jaw. Not every adult grows the full set of eight teeth on each side of the jaw.*

First incisor

Second incisor

Canine

First premolar

Second premolar

First and second molars

Third molar (wisdom tooth)

- **Milk teeth** are the 20 teeth that start to appear when a baby is about six months old.

- **When you are six,** you start to grow your 32 adult teeth – 16 top in the top row and 16 in the bottom.

- **Molars** are the (usually) six pairs of big, strong teeth at the back of your mouth. Their flattish tops are a good shape for grinding food.

- **The four rearmost molars,** one in each back corner of each jaw, are the wisdom teeth. These are the last to grow and sometimes they never appear.

- **Premolars** are four pairs of teeth in front of the molars.

- **Incisors** are the four pairs of teeth at the front of your mouth. They have sharp edges for cutting food.

- **Canines** are the two pairs of big, pointed teeth behind the incisors. Their shape is good for tearing food.

- **The enamel** on teeth is the body's hardest substance.
- **Dentine** inside teeth is softer but still hard as bone.
- **Teeth** sit in sockets in the jawbones.

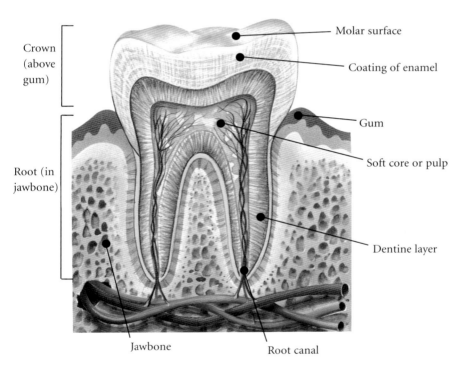

Crown (above gum)

Molar surface

Coating of enamel

Gum

Soft core or pulp

Root (in jawbone)

Dentine layer

Jawbone

Root canal

▲ *Teeth have long roots that slot into sockets in the jawbones, but they sit in a fleshy ridge called the gums. In the centre of each tooth is a living pulp of blood and nerves. Around this is a layer of dentine, then on top of that a tough shield of enamel.*

357

# Body systems

▲ *Fresh air and exercise are vital for keeping our body systems working to their best potential.*

- **Your body systems** are interlinked – each has its own task, but they are all dependent on one another.

- **The skeleton** supports the body, protects the major organs, and provides an anchor for the muscles.

- **The nervous system** is the brain and the nerves – the body's control and communications network.

- **The digestive system** breaks down food into chemicals that the body can use to its advantage.

- **The immune system** is the body's defence against germs. It includes white blood cells, antibodies and the lymphatic system.

- **The urinary system** controls the body's water balance, removing extra water as urine and getting rid of impurities in the blood.

- **The respiratory system** takes air into the lungs to supply oxygen, and lets out waste carbon dioxide.

- **The reproductive system** is the smallest of all the systems. It is basically the sexual organs that enable people to have children. It is the only system that is different in men and women.

- **The other body systems** are the hormonal system (controls growth and internal co-ordination by chemical hormones), integumentary system (skin, hair and nails), and the sensory system (eyes, ears, nose, tongue, skin, balance).

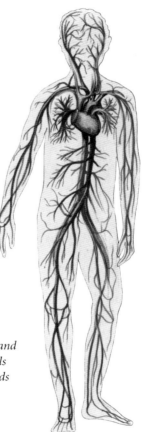

▶ *The cardiovascular system is the heart and the blood circulation. It keeps the body cells supplied with food and oxygen, and defends them against germs.*

> ...FASCINATING FACT...
> The reproductive system is the only system that can be removed without threatening life.

# Breathing

- **You breathe** because every single cell in your body needs a continuous supply of oxygen to burn glucose, the high-energy substance from digested food that cells get from blood.

- **Scientists** call breathing 'respiration'. Cellular respiration is the way that cells use oxygen to burn glucose.

- **The oxygen in air** is taken into your lungs, and then carried in your blood to your body cells.

- **Waste carbon dioxide** from your cells is returned by your blood to your lungs, to be breathed out.

- **On average** you breathe in about 15 times a minute. If you run hard, the rate soars to around 80 times a minute.

Breathing in          Breathing out

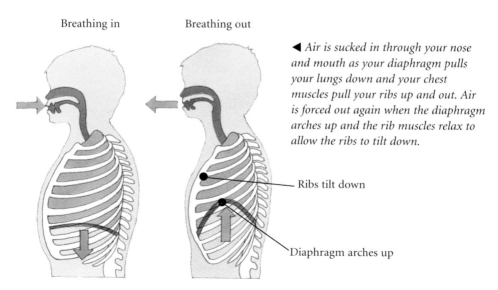

◄ Air is sucked in through your nose and mouth as your diaphragm pulls your lungs down and your chest muscles pull your ribs up and out. Air is forced out again when the diaphragm arches up and the rib muscles relax to allow the ribs to tilt down.

Ribs tilt down

Diaphragm arches up

● **Newborn babies** breathe about 40 times a minute.

● **If you live to the age of 80,** you will have taken well over 600 million breaths.

● **A normal breath** takes in about 0.4 litres of air. A deep breath can take in ten times as much.

● **Your diaphragm** is a dome-shaped sheet of muscle between your chest and stomach, which works with your chest muscles to make you breathe in and out.

● **Scientists** call breathing in 'inhalation', and breathing out 'exhalation'.

▶ *Wind musicians, such as this trumpeter, use their diaphragm and chest to control the air flowing in and out of their lungs. This allows them to produce a better quality sound.*

# The lungs

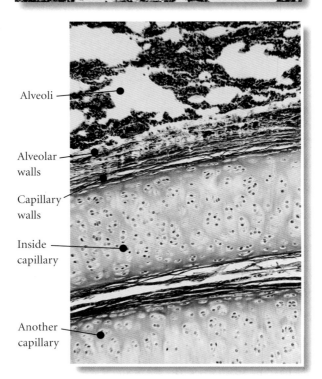

Alveoli

Alveolar
walls

Capillary
walls

Inside
capillary

Another
capillary

▲ *Taken through a powerful microscope, this*
*photo of a slice of lung tissue shows a blood vessel*
*and the very thin walls of an alveolus next to it.*

- **Your lungs** are a pair of
  soft, spongy bags inside
  your chest.

- **When you breathe** in, air
  rushes in through your
  nose or mouth, down your
  windpipe and into the
  millions of branching
  airways in your lungs.

- **The two biggest airways**
  are called bronchi
  (singular bronchus), and
  they both branch into
  smaller airways called
  bronchioles.

- **The surface of your
  airways** is protected by a
  slimy film of mucus, which
  gets thicker to protect the
  lungs when you have a
  cold.

- **At the end of each bronchiole** are bunches of minute air sacs called alveoli (singular alveolus).

- **Alveoli** are wrapped around with tiny blood vessels, and alveoli walls are just one cell thick – thin enough to let oxygen and carbon dioxide seep through them.

- **There are around 300 million alveoli** in your lungs.

- **The large surface area** of all these alveoli makes it possible for huge quantities of oxygen to seep through into the blood. Equally huge quantities of carbon dioxide can seep back into the airways for removal when you breathe out.

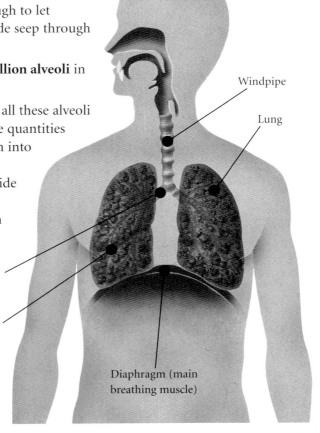

Windpipe

Lung

Main bronchus

Bronchial tubes

Diaphragm (main breathing muscle)

▶ *A front view of the lungs shows how they take up most of the room in the chest, being one of our most vital organs.*

# Circulation

- **Your circulation** is the system of tubes called blood vessels which carries blood out from your heart to all your body cells and back again.

- **Blood circulation** was discovered in 1628 by the English physician William Harvey (1578–1657), who built on the ideas of Matteo Colombo.

- **Each of the body's** 600 billion cells gets fresh blood continuously, although the blood flow is pulsating.

- **On the way out** from the heart, blood is pumped through vessels called arteries and arterioles.

- **On the way back** to the heart, blood flows through venules and veins.

- **Blood flows** from the arterioles to the venules through the tiniest tubes called capillaries.

- **The blood circulation** has two parts – the pulmonary and the systemic.

- **The pulmonary circulation** is the short section that carries blood which is low in oxygen from the right side of the heart to the lungs for 'refuelling'. It then returns oxygen-rich blood to the left side of the heart.

- **The systemic circulation** carries oxygen-rich blood from the left side of the heart all around the body, and returns blood which is low in oxygen to the right side of the heart.

- **Inside the blood,** oxygen is carried by the haemoglobin in red blood cells.

The pulmonary circulation takes blood to and from the lungs

Radial artery

Iliac vein

Femoral artery

Peroneal artery

For each outward-going artery there is usually an equivalent returning vein

The brain receives more blood than any other part of the body

Blood leaves the left side of the heart through a giant artery called the aorta

Blood returns to the heart through main veins called the vena cavae

Saphenous vein

◄ *Blood circulates continuously round and round your body, through an intricate series of tubes called blood vessels. Bright red, oxygen-rich blood is pumped from the left side of the heart through vessels called arteries and arterioles. Purplish-blue, low-in-oxygen blood returns to the right of the heart through veins and venules.*

▲ *Red blood cells can actually be brown in colour, but they turn bright scarlet when their haemoglobin is carrying oxygen. After the haemoglobin passes its oxygen to a cell, it fades to dull purple. So oxygen-rich blood from the heart is red, while oxygen-poor blood that is returning to the heart is a purplish-blue colour.*

**365**

# The heart

- **Your heart** is the size of your fist. It is inside the middle of your chest, slightly to the left.

- **The heart is a powerful pump** made almost entirely of muscle.

- **The heart contracts** (tightens) and relaxes automatically about 70 times a minute to pump blood out through your arteries.

- **The heart has two sides** separated by a muscle wall called the septum.

- **The right side** is smaller and weaker, and it pumps blood only to the lungs.

- **The stronger left side** pumps blood around the body.

- **Each side of the heart** has two chambers. There is an atrium (plural atria) at the top where blood accumulates (builds up) from the veins, and a ventricle below which contracts to pump blood out into the arteries.

- **Each side of the heart** (left and right) ejects about 70 ml of blood every beat.

- **There are two valves** in each side of the heart to make sure that blood flows only one way – a large one between the atrium and the ventricle, and a small one at the exit from the ventricle into the artery.

- **The coronary arteries** supply the heart. If they become clogged, the heart muscle may be short of blood and stop working. This is what happens in a heart attack.

. . . . FASCINATING FACT . . . .
During an average lifetime, the heart pumps
200 million litres of blood – enough to fill
New York's Central Park to a depth of 15 m.

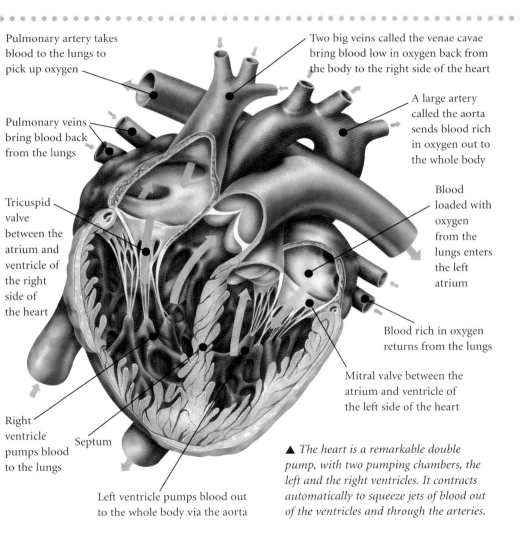

Pulmonary artery takes blood to the lungs to pick up oxygen

Two big veins called the venae cavae bring blood low in oxygen back from the body to the right side of the heart

A large artery called the aorta sends blood rich in oxygen out to the whole body

Pulmonary veins bring blood back from the lungs

Blood loaded with oxygen from the lungs enters the left atrium

Tricuspid valve between the atrium and ventricle of the right side of the heart

Blood rich in oxygen returns from the lungs

Mitral valve between the atrium and ventricle of the left side of the heart

Right ventricle pumps blood to the lungs

Septum

Left ventricle pumps blood out to the whole body via the aorta

▲ *The heart is a remarkable double pump, with two pumping chambers, the left and the right ventricles. It contracts automatically to squeeze jets of blood out of the ventricles and through the arteries.*

**367**

# Blood

- **Blood** is the reddish liquid that circulates around your body. It carries oxygen and food to body cells, and takes

carbon dioxide and other waste away. It fights infection, keeps you warm, and distributes chemicals that control body processes.

- **Blood is made up of** red cells, white cells and platelets, all carried in a liquid called plasma.

- **Plasma** is 90 percent water, plus hundreds of other substances, including nutrients, hormones and special proteins for fighting infection.

- **Blood plasma** turns milky immediately after a meal high in fats.

- **Blood platelets** are tiny pieces of cell that make blood clots start to form in order to stop bleeding.

◄ *A centrifuge is used to separate the different components of blood. The spinning action of the machine separates the heavier blood cells from the lighter plasma.*

◄ *Blood may look like a simple sticky red liquid, but it is actually a watery liquid containing millions of cells.*

● **Blood clots also** involve a lacy, fibrous network made from a protein called fibrin. Fibrin is set in action by a sequence of chemicals called factors (factors 1 through to 8).

● **The amount of blood** in your body depends on your size. An adult who weighs 80 kg has about 5 litres of blood. A child who is half as heavy has half as much blood.

● **A drop of blood** the size of the dot on this i contains around 5 million red cells.

● **If a blood donor** gives 0.5 litres of blood, the body replaces the plasma in a few hours, but it takes a few weeks to replace the red cells.

**369**

# Digestion

- **Digestion** is the process by which your body breaks down the food you eat into substances that it can absorb (take in) and use.

- **Your digestive tract** is basically a long, winding tube called the alimentary canal (gut). It starts at your mouth and ends at your anus.

- **If you could lay** your gut out straight, it would be nearly six times as long as you are tall.

- **The food you eat** is softened in your mouth by chewing and by chemicals in your saliva (spit).

- **When you swallow,** food travels down your oesophagus (gullet) into your stomach. Your stomach is a muscular-walled bag which mashes the food into a pulp, helped by chemicals called gastric juices.

- **When empty,** your stomach holds barely 0.5 litres, but after a big meal it can stretch to more than 4 litres.

- **The half-digested food** that leaves your stomach is called chyme. It passes into your small intestine.

- **Your small intestine** is a 6-m-long tube where chyme is broken down into molecules small enough to be absorbed through the intestine wall into the blood.

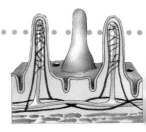

▲ *The small intestine is lined with tiny, finger-like folds called villi. On the surface of each villus are even tinier, finger-like folds called microvilli. These folds give a huge area for absorbing food.*

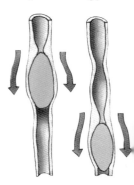

▲ *Swallowed food is pushed through the long, winding digestive tract by waves of contraction (tightening) that pass along its muscular walls. These waves are called peristalsis*

> **· · · FASCINATING FACT · · ·**
> On average, food takes 24 hours to pass right through your alimentary canal and out the other end.

- **Food that cannot be** digested in your small intestine passes on into your large intestine. It is then pushed out through your anus as faeces when you go to the toilet.

- **Digestive enzymes** play a vital part in breaking food down so it can be absorbed by the body.

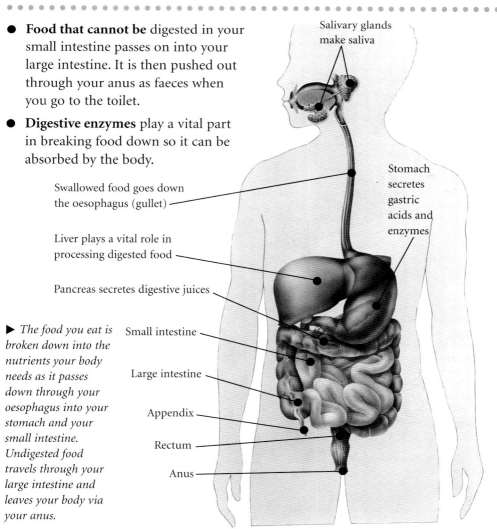

Salivary glands make saliva

Stomach secretes gastric acids and enzymes

Swallowed food goes down the oesophagus (gullet)

Liver plays a vital role in processing digested food

Pancreas secretes digestive juices

Small intestine

Large intestine

Appendix

Rectum

Anus

▶ *The food you eat is broken down into the nutrients your body needs as it passes down through your oesophagus into your stomach and your small intestine. Undigested food travels through your large intestine and leaves your body via your anus.*

371

# The liver

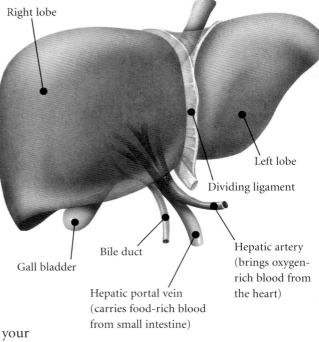

▶ *The liver is a large organ situated to the right of the stomach.*

Right lobe

Left lobe

Dividing ligament

Hepatic artery (brings oxygen-rich blood from the heart)

Bile duct

Gall bladder

Hepatic portal vein (carries food-rich blood from small intestine)

- **The liver** is your body's chemical processing centre.

- **The liver is your body's biggest internal organ,** and the word hepatic means 'to do with the liver'.

- **The liver's prime task** is handling all the nutrients and substances digested from the food you eat and sending them out to your body cells when they are needed.

- **The liver turns** carbohydrates into glucose, the main energy-giving chemical for body cells.

- **The liver keeps** the levels of glucose in the blood steady. It does this by releasing more when levels drop, and by storing it as glycogen, a type of starch, when levels rise.

- **The liver packs off** excess food energy to be stored as fat around the body.

▲ *The liver filters harmful substances such as alcohol and food additives to keep the body safe.*

● **The liver breaks down** proteins and stores vitamins and minerals.

● **The liver produces bile,** the yellowish or greenish bitter liquid that helps dissolve fat as food is digested in the intestines.

● **The liver clears the blood** of old red cells and harmful substances such as alcohol, and makes new plasma.

● **The liver's chemical processing units**, called lobules, take in unprocessed blood on the outside and dispatch it through a collecting vein.

**373**

# Carbohydrates

- **Carbohydrates** in food are your body's main source of energy. They are plentiful in sweet things and in starchy food such as bread, cakes, biscuits and potatoes.

- **Carbohydrates** are burned by the body in order to keep it warm and to provide energy for growth and muscle movement, as well as to maintain basic body processes.

- **Carbohydrates** are among the most common of organic (life) substance – plants, for instance, make carbohydrates by taking energy from sunlight.

- **Carbohydrates** include chemical substances called sugars. Sucrose (the sugar in sugar lumps and caster sugar) is just one of these sugars.

- **Simple carbohydrates** such as glucose, fructose (the sweetness in fruit) and sucrose are sweet and soluble (they will dissolve in water).

- **Complex carbohydrates** (or polysaccharides) such as starch are made when molecules of simple carbohydrates join together.

▼ *Bread is especially rich in complex carbohydrates such as starch, as well as simpler ones such as glucose and sucrose.*

▲ *Carbohydrates give us the instant energy we need to help us lead a full and active life.*

- **A third type of carbohydrate** is cellulose.

- **The carbohydrates** you eat are turned into glucose for your body to use at once, or stored in the liver as the complex sugar glycogen (body starch).

- **The average adult** needs 2000 to 4000 Calories a day.

- **A Calorie** is the heat needed to warm 1 litre of water by 1°C.

**375**

# Diet

- **Your diet** is what you eat. A good diet includes the correct amount of proteins, carbohydrates, fats, vitamins, minerals, fibre and water.

- **Most of the food** that you eat is fuel for the body, provided mostly by carbohydrates and fats.

- **Carbohydrates** are foods made from kinds of sugar, such as glucose and starch. They are found in foods such as bread, rice, potatoes and sweet things.

- **Fats** are greasy foods that will not dissolve in water. Some, such as the fats in meat and cheese, are solid. Some, such as cooking oil, are liquid.

- **Fats are not** usually burned up straight away, but are stored around your body until they are needed.

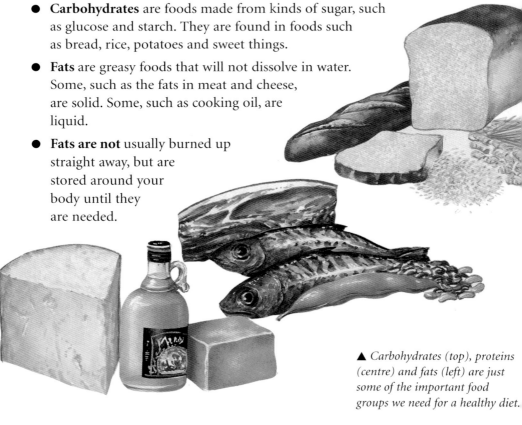

▲ *Carbohydrates (top), proteins (centre) and fats (left) are just some of the important food groups we need for a healthy diet.*

- **Proteins** are needed to build and repair cells. They are made from special chemicals called amino acids.

- **There are 20** different amino acids. Your body can make 11 of them. The other nine are called essential acids and they come from food.

- **Meat and fish** are very high in protein.

- **A correctly balanced vegetarian diet** of eggs, milk and cheese can provide all the essential amino acids.

▲ *Fresh fruit and vegetables provide us with an assortment of vital vitamins and minerals.*

- **Fibre or roughage** is supplied by cellulose from plant cell walls. Your body cannot digest fibre, but needs it to keep the bowel muscles exercised.

▶ *These foods contain fibre, which helps keep the digestive system healthy.*

377

# Excretion

- **Digestive excretion** is the way your body gets rid of food that it cannot digest.

- **Undigested food** is prepared for excretion in your large intestine or bowel.

- **The main part** of the large intestine is the colon, which is almost as long as you are tall.

- **The colon** converts the semi-liquid 'chyme' of undigested food into solid waste, by absorbing water.

- **The colon** soaks up 1.5 litres of water every day.

- **The colon walls** also absorb sodium and chlorine and get rid of   bicarbonate and potassium.

▲ *To work well, your bowel needs plenty of roughage – the indigestible cellulose plant fibres found in food such as beans and wholemeal bread. Roughage keeps the muscles of the bowel properly exercised.*

- **Billions of bacteria** live inside the colon and help turn the chyme into faeces. These bacteria are harmless as long as they do not spread to the rest of the body.

- **Bacteria in the colon** make vitamins K and B – as well as smelly gases such as methane and hydrogen sulphide.

▶ *This is an X-ray of the colon. Patients drink a liquid called barium to enable their doctor to see the colon more clearly and check it is in working order.*

- **The muscles of the colon** break the waste food down into segments ready for excretion.

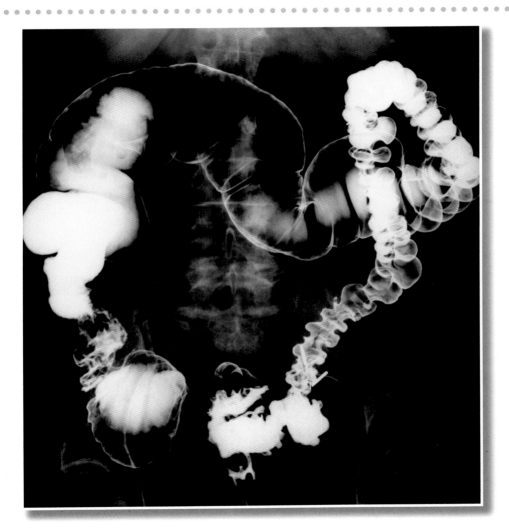

# The kidneys

- **The kidneys** are a pair of bean-shaped organs inside the small of the back.

- **The kidneys** are the body's water control and blood-cleaning plants.

- **The kidneys** are high-speed filters that draw off water and important substances from the blood. They let unwanted water and waste substances go.

- **The kidneys filter** about 1.3 litres of blood a minute.

- **All the body's blood** flows through the kidneys every ten minutes, so blood is filtered 150 times a day.

- **The kidneys manage** to recycle or save every re-useable substance from the blood. They take 85 litres of water and other blood substances from every 1000 litres of blood, but only let out 0.6 litres as urine.

- **The kidneys** save nearly all the amino acids and glucose from the blood and 70 percent of the salt.

- **Blood entering each kidney** is filtered through a million or more filtration units called nephrons.

- **Each nephron** is an incredibly intricate network of little pipes called convoluted tubules, wrapped around countless tiny capillaries. Useful blood substances are filtered into the tubules, then re-absorbed back into the blood in the capillaries.

- **Blood enters each nephron** through a little cup called the Bowman's capsule via a bundle of capillaries.

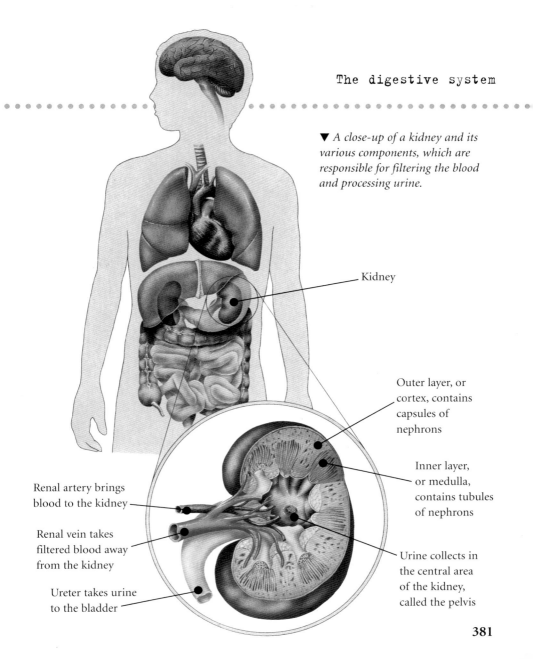

▼ *A close-up of a kidney and its various components, which are responsible for filtering the blood and processing urine.*

Kidney

Outer layer, or cortex, contains capsules of nephrons

Inner layer, or medulla, contains tubules of nephrons

Renal artery brings blood to the kidney

Renal vein takes filtered blood away from the kidney

Ureter takes urine to the bladder

Urine collects in the central area of the kidney, called the pelvis

**381**

# The eye

- **Your eyes** are tough balls that are filled with a jelly-like substance called vitreous humour.

- **The cornea** is a thin, glassy dish across the front of your eye. It allows light rays through the eye's window, the pupil, and into the lens.

- **The iris** is the coloured, muscular ring around the pupil. The iris narrows in bright light and widens when light is dim.

- **The lens** is just behind the pupil. It focuses the picture of the world on to the back of the eye.

- **The back of the eye** is lined with millions of light-sensitive cells. This lining is called the retina, and it registers the picture and sends signals to the brain via the optic nerve.

- **There are two kinds** of light-sensitive cell in the retina – rods and cones. Rods are very sensitive and work in even dim light, but they cannot detect colours. Cones respond to colour.

- **Some kinds of cone** are very sensitive to red light, some to green and some to blue. One theory says that the colours we see depend on how strongly they affect each of these three kinds of cone.

- **Each of your two eyes** gives you a slightly different view of the world. The brain combines these views to give an impression of depth and 3-D solidity.

- **Although each eye** gives a slightly different view of the world, we see things largely as just one eye sees it. This dominant eye is usually the right eye.

...FASCINATING FACT...
The picture received by your retina looks large and real –
yet it is upside down and just a few millimetres across.

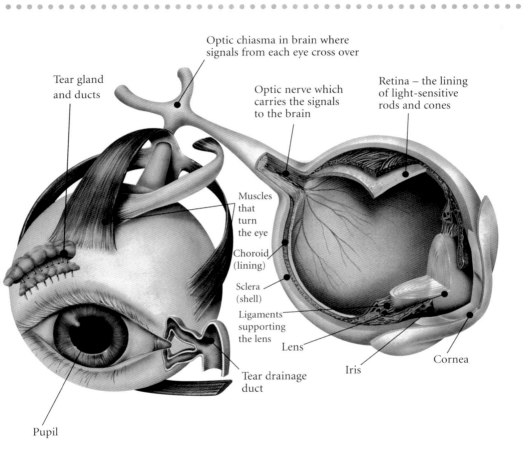

Optic chiasma in brain where
signals from each eye cross over

Tear gland
and ducts

Optic nerve which
carries the signals
to the brain

Retina – the lining
of light-sensitive
rods and cones

Muscles
that
turn
the eye

Choroid
(lining)

Sclera
(shell)

Ligaments
supporting
the lens

Lens

Iris

Cornea

Tear drainage
duct

Pupil

▲ *This illustration shows your two eyeballs, with a cutaway to reveal
the cornea and lens (which projects light rays through the eye's
window) and the light-sensitive retina (which registers them).*

# The ear

- **Pinnae** (singular, pinna) are the ear flaps you can see on the side of your head, and they are simply collecting funnels for sounds.

- **A little way inside your head,** sounds hit a thin, tight wall of skin, called the eardrum, making it vibrate.

- **When the eardrum vibrates,** it shakes three little bones called ossicles. These are the smallest bones in the body.

- **The three ossicle bones** are the malleus (hammer), the incus (anvil) and the stapes (stirrup).

- **When the ossicles vibrate,** they rattle a tiny membrane called the oval window, intensifying the vibration.

- **The oval window** is 30 times smaller in area than the eardrum.

- **Beyond the oval window** is the cochlea – a winding collection of three, liquid-filled tubes, which looks a bit like a snail shell.

- **In the middle tube** of the cochlea there is a flap which covers row upon row of tiny hairs. This is called the organ of Corti.

- **When sounds make** the eardrum vibrate, the ossicles tap on the oval window, making pressure waves shoot through the liquid in the cochlea and wash over the flap of the organ of Corti, waving it up and down.

- **When the organ of Corti waves,** it tugs on the tiny hairs under the flap. These send signals to the brain via the auditory nerve, and you hear a sound.

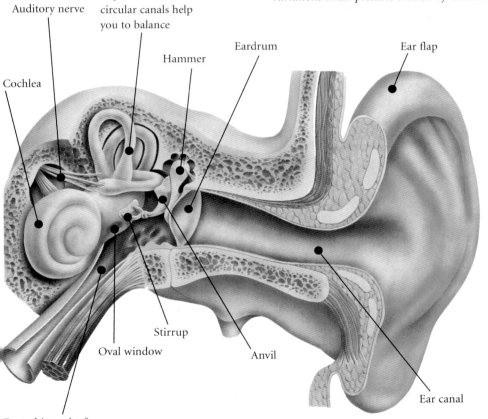

▼ *Most of your ear is hidden inside your head. It is an amazingly complex and delicate structure for picking up the tiny variations in air pressure created by a sound.*

Auditory nerve

Liquid-filled semi-circular canals help you to balance

Hammer

Eardrum

Ear flap

Cochlea

Stirrup

Oval window

Anvil

Ear canal

Eustachian tube for relieving air pressure

**385**

# Smell

- **Smells are scent molecules** which are taken into your nose by breathed-in air. A particular smell may be noticeable even when just a single scent molecule is mixed in with millions of air molecules.

- **The human nose** can tell the difference between more than 10,000 different chemicals.

- **Dogs can pick up** smells that are 10,000 times fainter than the ones humans are able to detect.

- **Inside the nose,** scent molecules are picked up by a patch of scent-sensitive cells called the olfactory epithelium.

▲ *Scents are closely linked to emotions in the brain, and perfume can be a powerful way of triggering feelings.*

- **Olfactory** means 'to do with the sense of smell'.

- **The olfactory epithelium** contains over 25 million receptor cells.

- **Each of the receptor cells** in the olfactory epithelium has up to 20 or so scent-detecting hairs called cilia.

- **When they are triggered** by scent molecules, the cilia send signals to a cluster of nerves called the olfactory bulb, which then sends messages to the part of the brain that recognizes smell.

- **The part of the brain** that deals with smell is closely linked to the parts that deal with memories and emotions. This may be why smells can evoke vivid memories.

- **By the age of 20,** you will have lost 20 percent of your sense of smell. By 60, you will have lost 60 percent of it.

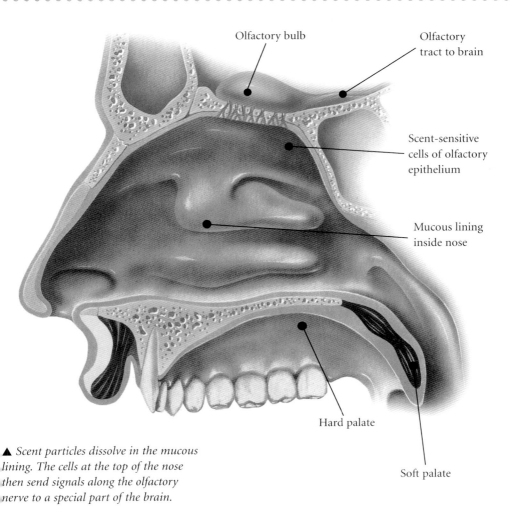

Olfactory bulb

Olfactory
tract to brain

Scent-sensitive
cells of olfactory
epithelium

Mucous lining
inside nose

Hard palate

Soft palate

▲ Scent particles dissolve in the mucous
lining. The cells at the top of the nose
then send signals along the olfactory
nerve to a special part of the brain.

387

# Taste

▲ *As well as tasting the flavour of ice cream, the tongue can also tell that it is cold and smooth.*

- **The sense of taste** is the crudest of our five senses, giving us less information about the world than any other sense.

- **Taste** is triggered by certain chemicals in food, which dissolve in the saliva in the mouth, and then send information to a particular part of the brain via sensory nerve cells on the tongue.

▶ *Certain parts of the tongue are more sensitive to one flavour than to others, as shown in this diagram.*

● **Taste buds** are receptor cells found around tiny bumps called papillae on the surface of your tongue.

● **Taste buds** are sensitive to four basic flavours: sweet, sour, bitter and salty.

● **The back of the tongue** contains big round papaillae shaped like an upside-down V. This is where bitter flavours are sensed.

● **The front of the tongue** is where fungiform (mushroom-like) papillae and filiform (hairlike) papillae carry taste buds that detect sweet, sour and salty flavours.

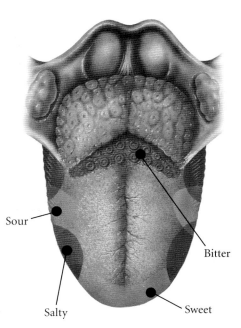

Sour

Bitter

Salty

Sweet

● **As well as taste,** the tongue can also feel the texture and temperature of food.

● **Your sense of taste** works closely together with your sense of smell to make the flavour of food more interesting.

● **Strong tastes,** such as spicy food, rely less on the sense of smell than on pain-sensitive nerve endings in the tongue.

● **People can learn** to distinguish more flavours and tastes than normal, as is the case with tea- or wine-tasters.

# Touch

- **Touch,** or physical contact, is one of five sensations that are spread all over your body in your skin. The others are pressure, pain, heat and cold.

- **There are sense receptors** everywhere in your skin, but places like your face have more than your back.

- **There are 200,000** hot and cold receptors in your skin, plus 500,000 touch and pressure receptors, and nearly 3 million pain receptors.

- **Free nerve-endings** are rather like the bare end of a wire. They respond to all five kinds of skin sensation and are almost everywhere in your skin.

- **There are specialized receptors** in certain places, each named after their discoverer.

▲ *The fingertips are where your sense of touch is most sensitive.*

> **FASCINATING FACT**
> Your brain knows just how hard you are touched from how fast nerve signals arrive.

▲ *As we grow up, we gradually learn to identify more and more things instantly through the sense of touch.*

- **Pacini's corpuscles** and Meissner's endings react instantly to sudden pressure.

- **Krause's bulbs,** Merkel's discs and Ruffini's endings respond to steady pressure.

- **Krause's bulbs** are also sensitive to cold.

- **Ruffini's endings** also react to changes in temperature.

**391**

# Skin

▲ *Skin colour varies from person to person because of melanin, a pigment which protects skin from the sun's harmful rays. The more melanin you have in your skin, the darker it is.*

- **Skin is your protective coat,** shielding your body from the weather and from infection, and helping to keep it at just the right temperature.

- **Skin is your largest sense receptor**, responding to touch, pressure, heat and cold.

- **Skin makes** vitamin D for your body from sunlight.

- **The epidermis** (the thin outer layer) is just dead cells.

...**FASCINATING FACT**...
Even though its thickness averages just 2 mm, your skin gets an eighth of all your blood supply.

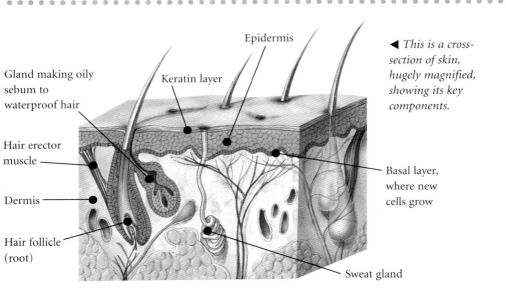

Epidermis

Keratin layer

Gland making oily sebum to waterproof hair

Hair erector muscle

Dermis

Hair follicle (root)

◀ *This is a cross-section of skin, hugely magnified, showing its key components.*

Basal layer, where new cells grow

Sweat gland

- **The epidermis is made mainly** of a tough protein called keratin – the remains of skin cells that die off.

- **Below the epidermis** is a thick layer of living cells called the dermis, which contains the sweat glands.

- **Hair roots** have tiny muscles that pull the hair upright when you are cold, giving you goose bumps.

- **Skin is 6 mm thick** on the soles of your feet, and just 0.5 mm thick on your eyelids.

- **The epidermis** contains cells that make the dark pigment melanin – this gives dark-skinned people their colour and fair-skinned people a tan.

# Hair

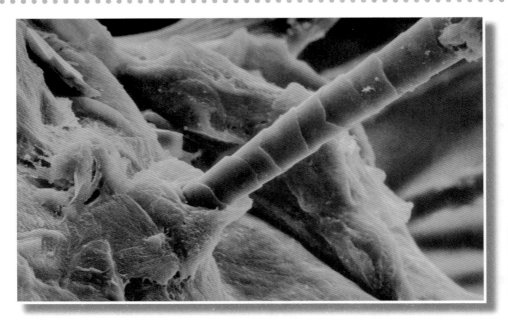

▲ *This highly magnified photograph shows a human hair growing from inside the skin.*

- **Humans are one of** very few land mammals to have almost bare skin. But even humans have soft, downy hair all over, with thicker hair in places.

- **Lanugo** is the very fine hair babies are covered in when they are inside the womb, from the fourth month of pregnancy onwards.

- **Vellus hair** is fine, downy hair that grows all over your body until you reach puberty.

- **Terminal hair** is the coarser hair on your head, as well as the hair that grows on men's chins and around an adult's genitals.

- **The colour of your hair** depends on how much there are of pigments called melanin and carotene in the hairs.

- **Hair is red or auburn** if it contains carotene.

- **Black, brown and blonde hair** get its colour from black melanin.

- **Each hair** is rooted in a pit called the hair follicle. The hair is held in place by its club-shaped tip, the bulb.

- **Hair grows** as cells fill with a material called keratin and die, and pile up inside the follicle.

- **The average person** has 120,000 head hairs and each grows about 3 millimetres per week.

▲ *The colour of your hair depends upon melanin made in melanocytes at the root.*

395

# Birth

- **Babies are usually born** 38–42 weeks after the mother becomes pregnant.

- **A few days or weeks before a baby is born,** it usually turns in the uterus (womb) so its head is pointing down towards the mother's birth canal (her cervix and vagina).

- **Birth begins** as the mother goes into labour – when the womb muscles begin a rhythm of contracting (tightening) and relaxing in order to push the baby out through the birth canal.

- **There are three stages** of labour. In the first, the womb muscles begin to contract or squeeze, bursting the bag of fluid around the baby. This is called breaking the waters.

▼ *A mother makes a special bond with her baby.*

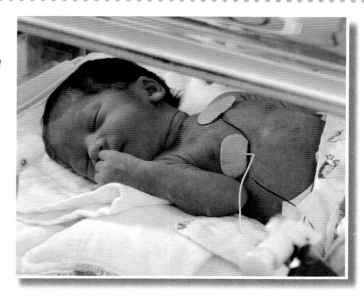

▲ *Babies that weigh less than 2.4 kg when they are born are known as premature. They are nursed in special care units.*

- **In the second stage** of labour, the baby is pushed out through the birth canal, usually by its head first, the body following quite quickly.

- **In the third stage** of labour, the placenta, which passed oxygen and nutrients from the mother's blood, is shed and comes out through the birth canal.

- **The umbilical cord** is the baby's lifeline to its mother. It is cut after birth.

- **A premature baby** is one born before it is fully developed.

- **A miscarriage** is when the developing baby is 'born' before the 28th week of pregnancy and cannot survive.

- **A Caesarian section** is an operation that happens when a baby cannot be born through the birth canal and emerges from the womb through a surgical cut made in the mother's belly.

397

# HISTORY

**Why did the ancient Egyptians mummify their dead kings?**

**Why was Joan of Arc burned at the stake?**

**What were the causes of World War I?**

The answers to these and many other questions can be found in this amazing section. Spanning the entire history of humankind and ranging across the globe, it provides a quick and easy way to learn about famous historical figures, wars and battles, peoples and lifestyles, myths and religion and the rise and fall of civilizations.

The first part, ancient history, covers the period from the dawn of humanity over four million years ago to the end of the Dark Ages around AD1000. The second part, modern history, begins with the Norman Conquest in 1066 and runs right up to the present day.

# Origins of mankind

- **Humans and apes** have so many similarities – such as long arms and fingers, and a big brain – that most experts think they must have evolved from the same creature.

- **The common ancestor** may be four-legged orang-utan-like creatures called dryopithecines that lived in trees 22–10 million years ago, like 'Proconsul' from East Africa.

- **The break came when** 'hominids' (human-like apes) began to live on the ground and walk on two legs.

- **Footprints** of three bipedal (two-legged) creatures from 4 million years ago were found preserved in ash at Laetoli, Tanzania.

- **The oldest hominid** is called *Ardipithecus ramidus*, known from 4.4 million years ago bone fragments found in Aramis, Ethiopia.

- **Many very early** hominids are australopiths ('southern apes'), for example, *Australopithecus anamensis* from 4.2 million years ago.

- **Australopiths** were only 1 m tall and their brain was about the same size as an ape's, but they were bipedal.

- **The best known** australopith is 'Lucy', a skeleton of *Australopithecus afarensis* of 3 million years ago, found in Kenya in 1974.

1

2

- **Lucy's discoverers** – Don Johanson and Maurice Tieb – called her Lucy because they were listening to the Beatles' song 'Lucy in the Sky with Diamonds' at the time.

- **Many early hominid** remains are just skulls. Lucy was an almost complete skeleton. She showed that hominids learned to walk upright before their brains got bigger.

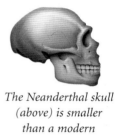

*The Neanderthal skull (above) is smaller than a modern human skull (below). Brain size has increased over thousands of years.*

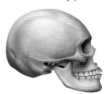

◀ *Experts once thought humans had evolved in a single line from australopiths, through* Homo habilis *(1),* Homo erectus *(2) and Neanderthal man (3) to humans (4). They now realize there were many branches.*

**401**

# Modern humans

- **The scientific name** for modern humans is *Homo sapiens sapiens*. The word *sapiens* is used twice to distinguish us from *Homo sapiens neanderthalis* (Neanderthal Man).

- **Unlike Neanderthals,** modern humans have a prominent chin and a flat face with a high forehead.

- **Some scientists** think that because we all share similar DNA, all humans are descended from a woman nicknamed 'Eve', who they calculate lived in Africa about 200,000 years ago. DNA is the special molecule in every body-cell that carries the body's instructions for life.

- **The oldest human** skulls are 130,000 years old and were found in the Omo Basin in Ethiopia and the Klasies River in South Africa.

- **About 30,000** years ago, modern humans began to spread out into Eurasia from Africa.

- **The earliest** modern Europeans are called Cro-Magnon Man, after the caves in France's Dordogne valley where skeletons from 35,000 years ago were found in 1868.

◀ *Both modern humans and Neanderthals used beautifully made spears for hunting.*

- **Modern humans** reached Australia by boat from Indonesia 50,000 years ago. They reached the Americas from Asia about the same time.

- **Modern humans** lived alongside Neanderthals for tens of thousands of years in the Middle East and Europe.

- **Modern humans** were probably the first creatures to speak what we would call language. Some scientists think language was a sudden genetic 'accident' that remained and developed because it gave humans a huge advantage.

- **With modern** humans came rapid advances in stone-tool technology, the building of wooden huts, a rise in population and a growing interest in art.

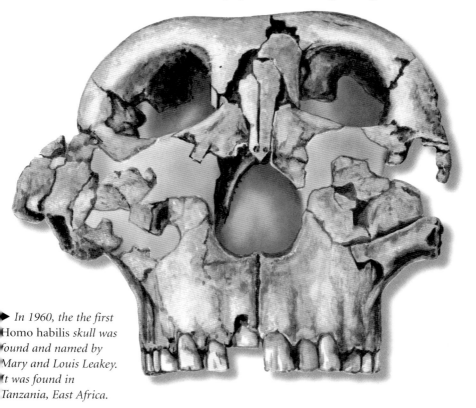

▶ *In 1960, the the first* Homo habilis *skull was found and named by Mary and Louis Leakey. It was found in Tanzania, East Africa.*

**403**

# The Stone Ages

- **The Stone Ages** were the periods of time before humans discovered metals and so used mainly stones for making tools.

- **Stone tools** were made by chipping away stones to make hammers, spear heads and arrow heads, knives and scrapers.

- **People** usually used local stone, but sometimes good stones were imported from a great distance.

- **Early Europeans** used mainly flint for their stone tools. Africans used quartz, chert, basalt and obsidian.

- **In Europe**, there were three Stone Ages – Old (Palaeolithic), Middle (Mesolithic) and New (Neolithic).

- **The Palaeolithic** began 2 million years ago, when various human ancestors gathered plants and hunted with stone weapons.

- **The Mesolithic** was the transition from the Old to the New Stone Age – after the Last Ice Age ended around 12,000 years ago.

- **The Neolithic** was the time when people began to settle down and farm. This occurred first in the Near East, about 10,000 years ago.

◀ A well-made, properly shaped stone tool could chop right through wood, meat, bone, and animal skin – even the toughest of hides.

- **In 1981,** a pebble shaped into a female form, half a million years old was found at Berekhat Ram in Israel's Golan Heights.

- **Venus figurines** are plump stone female figures from *c.*25,000 years ago, found in Europe, e.g. the Czech Republic.

► *Mesolithic people hunted with bows and arrows and flint-tipped spears.*

# The Bronze Age

- **The Bronze Age** is the period of prehistory when people first began to use the metal bronze.

- **Bronze is** an alloy (mix) of copper with about 10 percent tin.

- **The first metals** used were probably lumps of pure gold and copper, beaten into shape to make ornaments in Turkey and Iran about 6000BC.

- **Metal ores** (metals mixed with other minerals) were probably discovered when certain stones were found to melt when heated in a kiln.

- **Around 4000BC,** metalsmiths in southeast Europe and Iran began making copper axeheads with a central hole to take a wooden shaft.

- **The Copper Age** is the period when people used copper before they learned to alloy it with tin to make bronze. Metalworking with copper was flourishing in the early cities of Mesopotamia, in the Middle East, about 3500BC.

- **The Bronze Age** began several times between 3500 and 3000BC in the Near East, Balkans and Southeast Asia, when smiths discovered that, by adding a small quantity of tin, they could make bronze. Bronze is harder than copper and easier to make into a sharp blade.

▶ *A Bronze Age axe, 1500–700BC.*

- **Knowledge** of bronze spread slowly across Eurasia, but by 1500BC it was in use all the way from Europe to India.

- **The rarity** of tin spurred long-distance trade links – and the first mines, like the tin mines in Cornwall, England.

- **Bronze** can be cast – shaped by melting it into a clay mould (itself shaped with a wax model). For the first time people could make things any shape they wanted. Skilled smiths across Eurasia began to cast bronze to make everything from weapons to cooking utensils.

▶ *By 1000bc, beautiful metal swords and other weapons with sharp blades like this were being made all over Europe and western Asia.*

# The Iron Age

- **The Iron Age** is the time in prehistory when iron replaced bronze as the main metal.

- **The use of iron** was discovered by the Hittites in Anatolia, Turkey between 1500 and 1200BC. This discovery helped to make the Hittites immensely powerful for a few centuries.

- **Around 1200BC,** the Hittite Empire collapsed and the use of iron spread through Asia and central Europe. The Dorian Greeks became famous iron masters.

- **Tin is rare,** so bronze objects were made mostly for chieftains. Iron ore is common, so ordinary people could have metal objects such as cooking utensils.

- **Many ordinary** farmers could afford iron scythes and axes. With tough metal tools to clear fields and harvest crops quickly, farming developed much more rapidly.

- **Growth in population** put pressure on resources and warfare increased across Eurasia. Partly as a result, many northern European settlements developed into hillforts – hilltop sites protected by earth ramparts, ditches and stockades.

- **Around 650BC,** peoples skilled in iron-working, called Celts, began to dominate northern Europe.

> **...FASCINATING FACT...**
> In 1950, an Iron Age man was found in a peatbog at Tollund in Jutland, Denmark, perfectly preserved over 2000 years.

▶ *The easy availability of iron in the Iron Age meant that even a fairly poor man might have his own sword.*

- **Iron-working** reached China around 600BC. The Chinese used large bellows to boost furnace temperatures enough to melt iron ore in large quantities.

- **Iron tools** appearing in West Africa around 400BC were the basis of the Nok culture. Nok Farmers speaking Bantu languages spread south and east all over Africa.

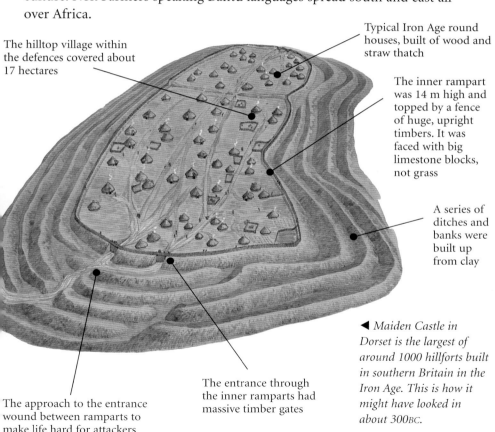

The hilltop village within the defences covered about 17 hectares

Typical Iron Age round houses, built of wood and straw thatch

The inner rampart was 14 m high and topped by a fence of huge, upright timbers. It was faced with big limestone blocks, not grass

A series of ditches and banks were built up from clay

The approach to the entrance wound between ramparts to make life hard for attackers

The entrance through the inner ramparts had massive timber gates

◀ *Maiden Castle in Dorset is the largest of around 1000 hillforts built in southern Britain in the Iron Age. This is how it might have looked in about 300BC.*

# Ancient Egypt

- **While dozens** of cities were developing in Mesopotamia, in Egypt the foundations were being laid for the first great nation.

- **From 5000 to 3300**BC, farmers by the river Nile banded together to dig canals to control the Nile's annual flooding and to water their crops.

- **By 3300**BC, Nile farming villages had grown into towns. Rich and powerful kings were buried in big, boxlike mud-brick tombs called *mastabas*.

- **Egyptian** townspeople began to work copper and stone, paint vases, weave baskets and use potter's wheels.

- **Early Egypt** was divided into two kingdoms – Upper Egypt, and Lower Egypt on the Nile delta. In 3100BC, King Menes of Upper Egypt conquered Lower Egypt to unite the two kingdoms, but a king of Egypt was always called King of Upper and Lower Egypt.

▶ *The ancient Egyptians built great cities and monuments along the Nile valley during the days of the Old Kingdom.*

▶ *The principal sites and cities of ancient Egyptian civilization.*

- **Menes founded** a capital for a united Egypt at Memphis.

- **With Menes,** Egypt's Dynasty I – the first family of kings – began. The time of Dynasties I and II, which lasted until 2649BC, is known by historians as the Archaic Period.

- **After the** Archaic Period came the Old Kingdom (2649–2134BC), perhaps the greatest era of Egyptian culture.

- **Craftsmen** made fine things, scholars developed writing and the calendar and studied astronomy and maths.

- **The greatest** scholar and priest was Imhotep, minister to King Zoser (2630–2611BC). Imhotep was architect of the first of the great pyramids, the Step Pyramid at Sakkara.

**411**

# Early China

● **In China**, farming communities known as the Yanshao culture developed by the HuangHe (Yellow River) 7000 years ago. By 5000BC, the region was ruled by emperors.

● **Early Chinese** emperors are known of only by legend. Huang-Ti, the Yellow Emperor, was said to have become emperor in 2697BC.

● **In about 2690BC,** Huang-Ti's wife, Hsi-Ling Shi, discovered how to use the cocoon of the silkworm (the caterpillar of the *Bombyx mori* moth) to make silk. Hsi-Ling was afterwards known as Seine-Than (the Silk Goddess).

● **By 2000BC,** the Chinese were making beautiful jade carvings.

● **The Hsias family** were said to be one of the earliest dynasties of Chinese emperors, ruling from 2000 to 1750BC.

◀ *The Shang emperors were warriors. Their soldiers fought in padded bamboo armour.*

- **The Shangs** were the first definitely known dynasty of emperors. They came to power in 1750BC.

- **Shang emperors** had their fortune told every few days from cracks on heated animal bones. Marks on these 'oracle' bones are the oldest examples of Chinese writing.

- **Under the Shangs,** the Chinese became skilled bronze-casters.

- **In the Shang** cities of Anyang and Zengzhou, thick-walled palace temples were surrounded at a distance by villages of artisans.

- **Shang emperors** went to their tombs along with their servants and captives, as well as entire chariots with their horses and drivers.

▲ *Silkworms (the larvae, or young, of the* Bombyx mori *moth) feed on mulberry leaves. Silk was invented in China, and for many years the method of making it was kept a closely guarded secret.*

**413**

# Aryan India

- **The Aryans** were a lighter-skinned herding people from southern Russia, ancestors to both Greeks and Indians.

- **About 2000BC,** the Aryan people began to sweep through Persia and on into India, where they destroyed the existing Indus civilization.

- **The Aryans** were tough warriors who loved music, dancing and chariot racing, but they slowly adopted Dravidian gods and settled in villages as farmers.

▶ *The dark-skinned Dravidian people who were living in India when the Aryans arrived became the servant class.*

- **Aryan people** were originally split into three categories: *Brahmins* (priests) at the top, *Kshatriya* (warriors) in the middle and *Vaisyas* (merchants and farmers) at the bottom.

- **When they** settled in India, the Aryans added a fourth category – the conquered, dark-skinned Dravidians, who became their servants.

- **The Aryans** gave India the language of Sanskrit.

- **From the** four Aryan classes, the elaborate system of castes (classes) in today's India developed.

- **Ancient Sanskrit** is closely related to European languages such as Latin, English and German.

- **The Aryans** had no form of writing, but they passed on history and religion by word of mouth in spoken *Books of Knowledge*, or *Vedas*.

- **The Brahmins** created the first Hindu scriptures as *Vedas*, including the *Rig-Veda*, the *Sama-Veda* and *Yajur-Veda*.

▲ *Sanskrit is the oldest literary language of India, and simply translated it means 'refined' or 'polished'. It forms the basis of many modern Indian languages such as Hindi and Urdu. Urdu is also the national language of Pakistan.*

**415**

# The Assyrians

- **The Assyrians** came originally from the upper Tigris valley around the cities of Ashur, Nineveh and Arbela.

- **About 2000BC,** Assyria was invaded by Amorites. Under a line of Amorite kings, Assyria built up a huge empire. King Adadnirari I called himself 'King of Everything'.

- **The Old Assyrian Empire** lasted six centuries, until it was broken by attacks by Mitannian horsemen.

- **From 1114 to 1076BC,** King Tiglath Pileser I rebuilt Assyrian power by conquest, creating the New Assyrian Empire.

◄ *Assyrian stone carvings were skillfully done. Many, such as this one showing a genie, decorated palace walls.*

...**FASCINATING FACT**...
King Assurbanipal's (668–627BC) palace was filled with books and plants from all over the world.

- **The New Assyrian Empire** reached its peak under Tiglath-Pileser III (744–727BC) and was finally overthrown by the Medes and Babylonians in 612BC.

- **The Assyrians** were ruthless warriors. They grew beards and fought with bows, iron swords, spears and chariots.

- **The Assyrians** built good roads all over their empire, so that the army could move fast to quell trouble.

- **The Assyrians** built magnificent palaces and cities such as Khorsabad and Nimrud.

- **Arab warriors** rode camels into battle for the Assyrians.

*Wealthy Assyrians strove to outdo each other with elaborate clothing and luxurious houses.*

# Polynesians

▲ *Outriggers are a traditional boat of Polynesia, and are named after rigging that sticks out to the sides to aid stability. Easy to pull ashore, and perfect for shallow waters, they are ideal for island life.*

- **Polynesians** are the peoples who live on the many islands in the middle of the Pacific Ocean, from Hawaii to Easter Island and New Zealand.

- **There are** 10,000 islands in Polynesia and the rest of the eastern Pacific, with hundreds of different cultures and languages, each with its own history.

- **Many Polynesian** islands may well have been first settled 40,000 years ago by people from Southeast Asia.

> **...FASCINATING FACT...**
> The biggest moai statues on Easter Island are up to
> 12 m tall and weigh 90 tonnes.

- **2000 years ago**, a second wave of migrants moved east from Fiji, Samoa and Tonga to the Marquesas Islands.

- **In their** canoes the settlers took crops (coconuts, yams, taros and breadfruit) and livestock (pigs and chickens).

- **Every island** developed its own style of woodcarving.

- **About** AD400, the new Polynesians moved on to Hawaii and Easter Island.

- **Easter Islanders** created strange stone statues called *moais*, carved with stone tools because they had no metal.

- **The settlers** crossed the ocean in small double canoes and boats called outriggers.

▶ *There are about 600 huge stone* moai *statues on Easter Island, on platforms called* ahus. *No one knows what they were used for.*

# Persia

- **Iran** is named after the Aryan people who began settling there *c*.15,000BC. Two Aryan tribes – the Medes and Persians – soon became dominant.

- **In 670BC,** the Medes under King Cyaxeres joined forces with the Babylonians and finally overthrew the Assyrians.

- **In 550BC,** the Medes themselves were overthrown by the Persians. The Persian king, Cyrus II, was the grandson of the king of the Medes, Astyages.

- **Cyrus II** had an army of horsemen and very skilled archers. He went on to establish a great Persian empire after conquering Lydia and Babylon.

- **The Persian** Empire was ruled by the Achaemenid family until it was destroyed by Alexander the Great in 330BC.

- **The Persian** Empire reached its greatest extent under Darius I, who called himself Shahanshah ('King of kings'). Darius introduced gold and silver coins, and also brought chickens to the Middle East.

▲ *Darius the Great ruled Persia from 521 until 486BC.*

- **Darius** built a famous road system and split his empire into 20 *satrapies* (regions), each ruled by a *satrap.*

- **'King's Ears'** were officials who travelled around the empire and reported any trouble back to the king.

- **The Persians** built luxurious cities and palaces – first at Susa, then in Darius's reign, at Persepolis.

● **Persian priests,** or *magi*, were known for their magic skills, and gave us the word 'magic'. A famous magus called Zarathustra, unusually, worshipped a single god – Ahuru Mazda. His god's evil enemy was Angra Mainyu.

◄ *Rich carvings adorned the walls at Persepolis – the great city and palace of Darius's reign.*

# Early Greece

- **Around 1200BC,** the Mycenaeans began to abandon their cities, and a people called the Dorians took over Greece.

- **Many Mycenaeans** fled overseas in a large battle fleet, and the Egyptians called them the Sea Peoples. Some ended up in Italy and may have been the ancestors of the Etruscan people there.

- **With the end** of Mycenaean civilization, Greece entered its Dark Ages as the art of writing was lost.

- **About 800BC,** the Greeks began to emerge from their Dark Ages as they relearned writing from the Phoenicians, a people who traded in the eastern Mediterranean.

- **The period** of Greek history from 800 to 500BC is called the Archaic (Ancient) Period.

- **In the Archaic Period,** the Greek population grew rapidly. States were governed by wealthy aristocrats.

◀ *Greek cargo ships carried oil, wheat and wine for trading. The sailors painted eyes on either side of the prow in the hope they would scare away evil spirits.*

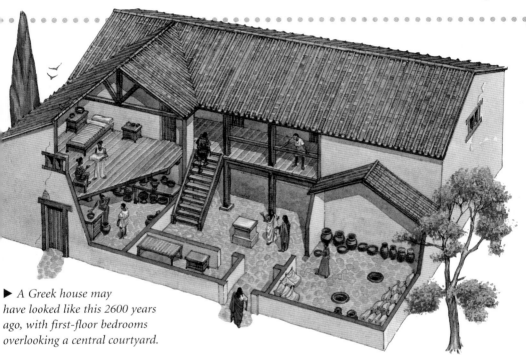

▶ *A Greek house may
have looked like this 2600 years
ago, with first-floor bedrooms
overlooking a central courtyard.*

- **The early Greeks** loved athletics and held four major events. They were called the Panhellenic Games and drew competitors from all over the Greek world.

- **The four Panhellenic Games** were the Olympic, Pythian, Isthmian and Nemean Games.

- **The Olympic Games** started in 776BC and were the most important. They were held every four years, at Olympia.

- **The Greek poet Homer** wrote his famous poems about the Trojan Wars around 700BC

# The Maya

- **The Maya** were a people who dominated Central America from 500BC to AD1524 (when they were conquered by Spanish invaders).

- **The Maya** began building large pyramids with small temples on top between 600BC and AD250.

- **Mayan civilization** peaked between AD250 and 900. This has become known as the Classic Period.

- **During the Classic Period,** Mayan civilization centred on great cities such as Tikal in the Guatemalan lowlands. They traded extensively – on foot and in dug-out canoes.

▶ *The Mayan pyramid at Chichén Itzá, in the Yucatán.*

- **Mayan people** in the Classic Period developed a clever form of writing in symbols representing sounds or ideas. They recorded their history on stone monuments called *stelae*.

- **Mysteriously**, **around** AD800, the Maya stopped making stelae and the Guatemalan cities were abandoned.

- **From AD800 to 1200,** the most powerful Mayan city was Chichén Itzá, in the Yucatán region of modern-day Mexico. From AD1200 to 1440 another city, Mayapán, came to the fore. After 1440, Mayan civilization rapidly broke up, following revolts by the leaders of some Mayan cities against Mayapán, and the division of Yucatán into separate warring states.

- **The Maya** were very religious. Deer, dogs, turkeys and even humans were often sacrificed to the gods in the temples on top of the pyramids.

- **Mayan farmers** grew mainly corn, beans and squash. From the corn, women made flat pancakes that are now called tortillas, and an alcoholic drink known as *balche*.

▶ *The Maya created complex calendars based on their detailed observation of the stars.*

425

# Alexander the Great

- **Alexander** the Great was a young Macedonian king who was one of the greatest generals in history. He built an empire stretching from Greece to India.

- **Alexander** was born in 356BC in Pella, capital of Macedonia. His father, King Phillip II, was a tough fighter who conquered neighbouring Greece. His mother was the fiery Olympias, who told him that he was descended from Achilles, the hero of the *Iliad*.

Alexander the Great

- **As a boy,** he was tutored by the famous philosopher Aristotle. A story tells how he tamed the unridable horse Bucephalus, which afterwards carried him as far as India.

- **When Alexander was 20**, his father was murdered by a bodyguard and he became king. Alexander quickly stamped out rebellion.

- **In 334BC,** Alexander crossed the narrow neck of sea separating Europe from Asia with his army. Within a year, he had conquered the Persian Empire.

- **In 331BC,** Alexander led his army into Egypt, where he was made pharaoh and founded the city of Alexandria. He trekked to the desert oasis of Siwah, where legend says an oracle proclaimed him son of the Greek god Zeus.

◀ *The key to Macedonian success was the phalanx – armoured soldiers standing in tightly packed rows bristling with long spears. Such a formation could withstand a cavalry attack, yet still move swiftly.*

...FASCINATING FACT...

An old legend said that anyone who untied a tricky knot in a town called Gordium would conquer Asia. Alexander instantly sliced through this Gordian knot with his sword.

- **In 327BC,** he married the lovely Bactrian princess, Roxane.

- **After capturing the city of Babylon** and finishing off the Persian king, Darius, Alexander led his conquering army into India. Here his homesick troops finally asked to go home.

- **In 325BC,** Alexander had ships built and carried his army down the Indus River and returned to Babylon. Within a year, he fell ill and died.

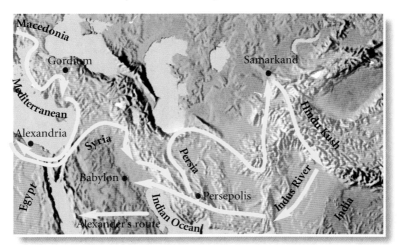

▲ *In just nine years and a series of brilliant campaigns, Alexander created a vast empire. No one knows exactly what his plans were. However, the teachings of his tutor Aristotle were important to him, and he had his own vision of different peoples living together in friendship.*

427

# The Roman Empire

- **For 200 years** after Augustus became emperor in 27BC, Roman emperors ruled over an empire so large and secure that citizens could talk of the *Pax Romana* (Roman Peace).

- **The Romans** built straight roads to move their troops about quickly. On the whole, they governed peacefully and also built hundreds of towns in the Roman manner.

- **After Augustus died,** in AD14, his stepson Tiberius succeeded him. Then came a succession of Augustus's descendants, including Gaius, Claudius and Nero.

  - **Gaius** (AD37–41) was known as Caligula ('little boots') because of the soldiers' boots he wore as a child.

  - **Soon after Caligula** became emperor, an illness left him mad. He spent wildly, had people whipped and killed, married and murdered his sister and elected his horse as a minister. Eventually he was murdered by soldiers.

  - **Claudius** (AD41–54) replaced Caligula. People thought he was stupid because he stuttered and was physically disabled. However, he proved the wisest and most humane of all emperors.

◄ *Gladiators were prisoners and criminals who were made to fight in big arenas called amphitheatres to entertain people.*

▶ *The orange area of this map shows the empire at its peak under the Emperor Trajan (AD98–117). It was divided into areas called provinces, such as Britannia (England and Wales) and Gallia (northern France). Each had its own Roman governor.*

▼ *Leading imperial officials wore flowing robes called togas.*

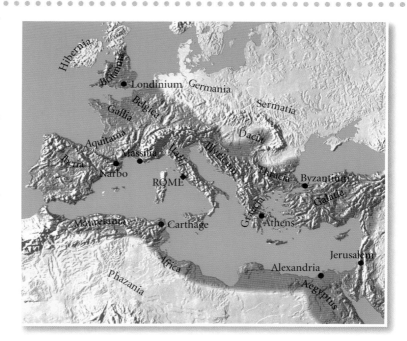

● **Claudius** was probably poisoned by his fourth wife Agrippina, who wanted power for her son Nero.

● **The power of Roman emperors** reached a peak under the 'Antonines' – Nerva, Trajan, Hadrian, Antoninus and Marcus Aurelius. They ruled AD96–180.

● **The Roman Empire** grew only a little after Augustus's death. Britain was conquered in AD43, and Emperor Trajan took Dacia (now Hungary and Romania).

**429**

# The Roman army

- **Rome** owed its power to its highly efficient army.

- **In a crisis,** Rome could raise an army of 800,000 men.

- **The Roman** army fought mainly on foot, advancing in tight squares bristling with spears and protected by large shields called *scutari*. They often put shields over their heads to protect them from arrows. This formation was called a *testudo* – or 'tortoise'.

- **Under** the Republic, the army was divided into legions of 5000 soldiers. Legions were made up of 10 cohorts. Cohorts, in turn, consisted of centuries containing 80-100 soldiers.

- **Each legion** was led by a *legatus*. A cohort was led by a *tribunus militum*. A century was led by a *centurion*.

- **All Roman** soldiers had a short sword (60 cm long) and carried two throwing spears. They also wore armour – first, vests of chain mail and a leather helmet; later, metal strips on a leather tunic and a metal helmet.

- **Roman** armies built huge siege engines and catapults when they had to capture a town.

- **After 100BC,** most Roman soldiers were professionals, who joined the army for life. Food accounted for about a third of their wages.

- **In training,** soldiers went on forced 30-km marches three times a month. They moved at 8 km per hour, carrying very heavy packs.

- **Soldiers** were flogged for misbehaviour. Mutiny was punished by executing one in ten suspects. This was called *decimation*.

▼ *Roman soldiers had to be tough – while on the march they carried all their weapons and armour, plus a pack full of clothes, food and tools for digging and building.*

◀ *The* testudo *formation proved highly effective for Roman foot-soldiers.*

**431**

# The first Britons

- **Britain has been inhabited** by human-like creatures for over 500,000 years. The oldest known settlement, at Star Carr in Yorkshire, dates back 10,000 years.

- **About 6–7000 years ago,** Neolithic farmers arrived from Europe. They began to clear the island's thick woods to grow crops and build houses in stone.

- **The early farmers** created round monuments of stones and wooden posts called *henges*. The most famous is Stonehenge in Wiltshire.

- *c.*2300BC, new people from the Rhine arrived. They are called Beakerfolk, after their beaker-shaped pottery cups. They were Britain's first metal-workers.

- **Legend has it** that the name Britain came from Brutus, one of the sons of Aeneas, who fled from Troy.

- *c.*700BC, Celts arrived, often living in hillforts.

- **Iron axes and ploughs** enabled huge areas to be cleared and farmed, and the population rose.

- **When Julius Caesar invaded,** in 55 and 54BC, the Celtic people of England, known as Britons, were divided into scores of tribes, such as the Catuvellauni and Atrebates.

- **Resistance from tribal leaders** such as Caratacus meant it took the Romans over a century to conquer the Britons.

- **The last revolt** was that of Queen Boudicca, in AD60.

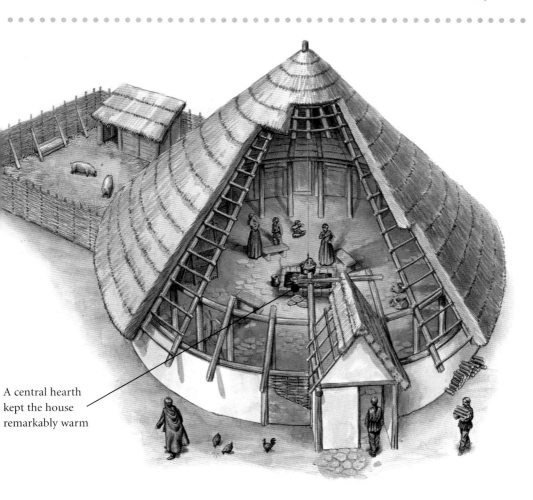

A central hearth
kept the house
remarkably warm

▲ *People of Bronze Age Britain lived in round houses like this,
with thick stone walls and a steeply-pitched, thatched roof.*

**433**

# Anglo-Saxons

- **The Angles**, Saxons and Jutes were peoples from Denmark and Germany who invaded Britain and settled there between AD450 and 600.

- **The Britons** resisted at first, but by 650 they were driven back into the west or made slaves.

- **The Angles** settled in East Anglia and the Midlands, the Saxons in Sussex, Essex and Wessex (Dorset and Hampshire).

- **Each tribe** had its own kingdom, yet by AD700 most people in the south thought of themselves as English.

- **Seven leading kingdoms** formed a 'heptarchy' – Essex, Kent, Sussex, Wessex, East Anglia, Mercia and Northumbria.

- **One king was *bretwalda*** (overlord), but the kingdoms vied for power.

- **When Ethelbert** of Kent was bretwalda, in AD597, St Augustine converted him to Christianity. Christianity spread rapidly throughout England. English monasteries became the universities of Europe. Masons from Gaul and Rome built stone churches.

- **Most Anglo-Saxons** were farmers. Others were warriors, as their famous epic poem of heroism, *Beowulf*, shows.

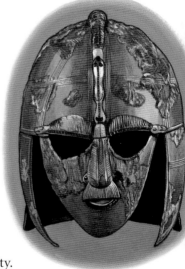

▲ *In 1939, the burial ship of the overlord Raedwald (died AD625) was discovered at Sutton Hoo in East Anglia. This helmet is one of the treasures it held.*

434

- **In the 700s,** Danish raiders conquered all of England but Wessex. They were pushed back by King Alfred, but attacks resumed in the reign of Ethelred II (AD978–1016).

- **The last Anglo-Saxon king** was Ethelred II's son, Edward the Confessor (1042-1066).

► *The Scandinavian Vikings who made continual raids on Britain were descended from earlier 'barbarian' peoples.*

◄ *Anglo-Saxon villages were made from materials such as wood, thatch and wattle (woven branches).*

**435**

# The Vikings

- **The Vikings** were daring raiders from Norway, Sweden and Denmark. Between AD800 and 1100, they swept in on the coasts of northwest Europe in their longships, searching for rich plunder to carry away.

- **People** were terrified by the lightning raids of the Vikings. A prayer of the time went, 'Deliver us, O Lord, from the fury of the Norsemen (Vikings). They ravage our lands. They kill our women and children'.

- **Vikings** prided themselves on their bravery in battle. Most fought on foot with swords, spears and axes. Rich Vikings rode on horseback.

- **Shock troops** called *berserkers* led the attack. *Berserk* is Norse for 'bare shirt' as they wore no armour. Before a battle, they became fighting-mad through drink and drugs and trusted in their god Odin to keep them safe.

- **The word 'Viking'** was only used later. People of the time called them Norsemen. The word Viking probably came from Vik, a pirate centre in Norway. When Norsemen went 'a-viking', they meant fighting as a pirate. Swedish Vikings who settled in eastern Europe may have been called Rus, and so Russia was named after them.

- **Not all Vikings** were pirates. At home, they were farmers and fishermen, merchants and craftworkers. Many went with the raiders and settled in the north of France, northern England and Dublin.

- **The Vikings** attacked mainly Britain and Ireland, but raided as far as Gibraltar and into the Mediterranean.

- **In Eastern Europe,** the Vikings' ships carried them inland up various rivers. They ventured far through Russia and the Ukraine, sometimes marauding as far south as Constantinople, which they called 'Miklagard', the big city.

● **The Norsemen** who settled in northern France were called Normans. The Norman king, William the Conqueror, who invaded England in 1066, was descended from their leader, Rollo.

▼ *At home, most Vikings were farmers. The women were left in charge when their husbands went raiding.*

▶ *A hammer like this one was used at many stages in a Viking's life – raised over the newborn, laid in the bride's lap at weddings, or carved on a grave. The hammer was the symbol of the great Viking god, Thor. Other major Viking gods were Odin and Frey. The Anglo-Saxons had the same gods and their names have given us some days of the week – Odin's or Wodin's day (Wednesday), Thor's day (Thursday) and Frey's or Frigg's day (Friday).*

437

# Holy Roman Empire

- **The Holy Roman Empire** was a mostly German empire, which lasted from AD800 until 1806.

- **The empire began** when Pope Leo III tried to gain the protection of Charlemagne, the King of the Franks, by reviving the idea of the Roman Empire.

- **Pope Leo III** is said to have taken Charlemagne by surprise in St Peter's church in Rome – on Christmas Day AD800 – and to have placed the crown of the empire on his head.

- **Charlemagne's Frankish Empire,** including France, Germany and Italy, became the Holy Roman Empire.

- **When Charlemagne died,** in AD814, the new Holy Roman Empire fell apart.

- **150 years later,** in AD962, the German king, Otto I, gained control of Italy as well as Germany and insisted the pope crown him Holy Roman Emperor.

- **Over the centuries,** the empire was continually beset by conflicts with both powerful Germans and the pope.

- **In 1076**, Pope Gregory VII and Emperor Henry IV were vying for control. Henry's subjects sided with the pope, so Henry had to give way.

- **Gregory forced Henry** to stand barefoot in snow for three days outside his castle in Tuscany to beg for a pardon.

- **The pope's Vatican** and other Italian cities gained almost complete independence from the emperor.

▲ *In 1250, the Holy Roman Empire extended from the North to the Mediterranean Sea. This is highlighted in brown. The Papal states (yellow), separated the Kingdom of the Two Scicilies, which also belonged to the Emperor.*

439

# The Norman invasion

- **On 5 January 1066,** the English king Edward the Confessor died. As he died, he named as his successor Harold Godwinson – the powerful earl of the kingdom of Wessex.

- **Harold's claim** to the English throne was challenged by William, the duke of Normandy in France, who claimed that Edward had already promised him the throne.

▲ *William's troops rapidly seized control of England. This was the last time the country was conquered by a foreign power.*

- **Harold's claim** was also challenged by Harold Hardraade, the king of Norway.

- **In autumn 1066**, Hardraade invaded northern England with Harold Godwinson's brother Tostig. His army was routed by Harold's at Stamford Bridge on 25 September.

- **On 27 September**, William's Norman army of 7000 crossed from France and landed at Pevensey in southern England.

- **Harold marched his army** south to meet the Normans, walking over 300 km to London in just five days.

▲ *The Normans commemorated their victory at the Battle of Hastings with a famous tapestry, made in England, now in Bayeux in France.*

- **Harold's tired army** met the Normans at Hastings in Sussex on 14 October, and took a stand by the Hoar Apple Tree on Caldbec Hill.

- **Harold's army** was mauled by William's archers, but axe-wielding English house-carles (infantry) put the Norman cavalry to flight. Harold was then killed – perhaps by an arrow. The English fought on for a while before fleeing.

- **After the battle**, William moved on London, where he was crowned king in Westminster Abbey on 25 December.

- **Within a few years**, the Normans had conquered England.

**441**

# Crusades

- **In the 11th century,** western Christian countries were threatened by the Muslim Seljuk Turks. In 1095, they were just outside Constantinople, capital of the Byzantine Empire and the centre of Christianity in the east. The emperor Alexander Comnenus appealed to the pope, Urban II, for help.

- **Urban II** held a meeting of church leaders at Clermont in France. He called for warriors to drive back the Turks and reclaim the Holy Land. This became a holy pilgrimage or Crusade. 'Crusade' comes from the Latin *crux*, meaning 'cross'.

- **Before the armies** could set out, 50,000 peasants began marching from western Europe on their own 'People's Crusade' to free the Holy Land. They had been stirred by tales of Turkish atrocities, spread by a preacher called Peter the Hermit. Many peasants died or got lost on the way; the rest were killed by Turks.

- **In 1096,** armies of French and Norman knights set out on the First Crusade. At Constantinople, they joined up with the Byzantines. Despite quarrelling on the way, they captured Jerusalem in 1099 and then set about massacring Jews and Turks.

◀ *When the Crusader knights set out to fight for control of Jerusalem, in the Holy Land, they went with different motives. Some were courageous men with a deep sense of honour and a holy purpose. Others were adventurers, out for personal gain or glory. This Crusader wears the famous uniform of the Knights Templars.*

- **After capturing Jerusalem**, the Crusaders divided the Holy Land into four parts or Counties, together known as Outremer (said 'oot-rer-mare'), which meant 'land beyond the seas'. The Crusaders ruled Outremer for 200 years and built great castles like Krak des Chevaliers in Syria.

- **Two bands of soldier-monks** formed to protect pilgrims journeying to the Holy Land – the Knights Hospitallers of St John and the Knights Templars. The Hospitallers wore black with a white cross. The Templars wore a red cross on white, which became the symbol of all Crusaders.

- **By 1144,** Crusader control in Outremer weakened, and the Turks advanced. King Louis VII of France and King Conrad of Germany launched a Second Crusade. But by 1187, Saladin had retaken most of Outremer.

- **In 1190,** the three most powerful men in Europe – Richard I of England, Philip II of France and Frederick Barbarossa (Holy Roman Emperor) – set off on the Third Crusade. Barbarossa died on the way and Philip II gave up. Only Richard went on, and secured a truce with Saladin.

- **In 1212,** thousands of children set off on a Children's Crusade to take back Jerusalem, led by French farm boy Stephen of Cloyes. Sadly, most were lured on to ships in Marseilles and sold into slavery or prostitution.

> **· · · FASCINATING FACT · · ·**
> The most famous Crusader was King Richard I of
> England, known as the Lionheart for his bravery.

443

# The Black Death

- **The Black Death** was the terrible epidemic of bubonic plague and pneumonia that ravaged Europe between 1347 and 1351.

- **The Black Death** was perhaps the worst disaster ever to have struck humanity.

- **Worldwide,** the Black Death killed 40 million people.

▲ *The Plague brought death so close to people that they began to think of it as a real person.*

- **The Black Death** killed 25 million people in Europe.

- **The disease** probably started in China. It was transmitted to Europeans when a Kipchak (Mongol) raiding party catapulted infected corpses into a Genoese trading centre in the Crimea.

- **The plague reached Genoa** in 1347 and spread west and north, reaching London and Paris in 1348.

- **The plague** was carried first by rat fleas that could also live on humans. It then changed to pneumonic plague, which was spread through coughs and sneezes.

- **After the Black Death,** fields were littered with bodies. Houses, villages and towns stood silent and empty.

- **Afterwards** there was such a shortage of labour that wages soared and many serfs gained their freedom.

▲ *Plague returned several times over the centuries, including London's Great Plague of 1665. Houses struck by this highly infectious scourge were marked with a cross.*

····**FASCINATING FACT**····
The Black Death killed more than one in
every four Europeans in just four years.

**445**

# The Hundred Years War

- **The Hundred Years War** was a long war between France and England, lasting from 1337 to 1453.

- **The war** was caused by disputes over Guyenne (English land in southwest France), English claims to the French throne, French support for the Scots and French efforts to block the English wool trade in Belgium.

- **1337:** French king Philip VI tried to take over Guyenne. English king Edward III, whose mother was sister to three French kings, retaliated by claiming the French throne.

  - **1340:** Edward won a great naval battle off Sluis, Belgium.

    - **1346:** Edward III's archers – outnumbered 3 to 1 – routed the greatest French knights at Crécy with their 2-m-long yew bows, and so hastened the end of knighthood.

    - **1347:** Edward III took the French port of Calais.

    - **1356:** Edward III's son, the Black Prince, won a great victory over the French at Poitiers.

    - **1415:** the last great English victory was Henry V's at Agincourt – 6000 English beat a French army of 30,000.

    - **The English** won most battles, but the French won the war because they had three times the resources.

◄ *The greatest knight of the war was Edward the Black Prince (1330–76), hero of the Battles of Crécy, Poitiers and Navarette.*

▲ *In the Battle of Agincourt (1415), the French failed to learn lessons from previous defeats and Henry V won a glorious victory.*

...FASCINATING FACT...
The tide turned for the French in 1429, when
Joan of Arc led them to victory at Orléans.

# The Wars of the Roses

- **The Wars of the Roses** were a series of civil wars fought in England in the 1400s as two branches of the Plantagenet family fought for the English throne.

- **On one side** was the house of York, with a white rose as its emblem. On the other was the house of Lancaster, with a red rose as its emblem.

- **The wars began** when Lancastrian king Henry VI became insane in 1453. With the country in chaos, Warwick the 'kingmaker' set up Richard, duke of York as Protector in Henry's place.

- **In 1455, Henry VI** seemed to recover and war broke out between Lancastrians and Yorkists.

  - **Richard was killed** at the Battle of Wakefield in 1460, but Henry VI became insane again.

  - **A crushing Yorkist victory** at Towton, near York, in 1461, put Richard's son on the throne as Edward IV.

  - **Edward IV** made enemies of his brothers Clarence and Warwick, who invaded England from France in 1470 with Henry VI's queen Margaret of Anjou and drove Edward out.

▲ The white – and red – roses were emblems of the rival houses of York and Lancaster. When Henry VII married Elizabeth of York, he combined the two to make the Tudor rose.

- **Henry VI** was brought back for seven months before Edward's Yorkists defeated the Lancastrians at Barnet and Tewkesbury. Henry VI was murdered.

- **When Edward IV died** in 1483, his son Edward V was still a boy. When young, Edward and his brother vanished – probably murdered in the Tower of London – and their uncle Richard III seized the throne.

- **Richard III** made enemies among the Yorkists, who sided with Lancastrian Henry Tudor. Richard III was killed at Bosworth Field on 22 August 1485. Henry Tudor became Henry VII and married Elizabeth of York to end the wars.

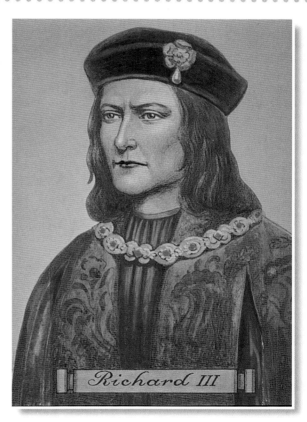

▲ *Richard was a harsh man, but not the evil monster portrayed in Shakespeare's play,* Richard III.

**449**

# Joan of Arc

- **St Joan of Arc** (c.1412–31) was the peasant girl who led France from defeat in the Hundred Years War and was burned at the stake for her beliefs.

- **Joan** was called Jeanne d'Arc in France. She called herself Jeanne la Pucelle (Joan the Maid).

- **Joan** was brought up in the village of Domrémy, near Nancy, northeastern France, as a shepherd girl.

- **By the age of 13,** Joan was having visions and believed that God had chosen her to help the French king Charles VII to beat the English.

- **Joan** tried to see the king but was laughed at until she was finally admitted to the king's court, in 1429.

▲ *Known traditionally as the Maid of Orléans, Joan was made a saint in 1920.*

- **To test Joan,** the king stood in disguise amongst his courtiers but Joan recognized him instantly. She also told him what he asked for in his secret prayers.

- **Joan was given** armour and an army to rescue the town of Orléans from the English and succeeded in just ten days.

- **Joan then** led Charles VII through enemy territory to be crowned at Rheims cathedral.

- **In May 1430,** Joan was captured by the English and accused of witchcraft.

- **Joan insisted** that her visions came from God, so a tribunal of French clergymen condemned her as a heretic. She was burned at the stake in Rouen on 30 May 1431.

▼ *It was said that a short-haired, armour-clad Joan, flying her own flag, pushed back the English at Orléans, in 1429. She then took the Dauphin to Rheims, to be crowned Charles VII.*

# The Renaissance

▼ *This portrayal of God's Creation of Man comes from the great Renaissance artist Michelangelo's famous paintings on the ceiling of the Sistine Chapel, in Rome.*

- **The Renaissance** was the great revolution in arts and ideas in Italy between the 1300s and the 1500s.

- **Renaissance** is French for 'rebirth', because it was partly about a revival of interest in the works of the classical world of Greece and Rome.

- **The Renaissance** began when many people started to doubt that the Church had all the answers.

- **Scholars** gradually developed the idea of 'humanism' – the idea that man is the focus of things, not God.

- **A spur** to the Renaissance was the fall of Constantinople in 1453. This sent Greek scholars fleeing to Italy, where they set up academies in cities like Florence and Padua.

- **Artists** in the Renaissance, inspired by classical examples, began to try and put people at the centre of their work – and to portray people and nature realistically rather than as religious symbols.

- **In the 1400s** brilliant artists like Donatello created startlingly realistic paintings and sculptures.

- **The three greatest artists** of the Renaissance were Michelangelo, Raphael and Leonardo da Vinci.

- **The Renaissance** saw some of the world's greatest artistic and architectural masterpieces being created in Italian cities such as Florence and Padua.

- **During the late 1400s**, Renaissance ideas spread to northern Europe.

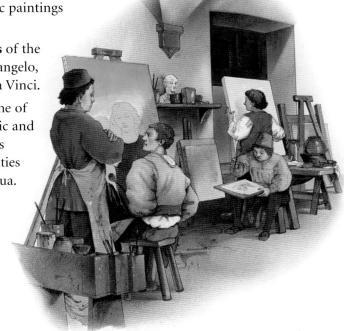

▶ *Many Renaissance painters ran studios where a team of artists worked on a 'production line' principle, so that the painter himself was not wholly responsible for the work.*

**453**

# Voyages of exploration

- **In the late 1300s,** the Mongol Empire in Asia collapsed and Ottoman Turks grew powerful in the Near East. Roads to China and the east were cut off.

- **Italian merchant cities** like Genoa and Venice needed another route. So bold sailors set out from Portugal and Spain to find a way to the east by sea.

▼ *Nearly all European explorers sailed in caravels. These ships were rarely more than 20–30 m long and weighed under 150 tonnes. But they could cope with rough seas and head into the wind, so could sail in most directions. They were also fast – vital when crossing vast oceans.*

Big square sails on the fore and main masts filled like parachutes for high-speed sailing

A lookout in the crow's nest often saw new land first

A triangular lateen sail on the mizzen (rear) mast helped the ship sail into the wind and manoeuvre along coasts

A raised section at the bow, called the forecastle, gave extra storm protection and extra accommodation

A small poop (raised deck) held the captain's cabin

The caravel's strong deck was a platform for guns and made it very storm-proof

The caravel had a deep, narrow hull and a strong, straight keel for speed and stability

454

- **At first,** they tried to go round Africa, and voyages ventured down Africa's unknown west coast.

- **Many early voyages** were encouraged by Portugal's Prince Henry (1394–1460), who set up a school of navigation at Sagres.

- **In 1488,** Bartholomeu Dias sailed round Africa's southern tip and into the Indian Ocean.

- **In 1497,** Vasco da Gama sailed round Africa to Calicut in India, and returned laden with spices and jewels.

- **Perhaps the greatest voyage** by a European was in 1492, when Genoese sail or Christopher Columbus set out across the open Atlantic. He hoped to reach China by travelling westwards around the world. Instead, he found the whole 'New World' – North and South America.

- **Columbus** only landed on Caribbean islands at first. Even when he reached South America on his last voyage, he thought he was in Asia. The first to realize it was an unknown continent was the Florentine explorer Amerigo Vespucci, who landed there in 1499. A map made in 1507 named North and South America after him.

- **In 1519–22,** Magellan's ship *Victoria* sailed across the Atlantic, round the southern tip of South America, across the Pacific and back round Africa to Spain. Although this Portuguese explorer was killed in the Philippines, his crew and ship went on to complete the first round-the-world voyage.

> **... FASCINATING FACT ...**
> Venetian John Cabot set out from Bristol, England in 1497 –
> and 'discovered' North America when he landed in Labrador.

# Elizabeth I

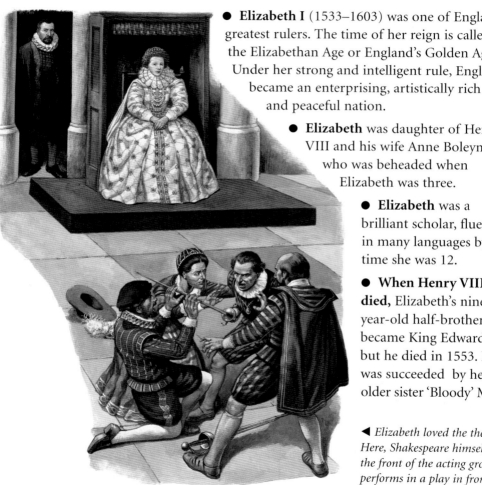

- **Elizabeth I** (1533–1603) was one of England's greatest rulers. The time of her reign is called the Elizabethan Age or England's Golden Age. Under her strong and intelligent rule, England became an enterprising, artistically rich and peaceful nation.

- **Elizabeth** was daughter of Henry VIII and his wife Anne Boleyn, who was beheaded when Elizabeth was three.

- **Elizabeth** was a brilliant scholar, fluent in many languages by the time she was 12.

- **When Henry VIII died,** Elizabeth's nine-year-old half-brother became King Edward VI, but he died in 1553. He was succeeded by her older sister 'Bloody' Mary.

◀ *Elizabeth loved the theatre. Here, Shakespeare himself (at the front of the acting group) performs in a play in front of the queen.*

► *William Shakespeare was one of several important English writers whose work flourished during Elizabeth I's reign.*

- **Mary** was staunchly Catholic. For a while Elizabeth was locked up, suspected of involvement in a Protestant plot.

- **Elizabeth** became queen in 1558, when Mary died.

- **At once Elizabeth** strengthened the Protestant Church of England by the Act of Supremacy in 1559.

- **Elizabeth** was expected to marry, and she encouraged foreign suitors when it helped diplomacy. But she remained single, earning her the nickname 'The Virgin Queen'.

- **Elizabeth** sent troops to help Protestants in Holland against their Spanish rulers, and secretly urged Francis Drake to raid Spanish treasure ships. In 1588 Spain sent an Armada to invade England. Elizabeth proved an inspiring leader and the Armada was repulsed.

- **Elizabeth's reign** is famed for the poetry and plays of men like Spenser, Marlowe and Shakespeare.

# Roundheads and Cavaliers

- **The English Civil War** (1642–49) was the struggle between 'Cavalier' supporters of King Charles I and 'Roundheads', who supported Parliament.

- **A key issue** was how much power the king should have. Charles wanted to be free to set taxes and his own brand of religion. Parliament demanded a say.

- **On the royalist side** were those, who wanted the English Church more Catholic; on the other were Puritans.

- **Puritans** were extreme Protestants. They believed that churches (and people) should be stripped of the wasteful luxury they saw in the Catholic Church and the aristocrats at the court of Charles's French, Catholic wife.

- **'Cavalier'** is from the French *chevalier* (horseman). It was meant as a term of abuse. Many Cavaliers were rich landowners.

- **Puritans** thought long hair indulgent, and the Roundheads got their name from their short-cropped hair. Many Roundheads were rich merchants and townspeople.

▶ *A Cavalier soldier. The term Cavalier was coined because many of Charles' supporters were seen as frivolous courtiers who loved fighting for its own sake.*

- **Many revolutionary groups** emerged among poorer people, such as the 'Diggers' and 'Levellers'.

- **The war** turned against the royalists when the parliamentarians formed the disciplined New Model Army.

- **Charles I** was beheaded in 1649.

- **Oliver Cromwell** (1599–1658) became Roundhead leader and signed Charles I's death warrant. In 1653, he made himself Lord Protector – England's dictator.

▶ *Many Cavaliers had long hair and wore colourful and elaborate clothes, after the style of the French court. Some, like Lovelace, were poets.*

459

# American independence

- **In 1763,** Britain finally defeated the French in North America, adding Canada to its 13 colonies – but wanted the colonists to help pay for the cost. The colonists resented paying taxes to a government 5000 km away.

- **To avoid costly wars** with Native Americans, George III issued a Proclamation in 1763 reserving lands west of the Appalachians for native peoples, and sent troops to keep settlers out, arousing colonists' resentment.

- **In 1764–5,** British prime minister George Grenville brought in three new taxes – the Sugar Tax on molasses, which affected rum producers in the colonies; the Quartering Tax, which obliged the colonists to supply British soldiers with living quarters; and the Stamp Tax on newspapers, playing cards and legal documents.

- **Colonists** tolerated sugar and quartering taxes, but the Stamp Tax provoked riots. Delegates from nine colonies met in New York to demand a say in how they were taxed, demanding 'No taxation without representation.'

- **As protests escalated,** Grenville was forced to withdraw all taxes but one, the tax on tea. Then, in 1773, a crowd of colonists disguised as Mohawk Indians marched on to the merchant ship *Dartmouth* in Boston harbour and threw its cargo of tea into the sea. After this 'Boston Tea Party', the British closed Boston and moved troops in.

- **A Congress of delegates** from all the colonies except Georgia met to demand independence, and appointed George Washington to lead an army to fight their cause.

- **In April 1775,** British troops seized military stores at Lexington and Concord near Boston and the war began.

The original 13 colonies of North America stretched from foggy Massachusetts in the north, 2500 km south to steamy Georgia. These 13 colonies became the first 13 states of the United States of America. The dates on the map show when they were founded. The green lines show today's states – these, of course, did not exist in 1775. In 1775, there were over 2.5 million people living in the colonies, with 450,000 in Virginia alone.

- **At first,** the British were successful, but the problems of fighting 5000 km from home told in the long run. In 1781, Washington defeated the British at Yorktown, Virginia and they surrendered.

- **In 1776,** the colonists drew up a Declaration of Independence, written by Thomas Jefferson. The British recognized independence in 1783, and in 1787 the colonists drew up a Constitution stating how their Union should be run. In 1789, George Washington was elected as the first president of the United States of America.

... FASCINATING FACT ...
The Declaration of Independence began with the now famous words:
'We hold these truths to be self-evident, that all men are created equal, that they are endowed by their Creator with certain inalienable rights, and that among these are Life, Liberty and the pursuit of Happiness.'

461

# The French Revolution

- **In 1789,** French people were divided among three 'Estates' – the nobles, clergy and middle class – plus the peasants. Nobles owned all the land, but were exempt from paying taxes, and the tax burden fell on the peasants.

- **In 1789,** France was bankrupt after many wars, and King Louis XVI was forced to summon Parliament, called the Estates General, for the first time in 175 years.

- **The three Estates** had met separately in the past, but now insisted on meeting in a National Assembly to debate how to limit the power of the king. The Assembly was dominated by the Third Estate, the middle class.

- **On 14 July 1789,** the poor people of Paris, tired of debates, stormed the prison fortress of the Bastille.

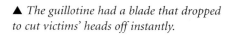

▲ *The guillotine had a blade that dropped to cut victims' heads off instantly.*

- **Fired by the fall of the Bastille,** peasants rose all over the country and refused to pay taxes. Parisian women marched to Versailles and dragged the king back to Paris.

- **The National Assembly** became more radical, ending serfdom and attacking the nobles and the Church. Many nobles fled the country in panic.

- **The Assembly speakers** who had the power to move the Paris mobs, like Georges Danton, came to the fore. The Assembly renamed itself the National Convention and set up the Committee of Public Safety to govern France by terror.

- **Many nobles** were sent to the guillotine and in 1793 Louis XVI and his queen, Marie Antoinette, were themselves guillotined.

- **This Reign of Terror** was presided over by Robespierre, who saw more and more of his rivals to the guillotine, including Danton. But in the end even Robespierre himself was guillotined, in July 1794.

- **With Robespierre gone,** conservatives regained control. Emphasis shifted to defending the revolution against foreign kings and to Napoleon's conquests.

▶ *When the French Revolution brought down the old ruling classes, crowds of ordinary people took to the streets to celebrate.*

**463**

# Industrial Revolution

- **The Industrial Revolution** refers to the dramatic growth in factories that began in the 1700s.

- **Before the Industrial Revolution**, most ordinary people were farmers who lived in small villages. Afterwards, most were factory hands and foremen living in huge cities.

- **The Revolution** began in Britain in the late 1700s – in France, the USA and Germany in the early 1800s.

- **The Farming Revolution** created a pool of cheap labour, while the growth of European colonies created vast markets for things like clothing.

- **The Revolution** began with the invention of machines for making cloth, like the spinning jenny.

- **The turning point** was the change from hand-turned machines like the spinning jenny, to machines driven by big water wheels – like Richard Arkwright's 'water powered spinning frame' of 1766.

  - **In 1771,** Arkwright installed water frames at Crompton Mill, Derby and created the world's first big factory.

◄ *In 1764, Lancashire weaver James Hargreaves created the 'spinning jenny' to help cottage weavers spin wool or cotton fibres into yarn (thread) on lots of spindles, turned by a single handle.*

- **In the 1780s**, James Watt developed a steam engine to drive machines – and steam engines quickly replaced water as the main source of power in factories.

- **In 1713**, Abraham Darby found how to use coke, rather than wood charcoal, to make huge amounts of iron.

- **In 1784**, Henry Cort found how to remove impurities from cast iron to make wrought iron – and iron became the key material of the Industrial Revolution.

▶ *Arkwright's water frame, powered by a water wheel, used four pairs of rotating rollers to stretch fibres before they were spun.*

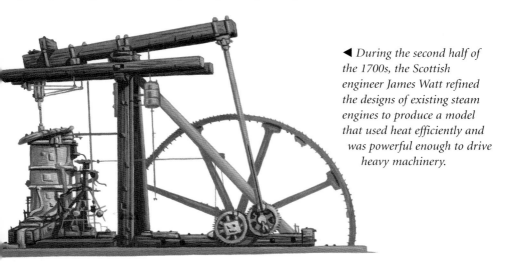

◀ *During the second half of the 1700s, the Scottish engineer James Watt refined the designs of existing steam engines to produce a model that used heat efficiently and was powerful enough to drive heavy machinery.*

**465**

# Napoleon

- **Napoleon Bonaparte** (1769–1821) was the greatest general of modern times, creating a French empire that covered most of Europe.

- **Napoleon** was quite short (157 cm) and was nicknamed le Petit Caporal ('the tiny corporal'). He was an inspiring leader, with a genius for planning and an incredibly strong will.

- **Napoleon** was born on the island of Corsica. At the age of nine he went to army school, and at fourteen he joined the French army.

- **The Revolution** gave Napoleon the chance to shine and by 1794, at just 25, he was a brigadier general.

▼ *The Battle of Waterloo, in 1815, was a hard-won conquest that finally ended Napoleon's bids for power. Leading the victors was British general Wellington, aided by the last-minute arrival of Prussian troops and by some serious French errors.*

▶ *Napoleon, with his right hand hidden, characteristically, inside his jacket.*

- **In 1796,** days after marrying Josephine de Beauharnais, Napoleon was sent with a small troop simply to hold up the invading Austrians. Instead, he drove them back as far as Vienna and conquered much of Austria.

- **By 1804,** Napoleon's conquests had made him a hero in France, and he elected himself as Emperor Napoleon I.

- **By 1812,** Napoleon had defeated all the major countries in Europe but Britain and decided to invade Russia.

- **Napoleon's invasion** of Russia ended in such disaster that it broke his power in Europe. Soon afterwards, he was defeated at Leipzig, Paris was occupied by his enemies and he was sent into exile on the isle of Elba.

- **Napoleon escaped** from Elba in March 1815 to raise another army, but this was defeated by Wellington's armies at Waterloo, Belgium in June.

- **After Waterloo**, Napoleon was sent to the island of St Helena in the mid-Atlantic, where he died, aged 51.

# The American Civil War

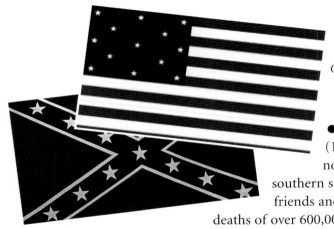

◀ *The Union flag had stars for all the 13 original states (top). The Confederates had their own version of the flag, also with 13 stars.*

- **The American Civil War** (1861–65) was fought between northern states (the Union) and southern states (the Confederacy). It split friends and families and resulted in the deaths of over 600,000 Americans.

- **The main cause** of the war was slavery. In 1850, slavery was banned in the 18 northern states, but there were 4 million slaves in the 15 southern states, where they worked on huge plantations.

- **The conflicts developed** over whether new states, added as settlers pushed westward, should be 'slave' or 'free' states.

- **In 1854,** slavers gained legal victories with the Kansas-Nebraska Act, which let new states decide for themselves.

- **In 1860,** the Abolitionist (anti-slavery) Republican, Abraham Lincoln, was elected as president.

- **The southern states** immediately broke away from the Union in protest, to form their own Confederacy.

- **As the war began,** the Confederates had the upper hand, fighting a mainly defensive campaign.

- **The turning point** came in July 1863, when an invading southern army, commanded by Robert E Lee, was badly defeated at Gettysburg in Pennsylvania.

- **The extra industrial resources** of the north slowly began to tell and General Grant attacked the south from the north, while Sherman advanced ruthlessly from the west.

- **Lee surrendered** to Grant in Appomattox Court House, Virginia, on 9 April 1865. Slavery was abolished, but a few days later Lincoln was assassinated.

▼ *The American Civil War has been described as the very first 'modern war'. It was basically a fight between two different philosophies of life – the forward-thinking, industrial, anti-slavery north versus the old-fashioned pro-slavery south, with its greater military resources.*

# The Crimean War

▲ *Around a third of the cavalrymen of the Light Brigade died making their heroic but useless charge.*

- **The Crimean War** was fought in the Crimea – to the north of the Black Sea – between 1854 and 1856.

  - **On one side** was Russia. On the other were Turkey, Britain, France, and Piedmont/Sardinia, while Austria gave political support.

    - **The main cause** of the war was British, French and Turkish worries about Russian expansion in the Black Sea.

      - **The war began** when Russia destroyed the Turkish fleet.

        - **Armies on both sides** were badly organized. Many British soldiers died of cholera before they even reached the Crimea and wounded soldiers suffered badly from cold and disease.

        - **During the Battle of Balaklava,** on 25 October 1854, a stupid mistake sent a gallant British cavalry charge straight on to the Russian guns. The heroic 'Charge of the Light Brigade' was made famous in a poem by Tennyson.

          - **Conditions** in the battle hospitals were reported in the first-ever war photographs and in the telegraphed news reports of W H Russell.

          - **Nurses** like Florence Nightingale and Jamaican Mary Seacole went to the Crimea to help the wounded.

          - **Lessons learned** in the Crimea helped to lay the foundations of modern nursing.

          - **The war** finally ended in 1856 with the Treaty of Paris, with few gains on either side.

# Victorian England

- **In 1837,** 18-year-old Victoria became the queen of England and reigned for 63 years until 1901 – the longest reign in British history.

- **Victoria's reign** is called the Victorian Age.

- **In the Victorian Age,** Britain became the world's largest industrial and trading power, and the British Empire reached its peak.

- **British factories and towns** mushroomed and railways were built throughout the country.

- **In 1851**, the Great Exhibition opened in a huge building of glass and iron, later called the Crystal Palace, to show British skills to the world.

- **In 1861**, Victoria's husband, Prince Albert, died and she went into mourning and wore black for the rest of her life.

▲ *Under Victoria, Britain came to wield control over the largest empire the world had ever seen, and made astonishing artistic, scientific and manufacturing advances.*

▶ *Benjamin Disraeli, twice prime minister in Victorian England (1868 and 1874–1880), and one of Victoria's favourite statesmen. Under Disraeli, the British Empire gained even more status when Victoria became Empress of India.*

- **The rapid expansion** of Victorian cities created vast slum areas where living conditions were appalling.

- **Social reformers** and writers such as Charles Dickens highlighted the problems of the slums. Slowly, Parliament passed laws to improve conditions for working people and to provide education for all.

- **The two great prime ministers** of the Victorian Age were the flamboyant Benjamin Disraeli (1804–81) and the dour William Gladstone (1809–98).

- **Victorian middle-class life** cultivated cosy moral values, but there was also a seamy side, with widespread prostitution and crime.

# World War I

- **World War I** (1914–18), the Great War, was the worst the world had seen (World War II would prove to be even worse), killing 10 million troops.

- **The war was caused** by the rivalry between European powers in the early 1900s. The assassination of Franz Ferdinand in Sarajevo in the Balkans, on 28 June 1914, made Austria start a war with Serbia. Russia came to Serbia's defence. Germany declared war on Russia and her ally France on 3 August.

- **The Germans** had a secret plan (the 'Schlieffen plan') for invading France. Instead of tackling the French head-on, as expected, they swept round to the north through neutral Belgium. This outrage drew Britain into the war.

- **As the Germans moved into France,** they came up against the British and French (the Allies). The opposing armies dug trenches – and stayed facing each other in much the same place for four years. The trenches, known as the Western front, stretched from the English Channel to Switzerland.

- **The war soon developed** an Eastern front, where the Central Powers (Austria and Germany) faced the Russians. The deaths of millions of Russians provoked the 1917 Revolution, which took Russia out of the war.

- **In the Alps,** the Central Powers were opposed by Italy. At Gallipoli in Turkey, British and Anzac (Australia and New Zealand) troops fought the Turks.

- **The Allies** relied on supplies from N. America, so the Germans used submarines to attack ships. The sinking of the *Lusitania* in May 1915, with 128 Americans out of 1198 casualties, brought the USA into the war.

- **In 1918,** there were 3.5 million Germans on the Western front and in March they broke through towards Paris.

- **In July 1918,** British tanks broke the German line at Amiens.

- **An Allied naval blockade** meant many people were starving in Germany. As more US troops arrived, the Germans were pushed back. At 11 o'clock on 11 November 1918, the Germans signed an armistice (peace).

◀ *Trenches were dug to protect troops from enemy gunfire, but became hell-holes, filled with water, rats and disease. Soldiers had to eat, sleep and stand guard ankle-deep in mud. Every now and then, they were ordered to 'go over the top' – climb out of their trenches and advance towards enemy lines. Out of the trench, they were exposed to enemy fire, and quickly mown down. Millions of soldiers on both sides died. On July 1 1916, 60,000 British soldiers were killed in just a few hours in the Battle of the Somme. The four-month Somme offensive killed 600,000 Germans, 400,000 British and 200,000 French – and advanced the Allies 7 km. The horror of war was conveyed in letters and poems by soldiers such as Siegfried Sassoon and Wilfred Owen.*

# The Spanish Civil War

- **In the 1920s,** a weak economy and political unrest led General de Rivera to run Spain as dictator, alongside King Alfonso XIII.

- **In 1930,** the army drove Rivera out. In 1931, a popular vote for a republic persuaded Alfonso to leave Spain.

- **Spain** was split. On the Left were socialists, communists and ordinary people who supported the republic. On the right were wealthy landowners, army officers, the Catholic Church, and the fascist Falange party, who wanted the king back.

▲ *General Franco, victor of the Civil War and right-wing dictator of Spain for almost 40 years.*

- **Complicating the picture** were Catalonians and Basques, who wanted to break away from Spain.

- **In February 1936**, elections put the Popular Front, formed by all the left-wing groups, in power.

- **In July 1936**, a wave of army revolts started in Morocco and threatened to topple the Popular Front. The Popular Front supporters armed themselves and a bitter civil war began, with terrible atrocities on both sides.

- **The forces of the Right** were called the Nationalists and were led by General Franco. They were supported by fascist (very right-wing) Germany and Italy.

476

- **The forces of the Left** were called the Republicans or Loyalists and were supported by Soviet Russia. Liberals from other countries, like the writer Laurie Lee, formed an International Brigade to fight for the Loyalists.

- **At first,** Loyalists held the northeast and the big cities, but they gradually fell back. In March 1939, Franco's forces captured Madrid, the last Loyalist stronghold.

- **Franco** was dictator of Spain until he died in 1975.

▲ *A recruiting poster for the fascist Falange party.*

# World War II

- **World War II** (1939–45) was the most terrible war ever fought. It not only killed 17 million soldiers – compared to 10 million in World War I – but also twice as many civilians, through starvation, bombings and massacres.

- **It was the first** truly global war – fought on the plains of Europe, in the jungles of Southeast Asia, on the deserts of Africa, among the islands of the Pacific, on (and under) the Atlantic Ocean, and in many other places.

- **It began** when Hitler's Germany invaded Poland on 1 September 1939. Great Britain thought the USSR would defend Poland but Hitler and Stalin made a pact. As Germany invaded Poland from the west, the USSR invaded from the east.

- **After a lull,** or 'Phoney War', in May–June 1940, the Germans quickly overran Norway and Denmark, then Luxembourg, the Netherlands, Belgium and France.

- **The British army** was trapped by the Channel coast, but the Germans held back, and 338,000 British troops got away from Dunkirk, France, on an armada of little boats.

'Never in the field of human conflict have so many owed so much to so few' – Churchill on the British fighter pilots.

▶ Winston Churchill (1874–1965) was the British prime minister whose courage and inspiring speeches helped the British withstand the German threat.

478

▶ *The bombing of Pearl Harbour by the Japanese forced the US to enter the war. Almost 4000 people were killed or injured by the attack, with the main targets being US war ships.*

- **By August 1940**, Germany launched air raids on England to prepare for an invasion. This was the Battle of Britain.

- **Fearing the USSR** would turn against him, Hitler launched a sudden invasion of the USSR on 22 June 1941. The USA joined the war when Japan bombed its fleet without warning in Pearl Harbor, Hawaii, on 7 Dec 1941.

- **Germany, Italy, Japan** and six other nations joined forces as the 'Axis'. Britain, the USA, USSR, China and 50 other nations were together called the Allies. In 1942, the Allies halted the Axis in Africa, invading Italy in 1943 and France in 1944. In 1945, the Allies drove into Germany from east and west. Germany surrendered on 7 May 1945. The terrible Pacific conflict ended when the USA dropped atom bombs on the Japanese cities Hiroshima and Nagasaki. Japan surrendered on 2 Sept 1945.

- **As the Allies** moved into Germany, they found the horror of Nazi death camps like Auschwitz and Buchenwald, where millions of Jews and others had been slaughtered by starvation and in gas chambers.

> ...FASCINATING FACT...
> The key to the early German successes was the Blitzkrieg
> ('lightning war') – a rapid attack with tanks and aeroplanes.

479

# The Cold War

- **The Cold War** was the rivalry between communist and non-communist countries after World War II – between the USSR and USA in particular.

- **It was called the Cold War** because the USSR and USA did not fight directly. But both supported countries that did, like the USA in Vietnam and the USSR in Korea.

- **The Iron Curtain** was the barrier between western Europe and communist eastern Europe.

- **The name Iron Curtain** was used by German propagandist Goebbels and adopted by Churchill.

- **The Berlin Wall** dividing communist East Berlin from the West was a powerful Cold War symbol. Dozens were shot trying to escape from the East over the wall.

- **The Cold War** was fought using both propaganda and art, and by secret means such as spies and secret agents.

◀ *For many, the tearing down of the Berlin Wall, in 1989, marked the end of the Cold War. Berliners had a huge party on the ruins.*

▶ *Fidel Castro, the prime minister of Cuba at the time of the 1962 missile crisis. The politics of Cuba's socialist revolutionary government was supported by the USSR and opposed by the USA.*

- **The USA and USSR** waged an arms race to build up nuclear bombs and missiles one step ahead of their rival.

- **Real war loomed** when US president Kennedy threatened the USSR as it attempted to build missile bases on the island of Cuba in 1962.

- **The Cold War** thawed after 1985, when Soviet leader Mikhail Gorbachev introduced reforms in the USSR and began to co-operate with the West.

- **In 1989,** the Berlin Wall came down. In 1989–90, many eastern European countries broke away from Soviet control.

481

# The break-up of the USSR

- **After Stalin died,** in 1953, many people were released from the Siberian prison camps, but the USSR, under its new leader Khrushchev, remained restrictive and secretive.

- **The KGB** was a secret police force. It dealt harshly with anyone who did not toe the communist line.

- **In the 1980s,** cracks began to appear in the communist machine.

- **In 1985,** Mikhail Gorbachev became Soviet leader and introduced policies of *perestroika* (economic reform), *glasnost* (government openness) and *demokratizatsiya* (increased democracy).

- **Gorbachev** also cut spending on arms, and improved relationships with the West.

- **In 1989,** a McDonalds restaurant opened in Moscow.

- **As people in the USSR** gained freedom, so people in communist eastern Europe demanded freedom. New democratic governments were elected in Hungary, Poland, Czechoslovakia, Romania and Bulgaria.

- **The republics** within the USSR wanted independence too, and in 1991 the USSR was dissolved and replaced by a Commonwealth of Independent States (CIS).

- **Gorbachev's reforms** angered Communist Party leaders, who staged a coup and imprisoned Gorbachev, but he was freed and the coup was brought down by Boris Yeltsin, who became the first president of Russia (once the largest republic in the USSR).

◀ *Mikhail Gorbachev.*

- **Under Yeltsin,** the state industries of the Soviet era were gradually broken up and Russia seemed to be moving towards Western-style capitalism. But the collapse of the Communist Party structure led to chaos, lawlessness and economic problems. In 2000, the Russians elected Vladimir Putin as president, a strong leader who they hoped would see them out of the crisis.

▲ *The Kremlin, in Moscow, dates back to the 1100s and is a walled collection of palaces and churches. Home to the tsars, it then became the seat of USSR government.*

483

# The European Union

- **The European Union** is an organization of 25 European countries, including France, Germany and the UK.

- **After World War II ended,** in 1945, Jean Monnet promoted the idea of uniting Europe economically and politically.

- **In 1952**, six countries formed the European Coal and Steel Community (ECSC), to trade in coal and steel.

- **The success of the ECSC** led the member countries to break down all trade barriers between them as part of the European Community (EC), in 1967.

- **1973–81:** six new countries join the EC, including the UK.

- **In 1992,** the 12 EC members signed a treaty at Maastricht in the Netherlands to form the European Union (EU).

- **The EU** added cooperation on justice and police matters and cooperation in foreign and security affairs to the economic links of the EC. These three links are called the 'Three Pillars' of the EU.

- **The EU** has four governing bodies – European Parliament, Council of the EU, European Commission, Court of Justice and Court of Auditors.

- **In 1999,** the EU launched the Euro, which is intended to become a single European currency.

▶ *The European Commission building in Strasbourg. The Parliament is in Brussels. The Court of Justice is in Luxembourg.*

# Index

## A

Abolitionist Republicans 468
absolute zero 340, 342
absorption 370, *370*
absorption, light 320, *321*
abyssal plain 126, 127
abyssal zone 212
Achaemenid family 420
Achilles 426
acid rain 106
acids, digestion *371*
acorns 158, 179
Act of Supremacy, Elizabeth I 457
Adadnirari I, king 416
Adams, John Couch 54
Adastrea 48
addax 324
adder, dwarf puff 324
advanced gas reactors 338
Aeneas of Troy 432
Aepyornis 265
aerial roots 149
aerials, television 332, 333
aerogels, density 346
Africa **136–137**, *136*
    exploration 455
    Iron Age 409
    Stone Age 404
    voyages of
    weathering 106
    World War II 478, 479
    zebu cattle 275
African elephant 290
African fringe-toed lizard 325
afterglow 16
age of the Earth **76–77**
aggregate fruits 158, 159
Agincourt, Hundred Years War 446, 447
Agrippa, empress 429
Ahuru Mazda, Persia 421
air **310–311**
    atmosphere *117*
    breathing 360, 361, *361*
    density 346
    epiphytes 164
    global warming 118

heat 342
leaves 151
lungs 362
photosynthesis 146, 152, 153
smell 386
sound 322, *322*, 323
states of matter 308
systems 359
weathering 106
air sacs 362
airways,
    lungs 362, 363
Alaska 101, 129
albatross 262
Albert, Prince 472
alcohol 373, *373*
alders 176, 177
Alexander Comnenus, emperor 442
Alexander the Great 420, **426–427**, *427*
Alexandria, Egypt 426
Alfonso XIII, king of Spain 476
Alfred the Great 435
algae 116, **188–189**, 212
    marine plants 168
Algeria 137
aliens 66
alimentary canal 370
Allies,
    World War I 475, *475*
    World War II 479
alloys 317, 406
almonds 158, 179
Alpha stars of constellations 24
alpine chough 227
Alps mountains 103
Alps, World War I 475
aluminium 299
alveoli 362, *362*, 363
Amalthea 48
Amazon river, South America 130
amber 303
amber fossils 91
America,
    rainforest 130, *130*
    wetlands 113
    World War I 475
American Civil War **468–469**

American independence **460–461**
amethyst *94*
Amiens, World War I 475
amino acids,
    diet 377
    kidneys 380
ammonia 49, 51, 305, *315*
ammonites 91
amoeba 209
Amorites 416
amorphous carbon 312
amphibians 77, 209, 215, **256–257**
amphitheatres 428
amplification 328
Ananke 48
Anatolia, Turkey 408
ancient Babylon 24
ancient Egypt **410–411**, *410, 411*
ancient Egyptians 24
ancient Greeks 26, 48, 53, 54, 58
ancient Romans 50
Andean condor 227
Andes mountains, South America 130, 131
    mountain building 102, 103
Andromeda galaxy 28, *28*
anemones 210
angiosperms 146, 164
anglerfish 212, 250
    tassel-finned 212
Angles 434
angling 245
Anglo-Saxons **434–435**, *435*
    Vikings 437
Angra Mainyu, Persia 421
animal waste 310
    carbon dioxide 310
    fossils 90, *90*
    magnetism 324
    oxygen 310
    remains 89
    swamps 112
ankle bones 351
Antarctic Circle 131
    deserts 110
Antarctic Treaty 141
Antarctica **140–141**, 143
Antares 22

spiny 270
antelope jack rabbit 324
antelopes 221, 222, 324
antennae,
    butterflies 238
    insects 236
anthers 156, 157
antibiotics 191
antibodies 359
antimatter 16
Antonines 429
Antoninus, emperor 429
ants **240–241**, *240*
    communication 232
    rainforest 221
    slavemaker 240
    tree 232
    wood 240
    woodland 218
    worker 236
anus 370, 371, *371*
anvil 384, 385
Anyang, China 413
Anzac, World War I 475
aorta 365, *367*
aphelion 72
*Apollo 11 67*
*Apollo* missions 66
appendicular skeleton 351
appendix 371
apples 158, 159, 197
Appomattox House, Virginia 469
Aquarius 26
Arab horses 288, 289
Arabs 417
arachnids 242
Aramis, Ethiopia 400
arapaima 244
Arbela 416
Archaeology,
    Maoris 438
*Archaeopteryx* 264, *264*
Archaic Period,
    Egypt 411
    Greece 422
Arctic fox 228, 229, 277
Arctic hare 229, 277
Arctic lupin 163
Arctic poppy 163
Arctic tern 234
Arcturuss 22
*Ardipithecus ramidus* 400
Argentavix 265

bridges 294
brightness,
  stars 22
  Venus 44
bristlecone pine 174
bristle-thighed curlews 234
Britain 432
  Anglo-Saxons 434
  Battle of 479
  Crimean War 471
  hillfort 409
  Industrial Revolution
    464
  Roman Empire 429
  Victorian 472
  Vikings 436
  World War I 474, 475,
    *475*
  World War II 478, 479
Britannia 429
British Empire,
  Victorian Age 472, *472,*
    473
British rule,
  North America 461
Britons **432–433**
broad-leaved trees 172, 176
  deciduous trees 184
  evergreens 180
  rainforest 165
broccoli 200
bromeliads 155
bronchi 362, 363
bronze 408
  China 413
Bronze Age **406–407**, *406,*
  433
Brussels sprouts 200
Brussels, Belgium 484
Brutus 432
bubonic plague 444
Bucephalus 426
Buchenwald, World War II
  479
buddleias 177
buds 146
  flower 147
buffalo 222, 223
  lion 287
bulbs
  garden 195
  herbs 204,
Bulgaria 482
bullhead 214

bulls 291, 292
burial,
  Egypt 410
  ships 434
burning,
  chemical reaction *161*
  temperature 341
burrowing anemones 210
bush 136
bushcats 294
buttercups 171
butterflies 156, 157, 163,
  236, **238–239**
  birdwing 221
  blue morpho 221
  monarch 238, 234
  woodland 219
buttes 110, 111
button mushrooms 192
bytes 335
Byzantine Empire 442

# C

cabbage 200
  savoy 200
  sea 200
cables,
  telecommunications 330,
    331
Cabot, John 455
cacti 166
Caesar, Julius,
  Britain 432
Caesarean section 397
Calais, Hundred Years War
  446
calcium 80, *81*
  bones 352, 353
calcium carbonate 109
Caledonian mountains
  103, 133
calendars 411, 425
calf bone *350*
California,
  climate 114
  North America 128
Caligula 428
Callisto 48
Calories 375
Caloris Basin, Mercury *43*
calves 291, 292, *292*
cambium,
  dicots,

trees 172, 173
camels 223
cameras 332, *332*
camouflage **276–277**
  cold climates 229
  flatfish 249
campion, sea 171
Canada 460
  coasts 123
  mountains 133
  polar bears 284
  rocks 88
Canadian Shield 128
canals, Mars 46
Cancer 26
canine teeth 356, *356*
canopy animals 220
canyons, ocean 126
Cape of Good Hope 136
capillaries,
  circulation 364
  kidneys 380
  lungs 362
Capricorn 26
caps 192
Caratacus, king 432
carats 94
caravels 454
carbohydrates **374–375**
  diet 376, *376*
  liver 372
carbon 80, 95
  bonds *150, 151*
  compounds 307
carbon dioxide 305, 359
  air 310, 311
  atmosphere 116
  blood 368
  breathing 360
  global warming 118, 119,
    *119*
  leaves 151
  lungs 363
  molecules 305
  photosynthesis 146, 150,
    152, 153
  Venus 44, *45*
  volcanoes 98
carbon monoxide 116
carbonate minerals 93
cardiovascular systems *359*
cargo bay 70, *71*
Caribbean
  islands 455

Caribbean plate 131
Caribbean Sea 128
caribou 228
Carme 48
carotene 395
carp 214
carpels 147
carrots 149
  vegetables 202, 203
cartilage 246
  airways *234*
  skeleton 350
carving,
  Assyrian 416
  Chinese 412
  Polynesian 419
Caspian Sea 135
cassava 202, 203
Cassini probe *51*
cast iron 317
casting 407, 413
Castro, Fidel 481
Catalonians, Spain 476
catapults 431
  English Civil War 458
  Spain 476
caterpillars 238, 239
catfish 244
cathode-ray tubes 302, 332
Catholic Church,
Catholics,
  Catuvellauni tribe 432
  Elizabeth I 457
cats,
  big 222, 227
  domestic 294, *294*, 295
  lion 286
  senses 272
  small 279
cattle 292
  Indian zebu 275
  sweat glands 275
cauliflower 200
Cavaliers **458–459**
Caverns 108, 109
caves **108–109**, 122
celandines 171
Celestial Police 58
celestial sphere **38–39**
cells,
  algae 188
  blood 368, *368*, 369, *369*
  bones 353
  breathing 360

**490**

## D

**492**

fruits **158–159**
  nuts 179
  rainforest 164
  seeds 161, 178
  sugars 152
fuel 147, *376*
  energy *345*
  heat *343*
  nuclear energy 338
  photosynthesis 150, 152, 153
  star birth 34
  supernovae 36
full Moon 62
Fuller, Buckmaster 313
fullerenes 312, 313
fungi **190–191**
  mushrooms 192, 193
  spores 161
funnel-web spider 243
fur 227, 228
  polar bears 285
furnace 316, 317, *317*, 341
furnaces *409*
fusion 74, 338

# G

Gaius, emperor 428
Galatea 54
galaxies *23*, **28–29**
  Big Bang 16, *17*
  black holes 18
  dark matter 20, *20*, *21*
  Milky Way 30, 31
  nebulae 32
  supernovae 36
  universe 14
galena *92*
Galilean moons 48
Galileo,
  Jupiter 48
Galileo space probe 49, 58
gall bladder *372*
Gallia 429
Gallipoli 475
gamma rays *339*
gannets 262
Ganymede 48
garden flowers **194–195**
  wildflowers 170
gardeners 194
gardens 201
garlic 204, 207

garnet 95, *95*
gas,
  ammonia 305, 315
  density 346
  molecules 343
  ununoctium 299
  water 314, *314*
gas clouds,
  Big Bang 16, *17*
  nebulae 32, 33, *33*
  planets 40
  star birth 34, *34*
gas planets 40
gases **308–309**
  air 310, *310*
  atmosphere 116, 117, *117*
  comets 60
  Earth's formation 75
  global warming 118, 119
  Jupiter 48
  Milky Way 31
  Saturn 50
  stars 22
  Sun 64
  Venus 44, 45
  volcanoes 98
  weathering 106
gasoline 340
Gaspra 58
gastric juices *370, 371*
Gaul 434
geckos 220
geese 215, 234
Gemini 26
gems 92, **94–95**, *95*
general relativity 348, 349
generations 208
generators,
  nuclear power *339*
genitals,
  hair 394
Genoa 454
geodesic dome 313
geoid 78, 79
George III, king of
  England 460
geostationary orbits 69
German language 415
Germany,
  Anglo-Saxons 434
  European Union 484
  Holy Roman Empire 438
  Industrial Revolution
    464

Spain 476
World War I 474 , 475,
  *475*
World War II 478, 479
Gettysburg, American Civil
  War 469
Ghiza, Egypt 411
giant kelp 168
giant redwood 160, 161
giant sequoia 174, 187
giant stick insect 237
Gibraltar 436
gills 192, 244, *244*, 257
gingkos 146, 161, 174
Gir forest, India 286
giraffes 222
  camouflage 276, 277
glaciers,
  Europe 132
gladiators *428*
Gladstone, William 473
glands 232
  digestion 371
  skin *393*
glass,
  lenses *319*
  light 318
glass lizard 261
gliding 262, 263
Global Positioning System
  68
global warming **118–119**
glow worms 233
glucose,
  breathing 360
  carbohydrates 374, *374*,
    375
  diet 376
  kidneys 380
  liver 372
glutens 198
gluteus maximus 355, *355*
glycogen 372, 375
gneiss rocks 85, 88
goats, mountain 226, 227
gobies 244, 210
Godwinson, Harold 440
Godwinson, Tostig 440
Goebbels 480
Golan Heights, Israel 405
gold 80, 92, *92*
  atoms 300
  Bronze Age 406
  elements *298*

Persia 420
gold of pleasure 197
golden hamsters 295
Gorbachev, Mikhail 481,
  482, *482*
Gordium 427
gorges 129
gorillas 233
gorse 170
gourds 197
grains 158
  cereals 198, 199
  crops 196, 197
Grand Canyon, North
  America 129, *129*
granite 85, 92
Grant, general 469
grapes 197
graphite 312, 313
grasses 149
  Arctic 162
  cereals 198
  crops 197
  fungi 191
  mushrooms 193
  wildflowers 171
grasshoppers 236
grassland life **222–223**
grasslands,
  Africa 136, *137*
  age of the Earth *76*
  Asia 134
  South America 131
gravel,
  deserts 110
  rivers 105
gravity 82
  Big Bang 16
  black holes 18
  dark matter 20
  Earth 74, 79
  Moon 346
  relativity 349
  weight 346
grayling 214, 215
great auk 265, 269
Great Australian Bight 123
Great Barrier Reef *138*, 139
Great Bear 24
great crested newt 257
Great Dark Spot, Neptune
  *54*, 55
Great Exhibition, Victorian
  Age 472

**497**

microscopes,
  lungs 362
  muscles 354
  Mars 46
  Mercury 43
organisms,
microvilli *370*
microwave radiation,
  Big Bang 16
microwaves 330
Middle East,
  Copper Age 406
  modern humans 402
  Persia 420
Middle Stone Age 404
Midlands, England 434
migrating animals *324*
migration 219, **234–235**,
  438
  butterflies 238
  ocean fish 248
  whales 273
milk 231
  bones *353*
  farm animals 292, 293
  mammals 270
  teeth 356
  whales 252
Milky Way *23*, **30–31**
  dark matter 20
  galaxies 28, 28
millet 197, 198
millipedes 218
minerals **92–93**, *92, 93*, 406
  Antarctica 141
  bones 352, *353*
  crust 84
  diet 376, *377*
  fossils 91
  gems 94, *94*, 95
  liver 372
  nuts 179
  photosynthesis 153
  roots 146, 147, 148, 149
  stem 146, 147
mines 141, 407
minke whale 253
Miranda 52
missions 70
mist *97*
mistletoe 149
  rainforest 164
Mitannians 416
mitral valve 367

moai statues 418, 419, *419*
mobile phones 330, 337
moccasin flower 171
modems 330, 336
Mohawk Indians 460
moisture 310, *310*
  atmosphere *117*
Mojave squirrel 324
molar teeth 356, *356*, *357*
molecular mass 305
molecules 152, **304–305**
  carbon 313
  colour 320, *320*
  compounds 306, *306*
  heat 342, *343*
  sound 322
  states of matter 308
  water 314, *314*, *315*
monarch butterflies 156,
  234, 238
monasteries,
  Britain 434
Mongol Empire 454
Mongols,
  Black Death 444
monkeys,
  communication 232
  rainforest 220
Monnet, Jean 484
monotremes 271, 230
monsoons,
  climate 115
Monterey pine trees 183
month 62
Monument Valley, USA
  110
Moon **62–63**
  Earth's formation 74
  gravity *346*
  relativity 349
  space exploration 66, *67*
  weight 346
  zodiac 26
moons,
  Jupiter 48
  Mars 47
  Neptune 54
  planets 40
  Pluto 56
  satellites 68
  Saturn 51
  Uranus 52
Morgan horses 288
Morocco 476

Moscow, Russia 483
  USSR 482
Mosses,
  Arctic 162
  desert plants 166
  spores 161, 191
moths 157, 164, 236, 238
  rainforest 221
  woodland 219
mould 190, 191
mountain goats 226, 227
mountain life **226–227**
mountain plants,
  conifers 175
mountain ranges **102–103**,
  *102, 103*
mountains,
  Africa 137
  Asia 134, 135
  climate 115
  Europe 132, 133
  North America 128, 129
  rivers 104
  South America 130
  undersea *126*, 127
mouth,
  breathing *360*
  digestion 370
  lungs 362
  taste 388
  teeth 356
movement,
  energy 345
  heat 342
  muscles 354
Mt Elbus, Europe 133
Mt Everest, Asia 135, *135*
Mt McKinley, North
  America 129
Mt Wilhelm, Papua New
  Guinea 139
mucus *362*, 387
muscle cells  355
muscle movement 374
muscles **354–355**
  birth 396
  breathing *360*, 361
  diet 377
  digestive tract 370, *370*
  excretion 378, *378*
  eyes 382, *383*
  heart 366
  lungs 363
  skeleton 350

skin 393, *393*
  systems 358
mushrooms 190, 191,
  **192–193**
  spores 161
musk ox 163
muskrats 219
mustangs 288
mustard 163
mycelium 191, 192, 193
Mycenae 422
myrtle 164

# N

Nac 60, 93
Nagasaki, Japan 479
Naias 54
Napoleon 463, **466–467**
narwhal 253
NASA 67
National Assembly 462,
  463
Nationalists, Spain 476
Native Americans 460
native elements *298*
natural satellites 68
Navarette 446
navigation 455
navigation satellites 68
Nazca plate 131
Nazis 479
Neanderthal man 401, 402
near Earth objects 58
Near East 454
  Bronze Age 406
  Stone Age 404
nebulae **32–33**
  star birth 34, *34*
nectar,
  butterflies 238
  hummingbirds 266
  pollination 156, 157
needle-like leaves 151, 176
  conifers 174, 175
  evergreens 180, 181
  pine trees 182
negative charge,
  electricity 326
  electrons 300, 303
  water 315
Neolithic period 404
  Britain 432
neon 310

supernovae 36
Venus 45
prickles 170
pride, lion 286, 287, *287*
priests 411, 415, 421
primary feathers 262
primrose 171
prisms 321
probes,
  asteroids 58
  Saturn *51*
  Uranus 52
  Venus 44
proboscis 290
Proclamation, North
  America 460
Proconsul 400
Proctista 188
pronghorn 222
protein 179
proteins 305
  blood 368, 369
  diet 376, *376*, 377
  liver 372
  skin 393
Protestants,
  Elizabeth I 457
  English Civil War 458
Proteus 54
proton-proton chain 22
protons
  atoms 300, *300*, 302, *302*, 303, *303*
  nuclear power 338
ptarmigans 228, 229
puberty 394
puffball fungi 191
pulmonary arteries *367*
pulmonary circulation 364, *365*
pulmonary veins *367*
pulp, teeth *357*
pumas 226, 227, *227*
pumpkins 196, 197
pupa 239
pupils 382, *383*
Puritans 458
Putin, Vladimir 483
pygmy goby 244
pyramids,
  Egypt 411
  Mayans 424
  Mexico 425
Pyranees 108

## Q

Qatar 143
quarks 16, 300
quarter horses 289
quartz,
  crust 84
  minerals 92, *92*
quartz tools 404
quasars,
  black holes 18
Quatering Tax 460
Quaternary Period 76
Queen Alexandra's
  birdwing butterflies 238
queen ants 240
queen termites 240
Queensland, Australia 139
Quito, South America 131

## R

rabbits,
  antelope jack 324
racehorses 289
racoons 219
radial artery *365*
radiation,
  atmosphere 117
  Big Bang 16
  Earth 73
  nebulae 32, *32*
radio signals,
  Saturn 51
  space probes *67*
radio waves,
  electromagnetic
  television 332
  telecommunications 330, *331*
radioactive waste 338
radioactivity 77, 90
radiocarbon dating 77, 90
Raedwald 434
rafflesia 154, 155, 164
rain,
  caves 108
  deserts 110
  Earth's formation 75
  rivers 104, 105
  weathering 106
rainforests,
  Africa 136, *136*
  Amazon 130, *130*

tropical **164–165**
ramparts 408, 409
Raphael 453
rapids 104
rarefactions 322
raspberries 159
rats,
  kangaroo 324
  water 215
rattan vine 146
razor clams 210
Reaction Control System
  70
reactors 338
receivers 330
receptors,
  smell 386
rectum *371*
recycling aluminium *299*
red blood cells,
  blood 368, 369
  circulation 364, *365*
  liver 373
red deer 218
red kangaroo 280
Red List of Threatened
  Species 270
Red Sea 411
  Africa 137
  crust 85
redwoods 186
  California 187
  conifers 174
  giant 160, 161
  Mendocino 186
reflection,
  colour 320, 321, *321*
  light 318, *318*, 319
  sound 323
reflection nebulae 32
refraction 318, *319*, *319*
Reign of Terror 463
relativity 14, **348–349**
religion,
  Aryans 415
  Mexico 425
Renaissance **452–453**
renal artery *381*
renal vein *381*
reproduction 146
reproductive system 359
reptiles *77*, 209, **256–257**, 264, 270
  dinosaurs 258

lizards 260
republic 430
Republicans, Spain 477
resins,
  pine trees 182
resistance 340
respiration 152, 360
respiratory system 359
resurrection trees 166
retina 382, *383*
revolutions,
  France 466
  Industrial **464–465**
Rheims Cathedral 451, *451*
rhinoceros beetle 237
rhinoceroses 221, 223, *223*
ribs,
  breathing *360*
  skeleton *350*, 351
rice 152, 198
  crops 197
Richard III, king of
  England 449, 449
Richard the Lionheart 443
Richard, duke of York 448
ridge, ocean 127
ring nebulae 33
rings,
  Neptune *55*
  Saturn 51
  Uranus *52*
rings, tree 172
river dolphins 253
River Nile, Africa 137
river plants,
  algae 188
rivers **104–105**, *104*, 105, *314*
  Asia 135
  North America 129
  rocks 89, *89*
  seas 121
  wetlands 113
roads 417, 420, 428
Robespierre 463
rock cycle 89
rock pools 210
rockets
  asteroids 58
  Mars 46, 47
  Mercury 42
  planets 40
  Pluto 57
  relativity 348, 349

**505**

**506**

**510**

# Acknowledgements

All artworks are from Miles Kelly Artwork Bank

The Publishers would like to thank the following picture source
whose photograph appears in this book:

414 Lyndsey Hebberd/CORBIS

All other photographs from:

Corel
digitalSTOCK
ILN
PhotoDisc